The Second Legal Answer Book for Nonprofit Organizations

Nonprofit Law, Finance, and Management Series

The Second Legal Answer Book for Nonprofit Organizations

Bruce R. Hopkins

JOHN WILEY & SONS, INC.
New York • Chichester • Weinheim • Brisbane • Singapore • Toronto

Copyright © 1999 by John Wiley & Sons, Inc. All rights reserved.

Published simultaneously in Canada.

Library of Congress Cataloging-in-Publication Data:

Hopkins, Bruce R.
   The second legal answer book for nonprofit organizations / Bruce
R. Hopkins.
       p.   cm.—(Nonprofit law, finance, and management series)
   Rev. ed. of: Legal answer book for nonprofit organizations. 1996.
   Includes bibliographical references and index.
   ISBN 0-471-29612-0 (pbk. : alk. paper)
   1. Nonprofit organizations—Law and legislation—United States—
Miscellanea.   2. Nonprofit organizations—Taxation—Law and
legislation—United States—Miscellanes.   I. Hopkins, Bruce R.
Legal answer book for nonprofit organizations.   II. Title.
III. Series.
   KF1388.Z9H67   1998
   346.73'064—dc21   98-27289

Subscription Notice

This Wiley product is updated on a periodic basis with supplements to reflect important changes in the subject matter. If you purchased this product directly from John Wiley & Sons, Inc., we have already recorded your subscription for this update service.

If, however, you purchased this product from a bookstore and wish to receive (1) the current update at no additional charge, and (2) future updates and revised or related volumes billed separately with a 30-day examination review, please send your name, company-name (if applicable), address, and the title of the product to:

Supplement Department
John Wiley & Sons, Inc.
One Wiley Drive
Somerset, NJ 08875
1-800-225-5945

For customers outside the United States, please contact the Wiley office nearest you:

Professional & Reference Division
John Wiley & Sons Canada, Ltd.
22 Worcester Road
Rexdale, Ontario M9W 1L1
CANADA
(416) 675-3580
1-800-567-4797
FAX (416) 675-6599

John Wiley & Sons, Ltd.
Baffins Lane
Chichester
West Sussex, PO19 1UD
UNITED KINGDOM
(44) (243) 779777

Jacaranda Wiley Ltd.
PRT Division
P.O. Box 174
North Ryde, NSW 2113
AUSTRALIA
(02) 805-1100
FAX (02) 805-1597

John Wiley & Sons (SEA) Pte. Ltd.
37 Jalan Pemimpin
Block B # 05-04
Union Industrial Building
SINGAPORE 2057
(65) 258-1157

About the Author

Bruce R. Hopkins is a lawyer in Kansas City, Missouri, having practiced law in Washington, D.C., for 26 years. He specializes in the representation of nonprofit organizations. His practice ranges over the entirety of legal matters involving nonprofit organizations, including issues pertaining to the application of intermediate sanctions, the commerciality doctrine, the use of joint ventures, acquisition of recognition of tax-exempt status, the representation of membership organizations and private foundations, holding of interests in for-profit businesses by tax-exempt organizations, review of annual information returns, and the return disclosure and distribution rules.

Mr. Hopkins served as chair of the Committee on Exempt Organizations, Tax Section, American Bar Association; chair, Section of Taxation, National Association of College and University Attorneys; and president, Planned Giving Study Group of Greater Washington, D.C. He was accorded the Assistant Commissioner's (IRS) Award in 1984. He also teaches a course on nonprofit organizations at the University of Missouri–Kansas City School of Law.

Mr. Hopkins is the series editor of Wiley's Nonprofit Law, Finance, and Management Series. In addition to *The Second Legal Answer Book for Nonprofit Organizations,* he is the author of *The Legal Answer Book for Nonprofit Organizations*; *The Law of Tax-Exempt Organizations,* seventh edition; *The Law of Fund-Raising,* second edition; *Charity, Advocacy, and the Law; The Nonprofit Law Dictionary; The Tax Law of Charitable Giving*; *A Legal Guide to Starting and Managing a Nonprofit Organization,* second edition; and is co-author, with Jody Blazek, of *Private Founda-*

tions: Tax Law and Compliance, with D. Benson Tesdahl; of *Intermediate Sanctions: Curbing Nonprofit Abuse;* and with Thomas K. Hyatt, of *The Law of Tax-Exempt Healthcare Organizations*. He also writes *The Nonprofit Counsel*, a monthly newsletter, published by John Wiley & Sons.

Mr. Hopkins earned his J.D. and LL.M. degrees at the George Washington University and his B.A. at the University of Michigan.

How to Use This Book

The Second Legal Answer Book for Nonprofit Organizations, like the original volume, is designed for nonprofit executives, board members, fundraising professionals, lawyers, and accountants who need quick and authoritative answers concerning the law governing nonprofit organizations. It is designed to help the reader not only better understand this law, but, more important, to show how to work with it and within its boundaries while maintaining and enhancing a tax-exempt organization's activities and effectiveness. This book uses simple, straightforward language and avoids technical jargon when possible. This question-and-answer format offers a clear and useful guide to understanding the complex, but extremely important, area of the statutes, regulations, and other law governing tax-exempt organizations. Citations are providing as research aids for those who need to pursue particular items in greater detail.

Numbering System: The question numbering system has been designed for ease of use. The questions are numbered consecutively within each chapter (e.g., 5:1, 5:2, 5:3).

Listing of Questions: The detailed List of Questions that follows the table of contents in the front of this book helps the reader locate areas of immediate interest. This listing serves as a detailed table of contents that provides both the question number and the page on which it appears.

Index: The index at the back of this book provides a further aid to locating specific information. All references in the index are to question numbers rather than page numbers.

In order to make a mistake, of course, one has to know the rules. Error is a function of competence. . . . If you know too well how to do something, you're less likely to fall into originality. Innovation depends upon competence; but competence depends on ignorance.

—*The Beast in the Nursery*
Adam Phillips (New York:
Pantheon Books, 1998)

Preface

The Preface for this book essentially was written in 1996—it can be found as the Preface to the companion book: *The Legal Answer Book for Nonprofit Organizations*. There, the origins of these books as to content and style are explained. In brief, the books were commissioned by the publisher and the format suggested by my mother.

Like the predecessor book, the substance of this one is practical advice. (As always, consult a lawyer for formal legal advice.) The content and tone is meant to be much like that used when speaking with clients. Each answer was prepared as though the client was on the other side of the desk.

Once again, the 13 chapters having been selected, a group of individuals was solicited to supply questions. This time, my "inquisitioners" included Jody Blazek, David Samuels, and Michael I. Sanders. Their contributions were very helpful and are very much appreciated; they, of course, are not responsible for the content of the answers. (Tom Hyatt was not allowed to submit any questions this time.)

During the writing, I was very sensitive to questions that frequently arose in the office and at seminars. Questions and answers were continually added and recorded down to the last minute. The book was basically completed when the Treasury Department and IRS issued the intermediate sanctions regulations in proposed form. This package of proposed rules is reflected in the book, thanks to some frenetic scrambles with page proofs in the waning hours.

Readers are encouraged to send in questions (or, if so moved, offer suggestions as to the content or wording of answers). These books will be periodically revised and updated, and comments will be gladly received.

The purpose here is to explain the law concerning nonprofit organizations to the nonlawyer. (Lawyers, however, are welcome to purchase and utilize the book.) There are summaries of the law in the book. There are also general explanations of how things legal in import ought to be done. Your author has been in practice in this branch of the law for nearly 30 years; a considerable portion of what is in the book is reflective of responses to the same questions that arise year in and year out. Some questions come from clients, others I routinely garner on the lecture circuit.

This end product has real value only if those who need it can use it to promptly resolve a problem or answer a question before them. It is intended to be a sourcebook that the nonprofit manager can pick up and, through one mechanism or another, immediately find the item of advice needed. To facilitate this book's usefulness, all of the questions answered in it are listed at the beginning. There also is an index. Endnotes have been kept to the minimum. (For more, see "How to Use This Book" on p. ix.) Those who need additional information on a matter can turn to one or more of the books in Wiley's Nonprofit Law, Finance, and Management Series.

The two Answer Books collectively contain 25 chapters and the answers to 787 questions. Your author will not be so immodest or pretentious to even remotely suggest that all the nonprofit manager needs to know about nonprofit organizations law is crammed into those answers. Still, the two books are designed to be handy and quick sources of needed legal information for the harried executive, officer, or board member of a nonprofit organization.

As the Preface to the companion book noted, the inspiration for it was the then-acquisitions editor at Wiley who managed this area, Marla J. Bobowick. Her successor and my current editor, Martha Cooley, has been supportive and encouraging in the preparation of this *Second Legal Answer Book.* She has been persuaded that it was the IRS's regulation publishing schedule and not me that was responsible for delays in the submission of manuscript.

Thanks, too, to the others at Wiley who helped in the production of the book, particularly Robin Goldstein and Elizabeth Knighton.

BRUCE R. HOPKINS

Kansas City, Missouri
December, 1998

Contents

List of Questions

CHAPTER 6   Social Welfare Organizations

Social Welfare Organizations in General

Tax Exemption Criteria

Overview of Return Contents

Revenue, Expenses, Balances, Assets

CHAPTER 1

Intermediate Sanctions

The federal tax law now includes the long-awaited and much heralded concept of *intermediate sanctions*—an emphasis on the taxation of those persons who engaged in impermissible private transactions with tax-exempt public charities and social welfare organizations, rather than revocation of the tax exemption of these entities. With this approach, tax sanctions—structured as penalty excise taxes—may be imposed on the disqualified persons who improperly benefited from a transaction and on organization managers who participated in the transaction knowing that it was improper. This body of law represents the most dramatic and important package of rules concerning exempt charitable organizations since Congress enacted the basic statutory scheme in this field in 1969. Intermediate sanctions hold the promise of transforming the private inurement and private benefit doctrines and are likely to impact the composition and functioning of many boards of directors.

Here are the questions most frequently asked by clients about the intermediate sanctions rules—and the answers to them.

Q 1:1   What does the term *intermediate sanctions* mean?

Before the intermediate sanctions rules were enacted, the Internal Revenue Service[1] had only two formal options when it found a substantial violation of the law of tax-exempt organizations by a public charity or a social welfare organization: do nothing or revoke the organization's tax exemption. However, these new rules provide the IRS with a third alternative—one that is more potent than doing nothing (including, perhaps, issuing some informal warning) and less draconian than revocation of tax exemption. It is, thus, an *intermediate* sanction.

In the instance of a transaction covered by these rules (Q 1:8), tax sanctions are to be imposed on the disqualified persons (Q 1:23) who improperly benefited from the transaction and perhaps on organization managers (Q 1:25) who participated in the transaction knowing that it was improper.

Q 1:2   What is the effective date of the intermediate sanctions rules?

The effective date of these rules generally is September 14, 1995.[2] However, the sanctions do not apply to any benefits arising from a transaction pursuant to a written contract that was binding on that date and continued in force through the time of the transaction, and the terms of which have not materially changed.[3]

Parties to transactions entered into after September 13, 1995, and before January 1, 1997, were entitled to rely on the rebuttable presumption of reasonableness (Q 1:21) if, within a reasonable period (such as 90 days) after entering into the compensation package, the parties satisfied the criteria that give rise to the presumption. After December 31, 1996, the rebuttable presumption arises only if the criteria are satisfied prior to payment of the compensation (or, to the extent provided by tax regulations, within a reasonable period thereafter).

Q 1:3   When were these rules enacted?

The intermediate sanctions law came into being on enactment of the Taxpayer Bill of Rights 2 (Act). This legislation was signed into law on July 30, 1996.[4]

Q 1:4   What is the legislative history of this legislation?

The Senate, on July 11, 1996, adopted the legislation as passed by the House of Representatives, on April 16, 1996, without change. The House vote was 425–0; the Senate voted by unanimous consent. There is no report of the Senate Finance Committee and no conference report. Thus, the report of the House Committee on Ways and Means, dated March 28, 1996 (House Report),[5] constitutes the totality of the legislative history of the intermediate sanctions rules.

Q 1:5   Have the Treasury Department and the IRS issued guidance as to these rules?

Yes, although the guidance is in proposed form as of late 1998. Proposed regulations were issued on July 30, 1998—on the second anniversary of the signing of the intermediate sanctions legislation (Q 1:3).[6]

COMMENT: The proposed regulations are not nearly as helpful as was hoped. For the most part, they merely restate what is in the statute and the legislative history, or can be found in the comparable rules in the private foundations context. Most of the interesting subtleties are embedded in the examples. Some areas of this body of law where guidance would be appropriate are completely unaddressed by the proposed regulations, such as the criteria for determining whether sales, lending, and rental transactions are reasonable (Q 1:18–Q 1:20). Guidance as to whether compensation is reasonable is skimpy (Q 1:16). Indeed, in one instance, the proposed regulations are in conflict with the legislative history (Q 1:23).

Q 1:6   What types of tax-exempt organizations are involved in these rules?

These sanctions apply with respect to public charities and tax-exempt social welfare organizations. These entities are termed, for this purpose, *applicable tax-exempt organizations.*[7]

Generally, a public charity will have received a determination letter (ruling) from the IRS as to its tax-exempt status (Q 4:4). Social welfare organizations, however, are not required to obtain an IRS ruling in this regard (*id.*). Thus, a social welfare organization is an applicable tax-exempt organization if it has applied for and received recognition of exemption from the IRS, filed an application for recognition of exemption with the IRS, filed an information return (Chapter 11) as a social welfare organization with the IRS, or otherwise held itself out as a social welfare organization.[8]

These entities include any organization described in either of these two categories of exempt organizations at any time during the five-year period ending on the date of the transaction.

NOTE 1:   In a case of a transaction occurring before September 14, 2000, the lookback period begins on September 14, 1995, and ends on the date of the transaction.[9]

CAUTION 1:   This is one aspect of the intermediate sanctions law that should be closely monitored. There is discussion about broadening the concept of applicable tax-exempt organization. The most likely candidates for inclusion are tax-exempt labor organizations and/or business, professional, and trade associations and other business leagues (Chapter 5).

CAUTION 2:   Just because an organization is not an *applicable tax-exempt organization* does not mean that it is not caught up in these rules. This is because an exempt organization can be a disqualified person (Q 1:28).

NOTE 2:   It is not clear as to whether the extent to which governmental entities may be covered by these rules.

Q 1:7   Are there any exceptions to these rules?

No. That is, all public charities and social welfare organizations are applicable tax-exempt organizations. Private foundations (Chapter 9) are not included in this tax regime because a somewhat similar system—that involving self-dealing rules (Q 9:15–9:20)—is applicable to them. Also, a foreign organization that receives substantially all of its support from sources outside the United States is not an applicable tax-exempt organization.[10]

Q 1:8   To what types of transactions do these rules apply?

This tax scheme has as its heart the *excess benefit transaction*.[11] The definition of an *excess benefit transaction* is based on the contract law concept of *consideration*. It generally is any transaction in which an economic benefit is provided by an applicable tax-exempt organization (Q 1:6) directly or indirectly to or for the use of any disqualified person (Q 1:23), if the value of the economic benefit provided by the exempt organization exceeds the value of the consideration (including the performance of services) received for providing the benefit. This type of benefit is known as an *excess benefit*.[12]

Q 1:9   How is *value* measured?

The standard is that of *fair market value*. The fair market value of property, including the right to use property, is the price at which property or the right to use it would change hands between a willing buyer and a willing seller, neither being under any compulsion to buy, sell, or transfer property or the right to use it, and both having reasonable knowledge of relevant facts.[13]

Q 1:10   Can an economic benefit be treated as part of the recipient's compensation?

Yes, but with some qualifications. An economic benefit may not be treated as consideration for the performance of services unless the organization clearly intended and made the payments as compensation for services. Items of this nature include the payment of personal expenses, transfers to or for the benefit of disqualified persons, and non-fair-market-value transactions benefiting these persons.

In determining whether payments or transactions of this nature are in fact forms of compensation, the relevant factors include whether (1) the appropriate decision-making body approved the transfer as compensation in accordance with established procedures and (2) the organization and the recipient reported the transfer (other than in the case of nontaxable fringe benefits) as compensation on relevant returns or other forms. These returns or forms include the organization's annual information return filed with the IRS (Chapter 11), the information return provided by the organization to the recipient (Form W-2 or Form 1099), and the individual's income tax return (Form 1040).[14]

With the exception of nontaxable fringe benefits and certain other types of nontaxable transfers (such as employer-provided health benefits and contributions to qualified pension plans), an organization is not permitted to demonstrate at the time of an IRS audit that it intended to treat economic benefits provided to a disqualified person as compensation for services merely by claiming that the benefits may be viewed as part of the disqualified person's total compensation package. Rather, the organization is required to provide substantiation that is contemporaneous with the transfer of the economic benefits at issue.

Q 1:11   What does the phrase *directly or indirectly* mean?

The phrase *directly or indirectly* means the provision of an economic benefit directly by the organization or indirectly by means of a controlled entity. Thus, an applicable tax-exempt organization cannot avoid involvement in an excess benefit transaction by causing a controlled entity to engage in the transaction.[15]

Q 1:12   What does the phrase *for the use of* mean?

A benefit can be provided to a disqualified person even though the transaction is with a nondisqualified person. A benefit of this nature might be enhancement of reputation, augmentation of goodwill, or some form of marketing advantage.

Q 1:13   Is there any other definition of the term *excess benefit transaction?*

Yes. The term *excess benefit transaction* includes any transaction in which the amount of any economic benefit provided to or for the use of a disqualified person is determined in whole or in part by the revenues of one or more activities of the organization, but only if the transaction results in impermissible private inurement.[16] In this context, the excess benefit is the amount of impermissible private inurement. This category of arrangement is known as a *revenue-sharing transaction.*

A revenue-sharing transaction may constitute an excess benefit transaction regardless of whether the economic benefit provided to the disqualified person exceeds the fair market value of the consideration provided in return if, at any point, it permits a disqualified person to receive additional compensation without providing proportional benefits that contribute to the organization's accomplishment of its exempt purpose. If the economic benefit is provided as compensation for services, relevant facts and circumstances include the relationship between the size of the benefit provided and the quality and quantity of the services provided, as well as the ability of the party receiving the compensation to control the activities generating the revenues on which the compensation is based.[17]

NOTE: Under preexisting law, certain revenue-sharing arrangements have been determined by the IRS to not constitute private inurement. It is to continue to be the case that not all revenue-sharing arrangements are improper private inurement. However, the Department of the Treasury and the IRS are not bound by any particular prior rulings in this area.

Q 1:14   Are any economic benefits disregarded for these purposes?

Yes. One set of disregarded benefits is the payment of reasonable expenses for members of the governing body of an applicable tax-exempt organization to attend meetings of the governing body of the organization. This exclusion does not encompass luxury travel or spousal travel.[18]

An economic benefit provided to a disqualified person that the person receives solely as a member of or volunteer for an organization is disregarded for these purposes, if the benefit is provided to members of the public in exchange for a membership fee of no more than $75 annually. For example, if a disqualified person is also a member of the organization and receives membership benefits such as advance ticket purchases and a discount at the organization's gift shop that would normally be provided in exchange for a membership fee of $75 or less per year, the membership benefit is disregarded.[19]

An economic benefit provided to a disqualified person that the disqualified person receives solely as a member of a charitable class that the applicable tax-exempt organization intends to benefit as part of the accomplishment of the organization's exempt purposes is generally disregarded for these purposes.[20]

Q 1:15 In the context of compensation, how does one determine whether it is excessive?

Existing tax law standards (including those standards established under the law concerning ordinary and necessary business expenses)[21] apply in determining reasonableness of compensation and fair market value. This concept is essentially the same as that in the private foundation context (Q 9:16).

TIP: In this regard, an individual need not necessarily accept reduced compensation merely because he or she renders services to a tax-exempt, as opposed to a taxable, organization.

Compensation that is excessive is a form of excess benefit transaction; the portion that is considered excessive is an excess benefit.

Q 1:16 What are the tax law standards used in determining the reasonableness of compensation?

The criteria that have been fashioned in determining the reasonableness of compensation are the following:

1. Compensation levels paid by similarly situated organizations, both tax-exempt and taxable, for functionally comparable positions

2. The location of the organization, including the availability of similar specialties in the geographic area

3. Written offers from similar institutions competing for the services of the individual involved

4. The background (including experience and education) of the individual involved

5. The need of the organization for the services of a particular individual

6. The amount of time an individual devotes to the position

An additional criterion that intermediate sanctions have brought to this area of the law is whether the compensation was approved by an independent board.

COMMENT: The intermediate sanctions proposed regulations merely extend this guidance: "Compensation for the performance of services is reasonable if it is only such amount as would ordinarily be paid for like services by like enterprises under like circumstances."[22] Given the immense focus on compensation in relation to the excess benefit transaction standard, this meager offering in the regulations is nothing short of irresponsible.

The proposed regulations offer some interesting rules as to what *circumstances* are to be taken into account, particularly in terms of moments in time. The general rule is that the circumstances to be taken into consideration are those existing at the date when the contract for services was made. Where reasonableness of compensation cannot be determined under those circumstances, however, the determination is to be made based on all facts and circumstances, up to and including circumstances as of the date of payment. Here is the best rule of all in this regard: In no event shall circumstances existing at the date when the contract is questioned be considered in making a determination of the reasonableness of compensation.[23]

NOTE: There are court opinions holding that reasonableness can be ascertained taking into account developments occurring after the transaction was consummated. A court opinion issued one week be-

---

fore the proposed regulations were released found that an event that occurred two years after the transaction in question could be taken into account in determining reasonableness.[24]

Q 1:17   What items are included in determining the value of compensation?

Compensation for these purposes means all items of compensation provided by an applicable tax-exempt organization in exchange for the performance of services. These items include (1) all forms of cash and noncash compensation, such as salary, fees, bonuses, and severance payments; (2) all forms of deferred compensation that is earned and vested, whether or not funded, and whether or not paid under a deferred compensation plan that is a qualified plan, but if deferred compensation for services performed in multiple prior years vests in a later year, that compensation is attributed to the years in which the services were performed; (3) the amount of premiums paid for liability or other insurance coverage, as well as any payment or reimbursement by the organization of charges, expenses, fees, or taxes not covered ultimately by the insurance coverage; (4) all other benefits, whether or not included in income for tax purposes, including payments to welfare benefit plans on behalf of the persons being compensated, such as plans providing medical, dental, life insurance, severance pay, and disability benefits, and both taxable and nontaxable fringe benefits (other than certain working condition fringe benefits and de minimis fringe benefits), including expense allowances or reimbursements or foregone interest on loans that the recipient must report as income; and (5) any economic benefit provided by an applicable tax-exempt organization, whether provided directly or through another entity owned, controlled by or affiliated with the organization, whether the other entity is taxable or tax-exempt.[25]

Q 1:18   What are the tax law standards used in determining the reasonableness of rental arrangements?

Where an applicable tax-exempt organization rents property to a disqualified person, it is crucial that the amount of the rent, and the other terms and conditions of the transaction, be reasonable. There should be a lease, a reasonable term, probably a security deposit, and other terms and conditions that are customary with respect to the type of rental arrangement involved.

NOTE: The proposed regulations are silent on this point, other than to define the term *value* in the context of the right to use property (Q 1:9).

Q 1:19   What are the tax law standards used in determining the reasonableness of borrowing arrangements?

Where an applicable tax-exempt organization lends money to a disqualified person, it is crucial that the amount lent, and the other terms and conditions of the transaction, be reasonable. There should be a note, a reasonable term, a reasonable rate of interest, probably some form of security, and other terms and conditions that are customary with respect to the type of lending arrangement involved.

Terms and conditions must also be reasonable where an applicable tax-exempt organization is borrowing money from a disqualified person.

NOTE: The proposed regulations are silent on this point.

Q 1:20   What are the tax law standards used in determining the reasonableness of sales transactions?

Where an applicable tax-exempt organization sells property to a disqualified person, it is crucial that the amount received (Q 1:9), and the other terms and conditions of the transaction, be reasonable. The consideration received by the organization need not be only money; it is permissible for property to be exchanged and for the consideration to be represented by one or more notes.

NOTE: The proposed regulations are silent on this point, other than to define the term *fair market value* (Q 1:9).

Q 1:21   Who has the burden of proof in a dispute with the IRS as to whether a transaction involves an excess benefit?

In an administrative proceeding with the IRS, generally the burden of proof is on the disqualified person who participated in the transaction. However, there is a rebuttable presumption of reasonableness, with respect to a compensation arrangement with a disqualified person.

NOTE: This rebuttable presumption is not a matter of statute (that is, it is not in the Act; it is provided in the House Report. Also, it is reflected in the proposed regulations.

This presumption arises where the arrangement was approved by a board of directors or trustees (or a committee of the board) that

1. Was composed entirely of individuals who do not have a conflict of interest (Q 1:22) with respect to the arrangement,

---

NOTE: This committee may be composed of any individuals permitted under state law to so serve and may act on behalf of the board to the extent permitted by state law.[26] As will be noted, however, committee members who are not board members are likely to be organization managers (Q 1:25).

---

2. Obtained and relied on appropriate data as to comparability prior to making its determination, and
3. Adequately documented the basis for its determination.[27]

As to the first of these criteria, which essentially requires an *independent* board (as opposed to a *captive* board), a reciprocal approval arrangement does not satisfy the independence requirement. This arrangement occurs where an individual approves compensation of a disqualified person and the disqualified person, in turn, approves the individual's compensation (Q 1:22).

As to the second of these criteria, appropriate data includes compensation levels paid by similarly situated organizations, both tax-exempt and taxable, for functionally comparable positions; the location of the organization, including the availability of similar specialties in the geographic area; independent compensation surveys by nationally recognized independent firms; and written offers from similar institutions competing for the services of the disqualified person.[28]

NOTE: There is to be a safe harbor for organizations with annual gross receipts of less than $1 million when reviewing compensation arrangements. This requires data on compensation paid by five comparable organizations in the same or similar communities for similar services. A rolling average based on the three prior tax years may be used to calculate annual gross receipts.[29]

As to the third of these criteria, adequate documentation includes an evaluation of the individual whose compensation was being established, and the basis for determining that the individual's compensation was reasonable in light of that evaluation and data. The organization's written or electronic records must note the terms of the transaction that was approved, the date of approval, the members of the governing body (or committee) who were present during debate on the transaction or arrangement that was approved and those who voted on it, the comparability data obtained and relied on by the governing body (or committee) and how the data was obtained, and the actions taken with respect to consideration of the transaction by anyone who is otherwise a member of the governing body (or committee) but who had a conflict of interest with respect to the transaction or arrangement.[30]

The fact that a state or local legislative or agency body may have authorized or approved a particular compensation package paid to a disqualified person is not determinative of the reasonableness of the compensation paid. Likewise, this type of authorization or approval is not determinative of whether a revenue-sharing transaction violates the private inurement proscription (Q 1:13).

If these three criteria are satisfied, penalty excise taxes can be imposed only if the IRS develops sufficient contrary evidence to rebut the probative value of the evidence put forth by the parties to the transaction. For example, the IRS could establish that the compensation data relied on by the parties was not for functionally comparable positions or that the disqualified person in fact did not substantially perform the responsibilities of the position.

A similar rebuttable presumption arises with respect to the reasonableness of the valuation of property sold or otherwise transferred (or purchased) by an organization to (or from) a disqualified person if the sale or transfer (or purchase) is approved by an independent board that uses appropriate comparability data and adequately documents its determination.

Q 1:22   What does the phrase *conflict of interest* mean?

The proposed regulations define the term by defining what is *not* a conflict of interest. Thus, a member of a governing body (or a committee of it) does not have a conflict or interest with respect to a compensation arrangement or transaction if the member

1. Is not the disqualified person and is not related to any disqualified person participating in or economically benefiting from the compensation arrangement or transaction,

2. Is not in an employment relationship subject to the direction or control of any disqualified person participating in or economically benefiting from the compensation arrangement or transaction,

3. Is not receiving compensation or other payments subject to approval by any disqualified person participating in or economically benefiting from the compensation arrangement or transaction,

4. Has no material financial interest affected by the compensation arrangement or transaction,

5. Does not approve a transaction providing economic benefits to any disqualified person participating in the compensation arrangement or transaction, who in turn has approved or will approve a transaction providing economic benefits to the member.[31]

Q 1:23 What does the term *disqualified person* mean?

The term *disqualified person*, in this context, means

1. Any person who was, at any time during the five-year period ending on the date of the excess benefit transaction involved, in a position to exercise substantial influence over the affairs of the applicable tax-exempt organization involved (Q 1:6) (whether by virtue of being an organization manager or otherwise),

---

NOTE: If the five-year period ending on the date of the transaction would have begun on or before September 13, 1995, the period begins on September 14, 1995, and ends on the date of the transaction.[32]

---

2. A member of the family of an individual described in the preceding category, and

3. An entity in which individuals described in the preceding two categories own more than 35 percent of an interest.[33]

Q 1:24 What is the scope of this *substantial influence* rule?

An individual is in a position to exercise substantial influence over the affairs of an organization if he or she, individually or with others,

---

serves as the president, chief executive officer, or chief operating officer of the organization. An individual serves in one of these capacities, regardless of title, if he or she has or shares ultimate responsibility for implementing the decisions of the governing body or supervising the management, administration, or operation of the organization.[34]

An individual also is in this position if he or she, independently or with others, serves as treasurer or chief financial officer of the organization. An individual serves in one of these capacities, regardless of title, if he or she has or shares ultimate responsibility for managing the organization's financial assets and has or shares authority to sign drafts or direct the signing of drafts, or authorize electronic transfer of funds, from the organization's bank account(s).[35]

A person can be in a position to exercise substantial influence over a tax-exempt organization despite the fact that the person is not an employee of (and does not receive any compensation directly from) a tax-exempt organization but is formally an employee of (and is directly compensated by) a subsidiary—including a taxable subsidiary—controlled by the parent tax-exempt organization.

NOTE: There is a conflict between the legislative history of these rules (Q 1:4) and the proposed regulations (Q 1:5). The legislative history states that an individual having the title of *trustee, director,* or *officer* does not automatically have status as a disqualified person. The proposed regulations, however, provide that persons having substantial influence include any individual serving on the governing body of the organization who is entitled to vote on matters over which the governing body has authority.[36]

TIP: Although it has been the view of the IRS that all physicians who are on the medical staff of a hospital or similar organization are insiders for purposes of the private inurement proscription,[37] a physician is a disqualified person under the intermediate sanctions rules only where he or she is in a position to exercise substantial influence over the affairs of the organization.

There are some categories of persons who are deemed to not be in a position to exercise substantial influence. One is any other public charity.[38] Another is an employee of an applicable tax-exempt organization who receives economic benefits of less than the amount of compensation referenced for a highly compensated employee, is not a member of the family of a disqualified person (Q 1:26), is not an individual referenced above as considered to have this influence, and is not a substantial contributor to the organization.[39]

A person who has managerial control over a discrete segment of an organization may be in a position to exercise substantial influence over the affairs of the entire organization.[40]

Facts and circumstances that tend to show the requisite substantial influence include the fact that the person founded the organization; is a substantial contributor to the organization; receives compensation based on revenues derived from activities of the organization that the person controls; has authority to control or determine a significant portion of the organization's capital expenditures, operating budget, or compensation for employees; has managerial authority or serves as a key advisor to a person with managerial authority; or owns a controlling interest in a corporation, partnership, or trust that is a disqualified person.[41]

Facts and circumstances that tend to show an absence of substantial influence are where the person has taken a bona fide vow of poverty as an employee, agent, or on behalf of a religious organization; the person is an independent contractor (such as a lawyer, accountant, or investment manager or advisor), acting in that capacity, unless the person is acting in that capacity with respect to a transaction from which the person might economically benefit either directly or indirectly (aside from fees received for the professional services rendered); and any preferential treatment a person receives based on the size of that person's contribution is also offered to any other contributor making a comparable contribution as part of a solicitation intended to attract a substantial number of contributions.[42]

Q 1:25   What does the term *organization manager* mean?

An *organization manager* is a trustee, director, or officer of an applicable tax-exempt organization, as well as an individual having powers or responsibilities similar to those of trustees, directors, or officers of the organization, regardless of title.[43]

An individual is considered an *officer* of an organization if he or she (1) is specifically so designated under the articles of incorporation, bylaws, or other organizing documents of the organization or (2) regularly exercises general authority to make administrative or policy decisions on behalf of the organization. An individual who has authority merely to recommend particular administrative or policy decisions, but not to implement them without approval of a superior, is not an officer.[44]

NOTE: Independent contractors, acting in a capacity as lawyers, accountants, and investment managers and advisors, are not officers.[45]

COMMENT: Principles similar to those under the law pertaining to private foundations are to be followed in determining who is an organization manager (Q 9:5).

An individual who is not a trustee, director, or officer, and yet serves on a committee of the governing body of an applicable tax-exempt organization that is invoking the rebuttable presumption of reasonableness (Q 1:21) based on the committee's actions, is an organization manager for these purposes.[46]

Q 1:26   What does the term *member of the family* mean?

The term *member of the family* is defined as constituting the following:

1. Spouses, ancestors, children, grandchildren, great-grandchildren, and the spouses of children, grandchildren, and great-grandchildren—namely, those individuals so classified under the private foundation rules, and
2. The brothers and sisters (whether by the whole or half blood) of the individual and their spouses.[47]

NOTE: Thus, this term is defined more broadly in the public charity setting than is the case with private foundations (Q 9:7).

Q 1:27   What is the definition of a *controlled entity*?

The entities that are disqualified persons because one or more disqualified persons own more than a 35 percent interest in them are termed *35 percent controlled entities*.[48] They are

1. Corporations in which one or more disqualified persons own more than 35 percent of the total combined voting power,
2. Partnerships in which one or more disqualified persons own more than 35 percent of the profits interest, and
3. Trusts or estates in which one or more disqualified persons own more than 35 percent of the beneficial interest.

NOTE: The term *combined voting power* includes voting power represented by holdings of voting stock, actual or constructive, but does not include voting rights held only as a director or trustee. This rule is identical to that in the private foundation context (Q 9:8–9:10).

In general, constructive ownership rules apply for purposes of determining what are 35 percent controlled entities.[49]

Q 1:28 Can a tax-exempt organization be a disqualified person?

Yes. A tax-exempt organization, other than a public charity (Q 1:6), can be a disqualified person. All that is required is that an exempt organization be in a position to exercise substantial influence over the affairs of the applicable tax-exempt organization involved (Q 1:23–Q 1:24).

For example, in an instance of an association (Chapter 5) with a related foundation, the association can be a disqualified person with respect to the foundation. Likewise, a social welfare organization (Chapter 6) with a related educational foundation can be a disqualified person with respect to that foundation.

NOTE: Other than providing that a public charity cannot be a disqualified person, the proposed regulations are silent as to when or whether any other type of tax-exempt organization can be a disqualified person.

Q 1:29 What are the sanctions?

The intermediate sanctions themselves are in the form of tax penalties.[50]

A disqualified person who benefited from an excess benefit transaction is subject to and must pay an initial excise tax equal to 25 percent of the amount of the excess benefit. Again, the excess benefit is the amount by which a transaction differs from fair market value, the amount of compensation exceeding reasonable compensation, or (pursuant to tax regulations) the amount of impermissible private inurement resulting from a transaction based on the organization's gross or net income (Q 1:13).

NOTE: In addition, the matter must be rectified—corrected—by a return of the excess benefit, plus additional compensation, to the applicable tax-exempt organization (Q 1:30).

An organization manager who participated (Q 1:31) in an excess benefit transaction, knowing (Q 1:32) that it was this type of a transaction, is subject to and must pay an initial excise tax of 10 percent of the excess benefit (subject to a maximum amount of tax of $10,000), where an initial tax is imposed on a disqualified person. The initial tax is not imposed where the participation in the transaction was not willful (Q 1:33) and was due to reasonable cause (Q 1:34).

An additional excise tax may be imposed on a disqualified person where the initial tax was imposed and if there was no correction of the excess benefit transaction within a specified time period. This time period is the *taxable period*, which means—with respect to an excess benefit transaction—the period beginning with the date on which the transaction occurred and ending on the earlier of

1. The date of mailing of a notice of deficiency with respect to the initial tax, or
2. The date on which the initial tax is assessed.

In this situation, the disqualified person would be subject to and must pay a tax equal to 200 percent of the excess benefit involved.

Q 1:30   What does the term *correction* mean?

The term *correction* means undoing the excess benefit to the extent possible and taking any additional measures necessary to place the organization in a financial position not worse than that in which it would be if the disqualified person had been dealing under the highest fiduciary standards.[51]

Correction of the excess benefit occurs if the disqualified person repays the applicable tax-exempt organization an amount of money equal to the excess benefit, plus any additional amount needed to compensate the organization for the loss of the use of the money or other property during the period commencing on the date of the excess benefit transaction and ending on the date the excess benefit is corrected. Correction may also be accomplished, in certain circumstances, by returning property to the organization and taking any additional steps necessary to make the organization whole.[52]

NOTE: The proposed regulations do not state what these "certain circumstances" might be nor do they reveal what the "additional steps" might entail.

Q 1:31   What does the term *participation* mean?

The term *participation* includes silence or inaction on the part of an organization manager where he or she is under a duty to speak or act, as well as any affirmative action by the manager. An organization manager, however, will not be considered to have participated in an excess benefit transaction where the manager has opposed the transaction in a manner consistent with the fulfillment of the manager's responsibilities to the applicable tax-exempt organization.[53]

Q 1:32   What does the term *knowing* mean?

A person participates (Q 1:31) in a transaction, *knowing* that it is an excess benefit transaction, only if the person (1) has actual knowledge of sufficient facts so that, based solely on those facts, the transaction would be an excess benefit transaction, (2) is aware that the act under these circumstances may violate the excess benefit transactions rules, and (3) negligently fails to make reasonable attempts to ascertain whether the transaction is an excess benefit transaction, or the person is in fact aware that it is an excess benefit transaction.[54]

Knowing does not mean having reason to know. Evidence tending to show, however, that a person has reason to know of a particular fact or particular rule is relevant in determining whether the person had actual knowledge of the fact or rule. For example, evidence tending to show that a person has reason to know of sufficient facts so that, based solely on those facts, a transaction would be an excess benefit transaction is relevant in determining whether the person has actual knowledge of the facts.[55]

Q 1:33   What does the term *willful* mean?

Participation in a transaction by an organization manager is willful if it is voluntary, conscious, and intentional. No motive to avoid the restrictions of the law or the incurrence of any tax is necessary to make the participation willful. Participation by an organization manager, however, is not willful if the manager does not know (Q 1:32) that the transaction in which the manager is participating is an excess benefit transaction.[56]

Q 1:34   What does the term *reasonable cause* mean?

An organization manager's participation is due to *reasonable cause* if the manager has exercised his or her responsibility on behalf of the organization with ordinary business care and prudence.[57]

TIP: If a person, after full disclosure of the factual situation to a lawyer (including in-house counsel), relies on the advice of the lawyer—expressed in a reasoned written legal opinion—that a transaction is not an excess benefit transaction, the person's participation in the transaction will ordinarily not be considered knowing or willful and will ordinarily be considered due to reasonable cause, even if the transaction is subsequently held to be an excess benefit transaction. The absence of advice of legal counsel with respect to an act does not, by itself, give rise to an inference that a person participated in the act knowingly, willfully, or without reasonable cause.[58]

CAUTION: A written legal opinion is *reasoned* so long as it addresses the facts and applicable law. An opinion is not reasoned if it does nothing more than recite the facts and state a conclusion.[59]

Q 1:35   Can there be joint liability for these taxes?

Yes. If more than one organization manager or other disqualified person is liable for an excise tax, then all of these persons are jointly and severally liable for the tax.[60]

Q 1:36   If the executive of a charity or social welfare organization is receiving compensation that he or she believes to be unreasonable, should the executive voluntarily reduce the compensation or wait to see whether the IRS raises the issue?

An executive in this position should not rely on his or her "gut feelings" about the reasonableness of the compensation. The first step an individual in this position should take is to determine whether the compensation arrangement is even subject to these rules. If the compensation is set by a pre-1995 binding unaltered contract, the excess benefit transaction rules do not apply with respect to it (Q 1:2).

CAUTION: Of course, the payment of excessive compensation in these circumstances could still amount to private inurement (Q 1:45).

If these rules do apply, the second step is to have the organization procure an independent opinion on the subject. It may turn out that the executive was wrong in his or her judgment. However, if it develops that the compensation is in fact excessive, the executive should work with the organization's board of directors in causing the salary to be lowered to the highest appropriate amount, so as to avoid future excess benefit transactions.

It is not a good idea to wait to see what the IRS may do. This is a self-reporting system (Q 1:40). A delay will involve interest and perhaps penalties should the IRS become aware of the matter. Thus, the prudent approach, having reduced the compensation, is to pay the tax and correct the past transgression(s) by correcting (Q 1:30) the situation. This would be done by returning the excess benefit, plus a suitable amount of interest (Q 1:30), for the year(s) involved to the employer organization.

CAUTION: If the board is notified of this situation by the executive and does nothing, the board members could be personally liable for taxes (Q 1:29).

Q 1:37   If the IRS raises questions about an executive's compensation, should the executive voluntarily reduce his or her compensation in order to minimize the risk of imposition of the sanctions?

That usually would be a very bad idea. Assuming the compensation is subject to these rules (Q 1:2), a reduction in compensation in the face of an IRS inquiry would be an admission that the compensation has been too high. The better approach is to work with the board of directors of the employer organization to obtain outside advice and then proceed from there (Q 1:36).

If all else fails and the compensation is found to be excessive, the IRS may be approached to see whether there is any basis for abatement on the ground of reasonable cause (Q 1:34).

Q 1:38   If the board of directors approves an employment contract with an executive and later determines that the compensation provided in the contract is excessive, what steps, if any, should the board take prior to the expiration of the contract?

There is a lot here for the board to do and consider. First step: see whether the contract is sheltered by the effective date rules (Q 1:2). If it is, that is the end of the matter (although it could still amount to private inurement). If it is not, then the board should seek an outside evaluation of the compensation level and determine the portion of it (if any) that is considered excessive.

A contract that is covered by the intermediate sanctions rules and embodies unreasonable compensation is nonetheless a binding contract. Thus, unless there is a provision in the agreement that allows it—an excellent idea, by the way—the board cannot unilaterally adjust the compensation level. (That would be a breach of contract.) Rather, the board should work with the individual—who, after all, will bear the brunt of the penalties (Q 1:29)—and proceed as discussed earlier (Q 1:36).

NOTE: If the excess benefit transaction consists of the payment of compensation for services under a contract that has not been completed, termination of the employment or independent contractor relationship between the organization and the disqualified person is *not* required in order to correct.[61]

Q 1:39   Is there any relief from this tax scheme? Any basis for being excused from these penalties?

Yes, there is a limited form of relief. Congress has provided the IRS with the authority to abate the intermediate sanctions excise tax in certain circumstances, principally where a taxable event was due to reasonable cause and not to willful neglect, and the transaction at issue was corrected within the specified taxable period (Q 1:30, Q 1:33, Q:34).[62]

NOTE: There was a mistake in the original statute, owing to the fact that the term *first tier tax* was defined twice—and, in one instance, incorrectly. This temporarily precluded the IRS from having abatement authority. However, this matter was rectified by the technical corrections portion of the Taxpayer Relief Act of 1997.

Q 1:40   How are these taxes reported and paid?

Under the law in existence prior to the enactment of intermediate sanctions, charitable organizations and other persons liable for certain excise taxes must file returns by which the taxes due are calculated and reported. These taxes are those imposed on public charities for excessive lobbying and for political campaign activities, and on private foundations and/or other persons for a wide range of impermissible activities. These returns are on Form 4720.

In general, returns on Form 4720 for a disqualified person or orga-nization manager liable for an excess benefit transaction tax must be filed on or before the 15th day of the fifth month following the close of that person's tax year.

Q 1:41   Can an organization reimburse a disqualified person for these taxes?

Yes. However, any reimbursements by an applicable tax-exempt organi-zation of excise tax liability are treated as an excess benefit unless they are included in the disqualified person's compensation during the year in which the reimbursement is made. (This rule is consistent with that noted earlier (Q 1:10), which is that payments of personal expenses and other benefits to or for the benefit of disqualified persons are treated as compensation only if it is clear that the organization intended and made the payments as compensation for services.) The total compensation package, including the amount of any reimbursement, is subject to the requirement of reasonableness.[63]

Q 1:42   Can an organization purchase insurance for a disqualified per-son to provide coverage for these taxes?

Yes. But, again (Q 1:0), the payment by an applicable tax-exempt organi-zation of premiums for an insurance policy providing liability insurance to a disqualified person for excess benefit taxes is an excess benefit transaction unless the premiums are treated as part of the compensa-tion paid to the disqualified person and the total compensation (includ-ing premiums) is reasonable.[64]

Q 1:43   Does the payment of an intermediate sanctions tax have any impact directly on a tax-exempt organization?

There are two ways in which the payment of an intermediate sanc-tions tax can have an impact on a tax-exempt organization. One would occur when the payment of the tax triggers a reimbursement by the organization or coverage under an insurance policy that it has pur-chased (Q 1:41, 1:42).

The other way an impact can occur arises from the fact that applic-able tax-exempt organizations are required to disclose on their annual information returns (Chapters 11 and 12) the amount of the excise tax penalties paid with respect to excess benefit transactions, the nature of the activity, and the parties involved.

Q 1:44   Is there a limitations period, after which these taxes cannot be imposed?

Yes. A three-year statute of limitations applies, except in the case of fraud.[65]

Q 1:45   Do intermediate sanctions take precedence over other sanctions used by the IRS?

Basically, yes. Intermediate sanctions may be imposed by the IRS in lieu of or in addition to revocation of an organization's tax-exempt status.[66] In general, these intermediate sanctions are to be the sole sanction imposed in those cases in which the excess benefit does not rise to a level where it calls into question whether, on the whole, the organization functions as a charitable or social welfare organization.

In practice, the revocation of tax-exempt status, with or without the imposition of these excise taxes, is to occur only when the organization no longer operates as a charitable or social welfare organization, as the case may be. Existing law principles apply in determining whether an organization no longer operates as an exempt organization. For example, in the case of a charitable organization, that would occur in a year, or as of a year, the entity was involved in a transaction constituting a substantial amount of private inurement.

Q 1:46   Won't the private inurement doctrine have an impact on definitions of excess benefit transactions?

Absolutely. The concepts of private inurement and excess benefit transaction are much the same. Thus, a great amount of existing law as to what constitutes private inurement will be applied in determining what amounts to excess benefit transactions. Although this will be the case particularly with respect to compensation issues, it will also be true in the realms of lending, borrowing, and sales arrangements, and the like. Indeed, some of this law is specifically said by the legislative history to be predicated on the private inurement doctrine, such as the rules pertaining to revenue-sharing transactions (Q 1:13).

Q 1:47   Won't the private foundation rules as to self-dealing have a similar impact?

No question about it. Much of what the law terms self-dealing in the foundation context will be used in ascertaining what are excess benefit transactions. The definition of self-dealing, although more specific, has generated a large amount of law (including private letter rulings and the like), which undoubtedly will be used in shaping the contours of the concept of the excess benefit transaction. Moreover, the law underlying many of the private foundation terms—such as the definition of *disqualified person* (Q 1:23), transactions for the benefit of disqualified persons (Q 1:8), meaning of *organization manager* (Q 1:25), meaning of *member of the family* (Q 1:26), and the process of correction (Q 1:30)—is being followed in the development of the law of intermediate sanctions.

Q 1:48   Won't determinations as to what is an excess benefit shape the law of private inurement and self-dealing?

Very much so. Just as those two terms are influencing the meaning of excess benefit transaction (Q 1:8–Q 1:14), as the coming months bring findings of what is an excess benefit transaction, these determinations will in turn shape the meaning of private inurement and self-dealing. Thus, each of these three terms will be constantly influencing the reach and content of the other two. To a lesser degree, the private benefit doctrine will also be affected by this ongoing confluence of these various bodies of law.

CHAPTER 2

Competition and Commerciality

The most troublesome aspect of the operations of nonprofit organizations today, from the standpoint of the law, is the extent to which these activities compete with, or are perceived as competing with, the undertakings of for-profit organizations. Commercial activities by nonprofit organizations are cast as forms of unfair competition with for-profit organizations. In our complex society, competition of this type is inevitable. But this practice often tarnishes the view of nonprofit organizations in the eyes of many, including those who formulate federal tax law and policy.

The concepts of competition and commerciality in the legal context are confusing. There is very little statutory law on the point; likewise, there is almost nothing about the subject in the tax regulations. What law there is—and it is growing—is mostly found in court opinions and IRS private letter rulings.

Here are the questions most frequently asked by clients about this matter of competition and commerciality—and the answers to them.

COMPETITION

Q 2:1   Just what is this matter of nonprofit/for-profit competition all about?

Like any civil society, the United States has three basic sectors: a for-profit, commercial, business sector; a nonprofit sector; and a governmental sector. A healthy democratic society requires the presence of these three sectors, and that each of them function to the fullest extent within suitable bounds. Personal freedoms are enhanced and maintained to the extent of the vibrancy of these sectors.

By definition and necessity, this tripartite societal structure produces friction: the sectors clash. There is ongoing struggle over what the "suitable boundaries" of the sectors are. The resulting fights are over what functions belong in which sector. A most cursory of glances at what is occurring with respect to the U.S. health care delivery system illustrates the extent to which this battle can be waged.

For the most part, these are policy determinations to be resolved by lawmakers (those in all three branches of government). That is, there is very little in the way of formal legal constraints in this setting, other than those against transgressing the bounds of federal public policy, the dictates of constitutional law principles, or perhaps state law rules. Although this is the way the system is supposed to work, these struggles generate problems for nonprofit organizations.

It is a general precept that nonprofit organizations are supposed to remain "in their place." In many respects, the U.S. economic system is still based on principles of capitalism. This means that for-profit organizations are generally treated more favorably, as to this matter of clashes between the sectors, than nonprofit organizations. That is, it is generally thought to be inappropriate for nonprofit organizations to engage in activities that are engaged in by for-profit organizations. There is a preference here: if for-profits do it, nonprofits should not do it.

Conceptually, according to this mode of thinking, nonprofit organizations are not supposed to undertake activities that are being performed by for-profit organizations. Likewise, if for-profit organizations enter a field previously unoccupied by them but traditionally the province of nonprofit organizations, the nonprofits are expected to abandon the field. In general, then, nonprofit entities—and this is particularly the case with charitable organizations—are often expected to engage only in functions conceded to them by the for-profit sector.

Q 2:2   What is the problem with nonprofit/for-profit competition?

It is basically one of economics. Almost always, the nonprofit organization is tax-exempt. This means that taxes are not a part of the entity's costs of *doing business*. Assuming all other expenses are the same as that of the for-profit counterpart, the tax-exempt nonprofit entity can engage in the competitive activity with a lower cost of operations. To acquire customers and increase market share, a nonprofit organization can pass the decreased cost of operation along to customers in the form of lower prices. What can result is a nonprofit organization and a for-profit organization performing the same activity for public consumption (sale of a good or performance of a service), with the nonprofit entity charging a lower price.

Usually, the for-profit critics of competition involving nonprofit organizations charge *unfair* competition. When that word is used, the complainants are asserting that the pricing policies of nonprofit organizations are undercutting the sales of items by for-profit organizations. This use of exempt status to lower prices in competing with for-profits is at the heart of the complaints in this context about (unfair) competition.

A secondary complaint is based on the thought that a consumer, given the choice to purchase a good or service from a nonprofit entity or a for-profit entity, will select the former. This view holds that the consumer is more comfortable purchasing an item from a nonprofit organization; there seems to be a greater element of trust. This phenomenon—the grounds for assertions that nonprofit organizations ought not to be undertaking certain endeavors *at all*—is known as the *halo effect.*

Q 2:3   How common is this form of competition?

It is rather common, and the practice is growing. There are essentially two manifestations of competition between nonprofit and for-profit entities.

One arises where the very essence of what the nonprofit organization does is competitive with for-profit organizations. A clear example of this is, as noted, found in the health care field, where some hospitals and other forms of health care providers are nonprofit and some are for-profit (proprietary entities). Predictably, this is generating much debate as to whether nonprofit hospitals should remain tax-exempt at all or be exempt to a much more limited extent. Other areas in which there are counterparts in both sectors are schools, publishing entities, various types of consulting groups, and financial institutions.

NOTE: An example of this issue is the tax-exempt credit union.[1] There is an ongoing battle as to whether such entities should remain exempt, in view of the fact that many of their operations are competitive with for-profit financial institutions. These days, Congress is being lobbied hard on the subject, with the National Credit Union Administration arguing for the exemption and the American Bankers Association contending for its repeal. This dispute was studied by the Congressional Research Service, which observed that "many believe that an economically neutral tax system requires that financial institutions engaged in similar activities should have the same tax treatment."[2]

COMMENT: Another comparable debate has, so far, led to an op-posite conclusion. This concerns tax exemption for fraternal benefi-ciary associations.[3] A report from the Department of the Treasury concluded that the insurance products offered by these organiza-tions are essentially the same as those provided by commercial in-surers; it observed that the large fraternal beneficiary societies "conduct their insurance operations in a manner similar to com-mercial insurers." However, the report dismissed this commerciality, stating that these societies "do not use their exemption to com-pete unfairly with commercial insurers in terms of price or to operate inefficiently."[4]

Most of the criticism in this area falls, however, in the realm of the other manifestation of competition. This is where the nonprofit organi-zation is substantially engaging in tax-exempt (usually noncompeti-tive) activities, but is selectively engaging in one or more competitive functions. One of the most controversial contemporary illustrations of this point—which will be discussed more fully in another setting (Q 2:5)—is the matter of travel tours. The travel industry is incensed be-cause of the competitive tours being packaged and sold by exempt en-tities such as universities, colleges, alumni associations, and similar organizations, as educational experiences. Other examples are dis-cussed later (Q 2:5).

Q 2:4   Has Congress responded to these complaints about unfair com-petition?

Yes. The principal response has been formulation of the unrelated busi-ness income rules.[5] Congress enacted these rules almost 50 years ago. A major component of the Revenue Act of 1950, the rules were devised specifically to eliminate unfair competition between nonprofit and for-profit organizations.

This was done, or thought to be done, by placing the unrelated business activities of exempt organizations on the same tax basis as those conducted by for-profit organizations, where the two are in com-petition. The essence of this body of law is to separate the income of a tax-exempt organization into two categories: (1) income from related business and (2) income from unrelated business. The rationale is that by taxing the income from unrelated business, the pricing differential that can lead to unfair competition is removed. This is known as *level-ing the playing field*.

COMMENT: One wag, sympathetic with the nonprofit sector in this regard, once said that the for-profits are not interested in seeing the playing field leveled. Rather, it was noted, the for-profits do not want the nonprofits to even be *on* the field.

However, the existence or nonexistence of competition is not a statutory requirement for there to be unrelated business. Nonetheless, some courts place considerable emphasis on the factor of competition when assessing whether an undertaking is an unrelated business. This can also be the case when eligibility for tax-exempt status is under consideration.

NOTE: Some courts have rejected the thought that the unrelated business rules were enacted purely to eliminate this form of competition. Thus, one court wrote that "while the equalization of competition between taxable and tax-exempt entities was a major goal of the unrelated business income tax, it was by no means the statute's sole objective."[6] Another court observed that "although Congress enacted the . . . unrelated business income rules to eliminate a perceived form of unfair competition, that aim existed as a corollary to the larger goals of producing revenue and achieving equity in the tax system."[7]

There has also been some legislative activity in connection with commercial undertakings. The principal illustration of this approach was the decision by Congress in 1986 to eliminate the tax exemption for most prepaid health care plans, such as those offered by Blue Cross and Blue Shield organizations (Q 2:14). Moreover, Congress allowed the tax-exempt status of prepaid group legal plans[8] to expire in 1992.

Q 2:5   What are some of the contemporary illustrations of issues in this area of competition?

There are many of them. Most arise in the health care delivery field. As noted (Q 2:3), there is competition between nonprofit and for-profit hospitals, as well as other health care entities such as health maintenance organizations, homes for the aged, and rehabilitation facilities. More often, however, rather than overall operations, there are specific activities of a health care provider that are regarded as competitive.

An example is the sale of pharmaceuticals. If a nonprofit hospital sells pharmaceuticals to its patients, that is considered a related (nontaxable) business, even though it may be an activity competitive with for-profit pharmacies. Yet, where a nonprofit hospital sells pharmaceuticals to private patients of physicians who have offices in a medical building owned by the hospital, or sells them to members of the general public, the activity is generally regarded as an unrelated (taxable) business. These latter types of sales are competitive with commercial pharmacies.[9]

Another example is diagnostic laboratory testing services provided by nonprofit hospitals to physicians in their private practice. The general rule is that services of this nature constitute unrelated business activities where they are otherwise available in the community.[10] These services are competitive with commercial laboratories that test specimens from private office patients of the hospitals' staff physicians. However, where there are unique circumstances, such as situations in which other laboratories are not available within a reasonable distance from the area served by the hospital or are inadequate to conduct tests needed by nonpatients of the hospital, the laboratory testing services are related businesses.[11]

Another illustration of this type of competitiveness is the operation of health clubs and fitness centers by nonprofit hospitals. Of course, there are commercial entities of this nature. Where the fees for use of these facilities are sufficiently high to restrict their use to limited segments of the community, the operations are nonexempt ones or unrelated businesses, as being competitive with commercial health clubs. In contrast, if a health club or similar facility provides community-wide benefits or advances education in a substantial manner, the activity is a related business.[12]

There are commercial enterprises that maintain physical rehabilitation programs. Thus, a nonprofit organization doing the same thing may not be tax-exempt or may be operating an unrelated business. For example, in the context of life-style rehabilitation programs, the IRS ruled that the operation of a miniature golf course by a nonprofit organization, the purpose of which was the advancement of the welfare of young people, was an unrelated business because the course was operated commercially, that is, in a competitive manner.[13] Yet the IRS also ruled that a nonprofit organization, operating to improve the life of abused and otherwise disadvantaged children by means of the sport of golf, did not conduct an unrelated activity in the operation of a golf course inasmuch as the opportunity to socialize and master skills through the playing of golf was found to be "essential to the building of self-esteem and the ultimate rehabilitation of the young people" by means of the organization's programs.[14]

The higher education setting also provides examples of competition between nonprofit and for-profit organizations. As an illustration, the commercial travel industry is, of course, a provider of tours. Yet universities, colleges, and alumni and alumnae associations also offer tours, usually as an educational experience. The IRS endeavors to differentiate between tours that are related activities and those that are unrelated (competitive) because they are primarily social, recreational, or other forms of vacation opportunities.[15]

Schools, colleges, and universities (and other types of nonprofit organizations) frequently receive payments from corporations. These institutions wish to treat these corporate sponsorships as contributions. However, they also want to recognize these sponsors as donors. The difficulty is that when they say something commendatory about the sponsor, particularly as to the quality or pricing of its goods or services, the purported recognition may in fact be advertising. Generally, advertising by a nonprofit, tax-exempt organization is considered an exploitation of exempt resources. The provision of advertising services is generally a commercial, competitive activity.[16]

Other types of nonprofit organizations provide further illustrations of this point. For example, the sale of items to the public by a nonprofit museum from its gift shop is generally a related business on the grounds that the items sold generate interest in the museum's collection and promote visitation to it. However, that rationale can break down when items are sold nationally or even internationally by catalog or when the items that are sold are used in a utilitarian manner (such as furniture). Trade associations often sell items to members that they use in their trade (such as tools and manuals). These and other forms of sales activity by nonprofit organizations are often seen as enterprises that are competitive with for-profit organizations.[17]

Q 2:6   Is the law successful in eliminating forms of this type of competition?

Sometimes, but certainly not entirely. The IRS does the best it can in enforcing the law in this area. But the agency has three basic problems in this regard. First, the law is often very vague. Second, on many occasions when the IRS makes a determination that an activity is a nonexempt function or an unrelated business, the nonprofit organizations involved are able to persuade Congress to create statutory law overriding the IRS's position. This, in turn, leads to an expansion of the Internal Revenue Code and the need for more interpretation.[18] Third, the IRS today lacks the funds and personnel to effectively police the competitive and commercial activities of nonprofit organizations.

An often underappreciated phenomenon is that, in many respects, the law is changing. What may have been perceived as an unrelated activity in 1950 is considered a related activity 50 years later. This means that when the for-profit community alleges unfair competition, it is often related business activities, not unrelated ones, that are in dispute.

For example, universities, colleges, and schools can operate bookstores that sell many items that are also sold in commercial establishments. The same can be said for hospitals that maintain gift shops and food service operations. Some of the items are sold clearly in advancement of exempt purposes, such as the books a college sells that are required in its courses. However, a university bookstore or hospital gift shop can sell clothing, sundry items, flowers, and the like without having those activities treated as unrelated businesses. Nonetheless, these activities are in competition with for-profit establishments, often small businesses.

Some of this sales activity is sheltered by the convenience doctrine.

EXPLANATION: The convenience doctrine is a rule of law that states that a business conducted by a charitable or educational organization for the convenience of its patients or students is not taxable as an unrelated business.[19] This doctrine is thus of great utility to schools, colleges, universities, and hospitals.

Some of these activities, however, are considered exempt functions. Thus, for example, a college can sell sports clothing, coffee cups, and toilet paper, all bearing the institution's name and logo, and not pay any tax on the net proceeds because the sale of these items is an exempt function, in that it promotes interest in the college among the student body. Likewise, a hospital can sell floral arrangements and other gift items without paying tax on the resulting net income because the sale of these items is an exempt function, in that the health of the patients is promoted by virtue of visits by friends and family bearing gifts. Yet the sale of each of these categories of goods is competitive with for-profit businesses.

COMMENT: The proprietor of a floral shop across the street from a nonprofit hospital's gift shop is not comforted by these rationales, nor is the owner of a computer sales franchise next door to a university bookstore that is selling the same hardware and software items because computer usage is mandated by the university's professors.

A frequently overlooked aspect of this matter of competition between nonprofit and for-profit entities is the conduct of businesses that are regarded as nontaxable undertakings (sometimes even as related activities) because they are done in the name of fund-raising. However, the simple application of the term *fund-raising* to an activity does not convert it from a taxable to a nontaxable activity.

Special event fund-raising involves many competitive functions: sports tournaments, theater outings, concerts, dances, dinners, auctions, bake sales, car washes, and more. Although these activities are by no means inherently charitable, they usually escape taxation on the ground that they are not regularly carried on.[20]

CAUTION: Often, an organization is of the belief that a fund-raising event is not regularly carried on because it is conducted over a few-day period. Yet the organization may spend months preparing for the event. Although the approach has been rejected in the courts to date, the IRS is of the view that *preparatory time* should be taken into account in determining regularity.[21] When this is done, of course, a business that seemingly occupies only a short period of time can be transformed into one occupying a substantial portion of a year—and one that is taxable.

There are some statutory exceptions for fund-raising events. Excluded from taxation are sales of items that were donated to the exempt organization (a special rule very helpful to nonprofit thrift shops and organizations that conduct auctions on a regular basis),[22] businesses conducted substantially by volunteers,[23] qualified sponsorship payments,[24] use of premiums,[25] qualifying entertainment activities,[26] certain bingo games,[27] and certain rentals of mailing lists.[28] In some instances, revenue from fund-raising activities can be protected from taxation by structuring it as royalty revenue.[29]

Consequently, there are many opportunities under current law for nonprofit organizations to compete with for-profit ones, and not pay any income tax on the resulting revenue.

Q 2:7   Will this situation change?

Yes, although the timing of any significant change is impossible to predict. Because of pressure from small business lobbyists and the ongoing search for sources of revenue for the federal government, as well as some tax policy considerations, Congress is likely to legislate new rules as to qualification for exemption and unrelated income taxation.

COMMENT: It was noted earlier (Q 2:4) that the original unrelated business income rules were created for the purposes of "producing revenue and achieving equity in the tax system." Only when there is consensus in Congress again as to ways to achieve those goals in the contemporary setting will there be comprehensive reform of the law defining unrelated business activity.

There is persistent talk of hearings before the House Subcommittee on Oversight on this subject. Areas of inquiry will undoubtedly include travel tours, affinity cards, gambling, and use of the royalty exception. But these changes, if they occur, are far from imminent. In part, this is because the nonprofit sector has been very effective in warding off stringent reforms in this area.

COMMERCIALITY

Q 2:8   How does this matter of competition relate to commerciality?

To date, rather awkwardly. One of the greatest oddities in the law of tax-exempt organizations is that there is a two-track system of law operating in this area. There are the unrelated business income rules that, as noted, were fashioned largely in response to the thought that competition between nonprofit, tax-exempt and for-profit entities is unwarranted. There is also a growing body of law standing for the proposition that a nonprofit organization, particularly a charitable one, that operates in a commercial manner cannot qualify for tax-exempt status. This principle of law is known as the *commerciality doctrine*.[30]

The subjects of competition and commerciality by no means fully overlap. The matter of competition is taken into account chiefly in ascertaining whether an activity is a related business or an unrelated business. This determination is based on statutory law. As noted (Q 2:4), it involves a question as to whether a nonprofit entity and a for-profit entity are doing the same thing. These comparisons rarely lead to a decision as to a nonprofit organization's tax exemption.

In contrast, the commerciality doctrine goes to the heart of tax exemption issues. It bypasses the issues concerning unrelated income taxation. It is not based on statutory law but was conjured up by the courts, initially almost inadvertently. The doctrine sometimes takes competition into account but, when it does, only as one of several factors. It tends to focus on the manner in which an organization is operating.

NOTE: To date, the commerciality doctrine has been applied only in the context of public charities. There is no reason, however, that the doctrine could not be extended to the operations of social welfare organizations (Chapter 6), trade and business associations (Chapter 5), labor entities, and other types of nonprofit organizations.

Q 2:9   What is the commerciality doctrine?

The commerciality doctrine essentially is this: A nonprofit organization is engaged in a non-tax-exempt activity when that activity is engaged in in a manner that is considered *commercial*. An activity is a commercial one if it is conducted in the same manner in the world of for-profit organizations.

When a court sees an activity being conducted by a for-profit business and the same activity conducted in the same fashion by a charitable organization, it is often affronted. The court is then stirred by some form of intuitive offense at the thought that a nonprofit organization is doing something that "ought to" be done only in the for-profit sector. Therefore, the court concludes that the nonprofit organization is conducting that activity in a commercial manner. This conclusion then results in a finding that the commercial activity is a nonexempt function, often leading to the decision that the nonprofit organization is not entitled to tax exemption.

NOTE: The essence of the commerciality doctrine having been stated, it must also be said that, to date, it is being unevenly applied.

Q 2:10   Where did the doctrine come from?

It grew out of some loose language in early court opinions. The Supreme Court started it all back in 1924. A case before the Court concerned a tax-exempt religious order that, although operated for religious purposes, also engaged in activities that the government alleged destroyed the order's exemption: investments in securities and real estate, and sales of items such as chocolate and wine. The Court ruled that the order should remain tax-exempt. Nonetheless, it found it necessary to state the government's argument in the case, which was that the order was "operated also for business and *commercial* purposes." The Court rejected this portrayal of the order, writing that there was no "competition" and that while the "transactions yield[ed] some profit [it was] in the circumstances a negligible factor."[31]

This articulation of the government's argument by the Court is burdened with an unnecessary redundancy: why the use of both words *business* and *commercial*? In any event, the Supreme Court did not enunciate a commerciality doctrine. However, by simply employing the word *commercial*, the Court gave birth to the doctrine.

The doctrine was formalized by the Court in 1945. On that occasion it was reviewing a case concerning the tax exemption of a chapter of the Better Business Bureau, which was pursuing exempt status as an educational organization. The chapter was found not to qualify for exemption, inasmuch as it was engaging in the nonexempt function of promoting a profitable business community. The Court, in the closest it has come to expressly articulating the commerciality doctrine, wrote that the organization had a "commercial hue" and that its activities were "largely animated by this commercial purpose."[32]

The 1960s saw the commerciality doctrine flourish. This came about because of a number of cases concerning nonprofit publishing organizations. One case, decided in 1961, pertained to a publisher of religious literature that, as the court put it, generated "very substantial" profits. Rejected was the IRS's contention that profits alone precluded tax exemption. But then the court added these fateful words: "If, however, defendant [the IRS] means only to suggest that it [profits] is at least some evidence indicative of a *commercial* character we are inclined to agree." In finding the organization not to be tax-exempt, the court declined to apply the unrelated income tax rules. This court obviously thought that the organization's primary activities were unrelated, inasmuch as exemption was revoked, but, inexplicably, the word *commercial*, rather than *unrelated*, was used.[33]

In a 1962 case, another nonprofit publishing organization failed to receive tax exemption because the "totality of [its] activities [was] indicative of a business, and . . . [the organization's] purpose [was] thus a commercial purpose and nonexempt."[34] A 1964 case involving a religious organization that conducted training projects saw rejection of application of the commerciality doctrine, with the court observing that "we regard consistent nonprofitability as evidence of the absence of commercial purposes."[35] In a 1968 case that was overruled, a lower court determined that a publisher of religious materials could not be tax-exempt because it "was clearly engaged primarily in a business activity, and it conducted its operations, although on a small scale, in the same way as any commercial publisher of religious books for profit would have done."[36]

Several other commerciality doctrine cases followed. In 1980 a court said this: "Profits may be realized or other nonexempt purposes may be necessarily advanced incidental to the conduct of the commercial activity, but the existence of such nonexempt purposes does not require denial of exempt status so long as the organization's dominant purpose for conducting the activity is an exempt purpose, and so long as the nonexempt activity is merely incidental to the exempt purpose."[37] In 1981 a publisher of religious materials lost its tax exemption because it became embued with a "commercial hue" and evolved into a "highly efficient business venture."[38] An appellate court in 1984, even while overruling a lower court's decision that a religious publishing house was no longer exempt, found the opportunity to say that if an exempt organization's "management decisions replicate those of commercial enterprises, it is a fair inference that at least one purpose is commercial."[39]

Recent cases in which commerciality was used as a basis for denial of tax exemption include one involving an organization selling religious tapes,[40] one operating prisoner rehabilitation programs,[41] and one operating a number of canteen-style lunch trucks.[42]

There are several other commerciality doctrine cases depicting its evolution, but this is how the doctrine started and grew into its contemporary framework.

Q 2:11   What factors are looked at in determining commerciality?

The commerciality doctrine is not so fully articulated as to enable a crisp response. However, the most expansive explanation of the commerciality doctrine was provided in an appellate court case decided in 1991. The organization involved was a nonprofit entity associated with a church that operated, in advancement of church doctrine, vegetarian restaurants and health food stores. The lower court wrote, in denying exemption as a charitable and/or religious organization, that the entity's "activity was conducted as a business and was in direct competition with other restaurants and health food stores." The court added (in what, by then, was an understatement): "Competition with commercial firms is strong evidence of a substantial nonexempt purpose."[43]

The appellate court opinion in this case stated the factors relied upon in its finding of commerciality. They were that (1) the organization sold goods and services to the public (thereby making the establishments "presumptively commercial"), (2) the organization was in "direct competition" with for-profit restaurants and food stores, (3) the prices set by the organization were based on pricing formulas common in the retail food business (with the "profit-making price structure looming large" in the court's analysis and the court criticizing the organization for not having "below-cost pricing"), (4) the organization utilized promotional materials and "commercial catch phrases" to enhance sales, (5) the organization advertised its services and food, (6) the organization's hours of operation were basically the same as those of for-profit enterprises, (7) the guidelines by which the organization operated required that its management have "business ability" and six months' training, (8) the organization did not utilize volunteers but paid salaries, and (9) the organization did not receive any charitable contributions.[44]

Q 2:12   What is to be made of the commerciality doctrine?

The doctrine of commerciality certainly is here to stay and is expected to grow in importance. Thus, the focus should be on the reach and the elements of the doctrine.

On the basis of the definition of the doctrine as articulated by a court in 1991 (Q 2:11), the doctrine is obviously too encompassing. For example, many tax-exempt organizations properly sell goods or services to the public (such as in the fields of education, health care, and theater); too much emphasis was placed by the court on that factor in the decision. Yet the court was correct in emphasizing competition, motive for engaging in the activity, and pricing. Probably the factor of advertising was appropriately included, although many nonprofit organizations advertise their exempt functions (such as hospitals, colleges, symphonies, and ballets). Factors like hours of operation and payment of salaries seem nonsensical in the modern era.

In contrast, some of these factors are dismaying, if not old-fashioned and plainly silly. For example, what is to be made of the court's wish for "below-cost pricing"? How long can an entity function (in the absence of a large endowment) doing that?

COMMENT: One is reminded of the radio advertisement in which the owner of a business is excitedly announcing an upcoming spectacular sale, with prices slashed. Once he is finished, his very critical mother appears, admonishing him. She tells the public, in a heavy accent, "He's a nice boy but not too good with the math."

Equally discouraging is the reference to lack of contributions. This remains a bugaboo that should have been put to rest years ago. There is no requirement in the law that, to be charitable, an organization must be funded, primarily or at all, by gifts. Indeed, the law is clear that an

organization funded entirely by exempt function income or investment income can be charitable. The absence of contributions should
not be an element in evaluating the presence of commerciality. Another factor that is foolish, if not completely unrealistic today, is reliance on the lack of volunteer assistance in concluding that an
organization is commercial.

COMMENT: In fact, there are many nonprofit organizations that perform activities in a commercial manner using volunteers. These include theaters, symphonies, and ballets.

One of these elements that is particularly galling is the fact that the
nonprofit organization's employees have some expertise and training.
This country is long overdue in improving the quality of nonprofit organization operations in the realm of, for example, management, law, and
fund-raising. Much impressive progress in this regard is being made. Today there are more college programs, seminars, books, and the like than
ever before. In the midst of all of this, along comes a court, finding
knowledgeable employees of a nonprofit entity evidence that it is operating commercially!

So, while the commerciality doctrine is playing an increasing role
in determining eligibility for tax-exempt status, the law is still awaiting a
comprehensive and realistic definition of the doctrine.

Q 2:13   Are there other factors that are taken into account in determin-ing commerciality?

Yes, usually by the media. These critiques are often based on a fundamental misunderstanding of what is meant by a nonprofit, tax-exempt
organization. Two examples will suffice.

The *Kansas City Star*, piqued at the decision of the National Collegiate Athletic Association (NCAA) to leave that city and move to Indi-
anapolis, published six days in a row in October 1997 a series of articles
about the organization. The opening article proclaimed that, "for a les-
son in commercialism, you can't beat" the NCAA. According to the article, over the past 23 years, the NCAA's revenues have increased 8,000
percent. It has a $1.7 billion television contract, a staff of 250 individu-
als, a real estate subsidiary, a marketing division, and it licenses its
name and logo for use on clothing. It owns a Learjet. It is a "powerful
sports cartel that is addicted to making money."[45]

The *New York Times*, enervated by the celebration of the 50th anniversary of the Educational Testing Service (ETS), published an article about the organization in September 1997. It seems that the ETS has "quietly grown into a multinational operation complete with for-profit subsidiaries, a reserve fund of $91 million, and revenue last year of $411 million." This article portrayed ETS as an entity transformed into a "highly competitive business operation that is as much multinational monopoly as nonprofit institution, one capable of charging hefty fees, laying off workers and using sharp elbows in competing against rivals."[46]

These and other inflammatory analyses are likely to have a lot to do with the evolution and enlargement of the commerciality doctrine. Being, unfortunately, all too typical, these articles missed the point of what is meant by being a nonprofit organization. Check off the list: There is nothing in the federal tax law prohibiting an exempt organization from operating in more than one country, having one or more for-profit subsidiaries, having a reserve fund, charging fees, and entering into licensing and other contracts. The articles focus on factors that are reflective of a yearning for an earlier, simpler era when nonprofit organizations were mostly struggling charities, eking out a year-by-year existence with barely enough in the way of contributions and held together by a dedicated cadre of volunteers. Thus, commerciality is seen in the size of the organization, the fact it has a paid staff, and ownership of an airplane.

COMMENT: This view is even stretched to find commerciality in the fact that a nonprofit organization lays off workers and uses "sharp elbows" against rivals. Terminating an individual's employment can be no more than sound management practice. And anyone worried about sharp elbows in this context has not been paying any attention to hospitals, colleges, and universities lately.

These and like reports, of course, include legitimate factors to take into account in determining commerciality. These are the reasons for (but not necessarily for the extent of) expansion, increase in and use of revenues, the charging of "hefty fees," and maybe even being a monopoly.

The *New York Times* article stated that "competition with for-profit rivals is a trend that bedevils nonprofit institutions across the country." As noted at the outset, there is much truth to this statement. What is also "bedeviling" nonprofit organizations these days is the confusion about them that is fostered by muddled analyses such as these.

Q 2:14   Is Congress likely to legislate some form of the commerciality doctrine?

It is nearly inevitable that a version of the commerciality doctrine will find its way into the statutory law. It is basically a matter of time (Q 2:7).

In the meantime, Congress has already gingerly entered this fray. As noted (Q 2:4), by the mid-1980s, Congress arrived at the conclusion that, irrespective of their initial novelty and worthiness, prepaid health care plans were no longer entitled to tax exemption (usually as social welfare organizations) because they were operating in a commercial manner, like for-profit insurers. Thus, in 1986, Congress adopted the following rule: A nonprofit organization cannot be tax-exempt (as a charitable organization or a social welfare organization) if a substantial part of its activities is the provision of commercial-type insurance.[47] The term *commercial-type insurance* means any form of insurance that is available in the for-profit sector, that is, is obtainable commercially.

This is the only time that any version of a commerciality doctrine has been added to the Internal Revenue Code. It may well be a provision that Congress will expand by extending it to fields other than insurance.

COMMENT 1:   Even in this tentative foray into the mysteries of the meaning and shaping of the commerciality doctrine, Congress went too far. For example, the term *commercial-type insurance* was not, despite its origins, confined to *health* insurance. Thus, this statutory commerciality doctrine began to be applied in circumstances where charitable organizations needed various types of insurance in furtherance of their exempt programs (such as vehicle insurance for organizations that deliver meals to the elderly or provide transportation for the disabled) yet could not obtain the coverage because it was not available or because of its cost. Realizing its overreaching, Congress in 1996 wrote a rule exempting qualified *charitable risk pools* from the ambit of the law denying tax exemption to *commercial* insurers.[48]

COMMENT 2: Sending a conflicting signal in 1997, Congress repealed special exemptions from the commercial-type insurance rules it created in 1986 for the Teachers Insurance Annuity Association-College Retirement Equities Fund and the Mutual Fund of America. These entities. which manage funds only for charitable entities, were previously tax-exempt as charitable organizations.

NOTE: The commerciality doctrine is tucked away in a sentence in the tax regulations. There, the term *commercial* is used as part of the elements for determining whether a business is *regularly carried on*. Thus, the regulations state that specific business activities of an exempt organization are ordinarily deemed to be regularly carried on if they "manifest a frequency and continuity, and are pursued in a manner, generally similar to comparable commercial activities of nonexempt organizations."[49]

Q 2:15   What is the future of the commerciality doctrine?

For the short term, the doctrine will continue to be developed in the courts. At some point in time, as noted, Congress will be motivated to either write an expansive definition of the term or augment the existing rules that presently are confined to insurance (Q 2:14).

The nonprofit community can expect many more reports in the media such as those noted earlier (Q 2:13), as the debate over this type of competition intensifies. Nonprofit organizations are likely to lose this battle on one or more fronts, perhaps including restrictive federal and/or state statutory law changes. If this happens, the process will have been hastened and inflamed by misleading reports such as these, which reflect great ignorance of what it means to be a nonprofit organization and what such organizations are allowed to do as a matter of law.

Q 2:16   What should nonprofit organizations be doing in this regard in the interim?

A tax-exempt, nonprofit organization should examine its operations in light of the elements of the commerciality doctrine enumerated earlier (Q 2:11, Q 2:12). The organization should evaluate each program activity the way the IRS or a court might do, by asking these questions: (1) Is the program competitive with an activity in the for-profit sector? (2) Why is the program being carried on?[50] (3) If fees are charged for the provision of a good or service, how are the prices set? (4) Are prices calculated to return income in excess of related expenses (that is, generate a profit)? (5) Are exempt functions subsidized by contributions and/or grants (fund-raising) or by an endowment fund? (6) Does the organization advertise or otherwise promote its operations? and (7) Are the salaries paid to employees and fees paid to vendors and other independent contractors reasonable?[51] The organization should formulate the best possible answers to these questions from its standpoint (as always, staying within the bounds of veracity). It should be prepared to defend itself against charges of commerciality.

Once these rationales are devised, they should be reflected in all written materials developed by the organization. This is particularly important in respect to language in the articles of organization, annual information returns (Chapters 11 and 12), annual reports, footnotes in financial statements, promotional literature, newsletters, and minutes of the board of directors. In many instances, as part of assembling a case that an organization is operating in a commercial manner, an IRS examiner or judge will select quotations from an organization's own materials, using them against the organization.[52]

CHAPTER 3

Partnerships and Joint Ventures

It is difficult to think of a contemporary issue involving tax-exempt organizations, particularly public charities, that is more controversial than their involvement in partnerships and other forms of joint ventures. This issue has been at the top of the IRS's list of exempt organizations' hot topics for years, fueled largely by various structures designed in the field of health care. The recent surge in activities concerning the whole-hospital joint venture is the latest in a long string of these developments and is not likely to be the last. Although, usually, a tax-exempt organization knows when it is in a partnership, an exempt entity can be a participant in a joint venture without realizing it.

Here are the questions most frequently asked by clients about involvement in partnerships and joint ventures—and the answers to them.

PARTNERSHIPS BASICS

Q 3:1   What is the legal definition of a *partnership*?

A *partnership* is a form of *business enterprise* (Q 10:2, Q 10:3), recognized in the law as an *entity*, as are other enterprises, such as a corporation, limited liability company, or trust. It is usually evidenced by a document, which is a partnership agreement, executed between persons who are the partners. These persons may be individuals, corporations, and/or other partnerships. Each partner owns an interest in the partnership; these interests may or may not be equal.

In the federal tax law, the term *partnership* includes a "syndicate, group, pool, joint venture, or other unincorporated organization, through or by means of which any business, financial operation, or venture is carried on, and which is not . . . a trust or estate or a corporation."[1] A partnership must have at least two members,[2] who are its owners.

The concept of a partnership has long been given broad interpretation. In a classic example of this, a court defined a partnership as a relationship based on a "contract of two or more persons to place their money, efforts, labor, and skill, or some or all of them, in lawful commerce or business, and to divide the profit and bear the loss in definite proportions."[3] Thus, co-owners of income-producing real estate who operate the property (either through an agent or one or more of them) for their joint profit are operating a partnership.[4]

An entity that does not qualify for tax purposes as a partnership will undoubtedly be regarded as an *association*, which means that it is taxed as a corporation.[5] When that happens, certain tax attributes are lost (Q 3:5).

There are two basic types of partnerships: the *general partnership* and the *limited partnership*.

Q 3:2   What is a *general partnership*?

The difference between the two types of partnerships is delineated principally by the extent of the partners' liability for the acts of the partnership. Generally, liability for the consequences of a partnership's operations rests with the general partner or general partners. Moreover, a general partner is liable for satisfaction of the ongoing obligations of the partnership and can be called upon to make additional contributions of capital to it. Every partnership must have at least one general partner. Sometimes where there is more than one general partner, one of them is designated as the managing general partner.

Many partnerships are comprised of only general partners, who contribute cash, property, and/or services. This type of partnership is a *general partnership*. The interests of the general partners may or may not be equal. In many respects, a general partnership is akin to a *joint venture* (Q 3:6).

A general partnership is usually manifested by a partnership agreement.

Q 3:3   What is a *limited partnership*?

A *limited partnership* is one that has limited partners as participants. A limited partner is a person whose exposure to liability for the functions of the partnership is confined to the amount of that person's contribution to (investment in) the partnership.

Some partnerships need or want to attract capital from sources other than the general partner or partners. This capital can be derived from investors, who are limited partners. Their interest in the partnership is, as noted, limited in the sense that their liability is limited. The limited partners are involved to obtain a return on their investment and perhaps to procure some tax advantages.

Thus, a partnership with both general and limited partners is a limited partnership.

A limited partnership is usually manifested by a partnership agreement.

Q 3:4   Why is the partnership vehicle used?

As a general proposition, the partnership is used as a business enterprise because the parties bring unique resources to the relationship, and they want to blend these resources for the purpose of beginning and conducting a business. Another reason for the partnership form—particularly the limited partnership vehicle—is to attract financing for one or more projects. In some instances, the partnership vehicle is favored because of its tax status (Q 3:5).

Q 3:5   How are partnerships taxed?

Partnerships are not taxed. They are *pass-through entities*; this means that the entity's income, deductions, and credits are passed along to the partners.[6]

JOINT VENTURE BASICS

Q 3:6   What is the legal definition of a *joint venture*?

A *joint venture* is a form of *business enterprise* (Q 10:2, Q 10:3), recognized in the law as an *entity*, as are other enterprises, like a corporation or trust. Essentially, a general partnership (Q 3:2) and a joint venture are the same thing.

One court defined a *joint venture* as an association of two or more persons with intent to carry out a single business venture for joint profit, for which purpose they combine their efforts, property, money, skill, and knowledge, but they do so without creating a formal entity, namely, a partnership, trust, or corporation.[7] Thus, two or more entities (including tax-exempt organizations) may operate a business enterprise as a joint venture.[8]

However, the concept of a joint venture is broader than that of a general partnership. One of the ways this fact can be manifested is evident when the law treats an arrangement as a joint venture for tax purpose, even though the parties involved insist that their relationship is something else (such as parties to a management agreement or a lease).

NOTE: This issue can arise in the unrelated business income context, where a tax-exempt organization is asserting that certain income it is receiving is passive in nature (and thus not taxable) and the IRS is contending that the income (most frequently rent or royalty income) is being derived from active participation in a joint venture.

The federal tax law is inconsistent in stating the criteria for ascertaining whether a joint venture is to be found as a matter of law. According to the Supreme Court, "[w]hen the existence of an alleged partnership arrangement is challenged by outsiders, the question arises whether the partners really and truly intended to join together for the purpose of carrying on business and sharing in the profits or losses or both."[9] The Court added that the parties' "intention is a question of fact, to be determined from testimony disclosed by their 'agreement considered as a whole, and by their conduct in execution of its provisions.' "[10] In one instance, a court examined state law and concluded that the most important element in determining whether a landlord-tenant relationship or joint venture agreement exists is the intention of the parties. This court also held that the burden of proving the existence of a joint venture is on the party who claims that that type of relationship exists (such as the IRS).[11]

Yet, another court declared that "it is well settled that neither local law nor the expressed intent of the parties is conclusive as to the existence or nonexistence of a partnership or joint venture for federal tax purposes."[12] The court wrote that this is the test to follow: "whether, considering all the facts—the agreement, the conduct of the parties in execution of its provisions, their statements, the testimony of disinterested persons, the relationship of the parties, their respective abilities and capital contributions, the actual control of income and the purposes for which it is used, and any other facts throwing light on their true intent—the parties in good faith and acting with a business purpose intended to join together in the present conduct of the enterprise."[13]

This latter court wrote that the "realities of the taxpayer's economic interest rather than the niceties of the conveyancer's art should determine the power to tax."[14] The court added: "Among the critical elements involved in this determination are the existence of controls over the venture and a risk of loss in the taxpayer."[15] Finally, the court said that it is not bound by the "nomenclature used by the parties," so that a document titled, for example, a *lease* may in law be a partnership agreement.[16]

Q 3:7   Why is the joint venture vehicle used?

The joint venture vehicle is generally used when two or more persons share resources to advance a specific project or program. When the arrangement is formally established, it is often denominated a *general partnership* (Q 3:2). As noted, however, parties to a transaction can find themselves treated as being in a joint venture as a matter of law.

Moreover, the term *joint venture* is often broadly used. The term appears in the formal definition of a *partnership* (Q 3:1). It is often applied in other contexts, such as when the structure of a venture is based on use of a limited liability company.

Q 3:8   What is a *limited liability company?*

A *limited liability company* is a legal entity, recently recognized under state law. It is not a corporation, although it has the corporate attribute of limitation against personal liability. A limited liability company is treated as a partnership for tax purposes (Q 3:10).

Q 3:9   How are joint ventures taxed?

Joint ventures are not taxed. They are *pass-through entities*; this means that the entity's income, deductions, and credits are passed along to the partners. Thus, joint ventures are treated the same as partnerships for tax purposes (Q 3:5).

Q 3:10   How are limited liability companies taxed?

Limited liability companies are not taxed. They are, as noted, treated the same as partnerships for tax purposes (Q 3:5).

NOTE: Likewise, S corporations are treated as partnerships for tax purposes (Q 10:6).

TAX-EXEMPT ORGANIZATIONS AND PARTNERSHIPS

Q 3:11   Can a tax-exempt organization be involved in a general partnership?

There is no question that a tax-exempt organization can be involved in a general partnership. The principal tax law issues become, however, whether involvement in the partnership jeopardizes the entity's exempt status and/or causes it unrelated business income. To date, all of the law on the point concerns public charities[17] in general partnerships. Inasmuch as the law in this regard is the same as that pertaining to public charities in joint ventures, it will be discussed in that context (Q 3:22–Q 3:28).

Q 3:12   Can a tax-exempt organization be involved in a limited partnership?

Again, the answer is a definite yes. And, again, the tax issues are whether tax exemption would be threatened and/or unrelated business income generated. Here, too, the law to date has focused only on public charities in limited partnerships.

Resolution of these issues depends on whether the exempt organization is in a limited partnership as a limited partner or a general partner (Q 3:13, Q 3:14).

Q 3:13   Can a tax-exempt organization be involved in a limited partnership as a limited partner?

The answer is clearly yes, although there is little law on the point. When an exempt organization is a limited partner in a limited partnership, it is in the venture as an investor.[18] The law then is likely to focus primarily on whether the investment is a prudent one for the organization and whether its board is adhering to the requisite principles of fiduciary responsibility.[19]

Q 3:14   Can a tax-exempt organization be involved in a limited partnership as a general partner?

Yes. This brings the discussion to one of the most critical aspects of this subject: the impact of involvement in a limited partnership by a public charity as a general partner on the charity's tax-exempt status. For years, the IRS has had great concerns on this point. Indeed, it was not until 1998 that the IRS formally stated that a charitable organization may form and participate in a partnership and be or remain tax-exempt.[20]

NOTE: Nonetheless, the IRS has issued dozens of private letter rulings, technical advice memoranda, and general counsel memoranda stating that a public charity's involvement in a limited partnership will not endanger its exempt status.[21] Indeed, on one occasion the IRS ruled that the exempt status of a charitable organization should not be revoked because of its participation as a general partner in seven limited partnerships.[22] Moreover, the IRS has *never* issued a published private determination that involvement in a limited partnership would cause loss or denial of a charity's exempt status.

CAUTION: As to this last observation, there have been ruling requests in which the facts were altered to gain the IRS's favor in this regard, and there have been ruling requests involving charities in limited partnerships that have been withdrawn in anticipation of an adverse ruling. Further, the IRS provided guidance indicating when an involvement in a joint venture by a charity could lead to loss of its exemption (Q 3:27).

Q 3:15   What are the IRS's concerns about public charities as general partners in limited partnerships?

Despite the fact that the debate, in and out of the IRS, over participation by public charities in limited partnerships as general partners has been openly raging for more than 20 years, the IRS and some courts are still not enamored with the idea. The primary concern the IRS has in this context is the potential of private inurement and/or private benefit[23] accruing to the for-profit participants in the venture.

More specifically, it is the view of the IRS that substantial benefits can be provided to the for-profit participants in a limited partnership (usually the limited partners) involving a tax-exempt organization as the or a general partner. This concern has its origins in arrangements involving charitable hospitals and physicians practicing there, such as a limited partnership formed to build and manage a medical office building, with an exempt hospital as the general partner and investing physicians as limited partners.

Q 3:16   Why has this controversy lasted so long?

There are several reasons that this controversy about public charities in limited partnerships has spanned many years—and shows no sign of abating. One is the ongoing number, variation, and complexity of these arrangements. Another is the great prevalence of the use of limited partnerships in the health care setting; as the law in that sphere has ballooned,[24] so too has the general law concerning charities in partnerships.[25] Still another reason is that the IRS adopted a very hard-line stance in this area at the beginning.

Q 3:17   What was this original IRS hard-line position?

The original position of the IRS in this regard came to be known as the *per se rule*. Pursuant to this view, involvement by a charitable organization in a limited partnership as general partner meant *automatic* revocation or denial of tax exemption, irrespective of the structure or purpose of the partnership. The per se rule was grounded on the premise that substantial private economic benefit was being accorded the limited partners.

Here is the IRS in 1978, in first articulating this per se rule, advising a public charity: "If you entered [into] the proposed partnership, you would be a direct participant in an arrangement for sharing the net profits of an income producing venture with private individuals and organizations of a non-charitable nature. By agreeing to serve as the general partner of the proposed . . . project, you would take on an obligation to further the private financial interests of the other partners. This would create a conflict of interest that is legally incompatible with you being operated exclusively for charitable purposes."[26]

NOTE: This was the position the IRS staked out, even though the purpose of the partnership was to advance a charitable objective (the development and operation of a low-income housing project).

There were other instances of application of the per se rule in the late 1970s and into the 1980s. Some of these cases did not involve formal partnerships (Q 3:1). For example, an IRS private letter ruling issued in 1979 concerned the issue of whether certain fees derived by tax-exempt lawyer referral services were items of unrelated business income. The IRS ruled that the fees paid by lawyers to the organizations, based on a percentage of the fees received by the lawyers for providing legal services to clients referred to them by these exempt organizations, constituted unrelated income. The reason: The subsequently established lawyer-client relationship was a commercial undertaking, and the ongoing fee arrangement with the percentage feature placed the organizations in the position of being in a joint venture in furtherance of those commercial objectives.[27]

Q 3:18   What became of the IRS's per se rule?

The IRS's per se rule was rejected by a court in a very significant decision. The case concerned syndication of a play being staged at a tax-exempt theater.

OBSERVATION: Before continuing with a description of this case, it should be noted that, as a matter of fundamental litigation practice, the party advocating the rule of law being asserted (here, the IRS) endeavors to select a situation involving facts that are the most compelling from the standpoint of its position. Inexplicably, the IRS advanced its cause in a blatant violation of litigation strategy. The theater group sponsoring the play was truly struggling financially, the play was being staged at the Kennedy Center in Washington, D.C., and the production was an engaging drama in the form of a sympathetic portrayal of the Supreme Court!

Needing financial assistance, the theater group underwrote its production costs with funds provided by private investors. The IRS sought to revoke the organization's tax-exempt status for attempting to sustain the arts in this fashion but lost, both at trial and on appeal.[28] Again, the matter involved a limited partnership that was being used to further the exempt ends of the general partner. The courts in this case placed some emphasis on the facts that the partnership had no interest in the tax-exempt organization or its other activities, the limited partners had no control over the way in which the exempt organization operated or managed its affairs, and none of the limited partners nor any officer or director of a corporate limited partner was an officer or director of the charitable organization.

NOTE: Much later, the IRS pronounced this control element a "significant" factor in this type of analysis (Q 3:27).

Shortly after this litigation, the IRS began to relax its stance in these regards. This new view was manifested in a 1983 general counsel memorandum, in which the lawyers for the IRS opined that it is possible for a charitable organization to participate as a general partner in a limited partnership without jeopardizing its tax exemption.[29] The IRS's lawyers advised that two aspects of this matter should be reviewed: whether (1) the participation may be in conflict with the goals and purposes of the charitable organization and (2) the terms of the partnership agreement contain provisions that insulate the charitable organization from certain of the obligations imposed on a general partner. In this instance, the limited partnership (another low-income housing venture) was found to further the organization's charitable purposes and several specific provisions of the partnership agreement were deemed to provide the requisite insulation for the charitable organization/general partner. Thus, the organization was permitted to serve as the partnership's general partner and simultaneously retain its tax exemption.

This development paved the way for the contemporary set of rules pertaining to public charities as general partners in limited partnerships.

OBSERVATION: The official date marking the demise of the per se rule seems to be November 21, 1991, when the IRS office of general counsel wrote that the IRS "no longer contends that participation as a general partner in a partnership is *per se* inconsistent with [tax] exemption."[30]

Q 3:19   When can a tax-exempt organization be involved in a limited partnership as a general partner and still be tax-exempt?

The current position of the IRS as to whether a charitable organization will have its tax-exempt status revoked (or recognition denied) if it functions as a general partner in a limited partnership is the subject of a three-part test.[31]

Under this test, the IRS first looks to determine whether the charitable organization/general partner is serving a charitable purpose by means of participation in the partnership. If involvement in the partnership is serving a charitable purpose, the IRS applies the rest of the test. Should the partnership fail to adhere to the charitability standard, however, the charitable organization/general partner will be deprived of or be denied tax-exempt status.

The first element of this test is an aspect of the fundamental *operational test* that every exempt charity must meet. This test is an evaluation of the operations of the organization. In general, for tax purposes, the activities of a partnership are often considered to be the activities of the partners.[32] This aggregate approach is applied for purposes of the operational test.[33] Consequently, when a charitable organization is advancing charitable ends by means of a partnership (such as the construction and operation of a medical office building on the grounds of a hospital, the purchase and operation of a CAT scanner at a hospital, or low-income housing projects), it continues to satisfy the operational test and thus be exempt.

The rest of this test is designed to ascertain whether the charity's role as general partner inhibits the advancement of its charitable purposes. Here, the IRS looks to means by which the organization may, under the particular facts and circumstances, be insulated from the day-to-day responsibilities as general partner and whether the limited partners are receiving an undue economic benefit from the partnership. It is the view of the IRS that there is an inherent tension between the ability of a charitable organization to function exclusively in furtherance of its exempt functions and the obligation of a general partner to operate the partnership for the benefit of the limited partners. This tension is the same perceived phenomenon that the IRS, when it deployed the per se rule, chose to characterize as a "conflict of interest" (Q 3:17).

An application of this test is reflected in a private letter ruling made public in 1985,[34] which involved a charitable organization that became a general partner in a real estate limited partnership that leased all of the space in the property to the organization and a related charitable organization. The IRS applied the first part of the test and found that the partnership was serving charitable ends because both of the tenants of the partnership were charitable organizations.

TIP: The IRS general counsel memorandum underlying this private letter ruling noted that if the lessee organization that was not the general partner had been an exempt organization other than a charitable one, the charity/general partner would have forfeited its tax exemption.[35]

Upon application of the rest of the test, the IRS found that the charitable organization/general partner was adequately insulated from the day-to-day management responsibilities of the partnership and that the limited partners' economic return was reasonable.

Q 3:20   Are there any other aspects of this matter?

Yes. There seem to be other requirements that are added to the three-part test from time to time. For example, in one instance the IRS emphasized the facts that the charitable organization was "governed by an independent board of directors" composed of church and community leaders, and that it did not have any other relationship with any of the commercial companies involved in the project. The IRS added that there was not any information which indicated that the organization was controlled by or "otherwise unduly influenced" by the limited partners or any company involved in the development or management of the project.[36]

In recent years, nearly all of the federal tax law in this setting has developed as the result of innovative financing techniques, including partnerships, by or for the benefit of hospitals and other health care organizations, institutions, and systems. Among the legitimate purposes for involvement of a health care provider in a partnership recognized by the IRS are the raising of needed capital, the bringing of new services or a new provider to a community, the sharing of a risk inherent in a new activity, and/or the pooling of diverse areas of expertise.[37]

NOTE: In its most "official" pronouncement on these points, the IRS developed a fact situation in which a hospital became involved in a joint venture with a for-profit entity because the hospital concluded "that it could better serve its community if it obtained additional funding."[38]

The IRS, in evaluating these situations, looks to see "what the hospital gets in return for the benefit conferred on the physician-investors."[39] One of the curious aspects of this evolution of the rules is the apparent abandonment of the second prong of the three-part test (concerning insulation of the charity/general partner[40]): it is skimmed over in the most important pronouncements on the point by the IRS's lawyers[41] and is never mentioned in the IRS's formal summary of this area of the law.[42]

One other point: It has never been clear as to why the IRS formulated the per se test in the first instance, inasmuch as it has always been understood that public charities can be general partners in limited partnerships—this is in the Internal Revenue Code, in two places. One provision speaks of "a partnership of which an [exempt] organization is a member."[43] Another references "a partnership which has both a tax-exempt entity and a person who is not a tax-exempt entity as partners."[44] These pronouncements from Congress would be wholly superfluous in the case of public charities if their mere participation as a general partner in a limited partnership would deprive them of their exempt status.[45]

Q 3:21   How do the unrelated business income rules apply in the partnership context?

Normally, the unrelated business income rules become applicable to a tax-exempt organization because of a business activity conducted directly by that organization. However, these rules can also become activated when an unrelated business is conducted in a partnership of which an exempt organization is a member.

The rule applied in this context is a *look-through rule*: if a business regularly carried on by a partnership, of which a tax-exempt organization is a member, is an unrelated business with respect to the exempt organization, in computing its unrelated business taxable income the organization must include its share (whether or not actually distributed) of the gross income of the partnership from the unrelated business.[46] This rule applies irrespective of whether the tax-exempt organization is a general or limited partner.[47]

NOTE: With respect to partnership interests acquired after December 17, 1987, through partnership years ending on December 31, 1993, or thereafter in 1994, a tax-exempt organization's share (whether or not distributed) of the gross income of a publicly traded partnership[48] must be treated as gross income derived from an unrelated business.[49] This rule for pre-1994 holdings is the same as that for S corporation stock today (Q 10:18).

TAX-EXEMPT ORGANIZATIONS AND JOINT VENTURES

Q 3:22   Can a tax-exempt organization be involved in a joint venture?

There is no question that a tax-exempt organization can be involved in a joint venture. The principal tax law issues become—just as in the case of involvement in partnerships (Q 3:11)—whether involvement in the joint venture jeopardizes the entity's exempt status and/or causes it to receive unrelated business income. To date, nearly all of the law on the point concerns public charities[50] in joint ventures.

There are two types of these involvements. One occurs where the public charity *intends* to be in a joint venture. The other occurs where the joint venture arrangement is imposed on the parties as a matter of law.

Q 3:23   Why would a public charity want to participate in a joint venture?

The basic reason that a public charity (or other type of tax-exempt organization) wants to participate in a joint venture is to carry out a single project or program, using the efforts, money, and/or expertise of one or more other parties. It is a resource-gathering, resource-sharing operation. Often, the other party or parties are not exempt organizations.

Q 3:24   What does a public charity in a joint venture have to do to acquire or retain tax-exempt status?

The basic rule is that a public charity (or other type of exempt organization) may enter into a joint venture with a for-profit organization (or other entity), without adversely affecting the charity's tax-exempt status, as long as doing so furthers exempt purposes and the joint venture agreement does not prevent it from acting exclusively to further those purposes. A joint venture does not present the private inurement or private benefit problems that are associated with participation by exempt organizations in limited partnerships, because there are no limited partners receiving economic benefits (Q 3:3). In contrast, an involvement in a joint venture by a tax-exempt organization would lead to loss or denial of tax exemption if the primary purpose of the exempt organization is to participate in the venture and if the function of the venture is unrelated to the exempt purposes of the tax-exempt organization.

An example of an involvement in a joint venture that does not adversely affect a public charity's exempt status is a charitable organization participating in a venture with a for-profit entity to own and operate an ambulatory surgical center.[51] Another is a charitable organization in a venture with a for-profit entity for the purpose of organizing and operating a free-standing alcoholism/substance abuse treatment center.[52] Still another involves a charitable hospital that participates with a for-profit organization in a venture for the purpose of providing magnetic resonance imaging services in an underserved community.[53]

A tax-exempt organization may enter into a joint venture with another tax-exempt organization, in furtherance of the exempt purposes of both of them.[54]

As will be discussed (Q 3:27), a joint venture of this nature may be structured by use of a limited liability company.[55]

Q 3:25   How can a tax-exempt organization be considered involved in joint venture against its will?

The joint venture form is usually imposed on a relationship with one or more other parties involving a tax-exempt organization where the revenue received by the exempt organization from the relationship is to be taxed. This can happen because of the sweep of the definition of the term *joint venture* (Q 3:6).

A classic example of this comes from the practice of crop-share leasing, where the exempt organization wants the relationship to be that of landlord-tenant and the IRS wants it to be cast as a joint venture. (The IRS is not prevailing in these cases.)

This dichotomy was illustrated in a case involving a charitable organization and its tenant-farmer.[56] The specific question before the court was whether the rent, equaling 50 percent of the crops and produce grown on the farm, constituted rent that was excludable as unrelated business income.[57] The court looked to state law to ascertain the meaning to be given the term *rent*. It observed that the written contracts at issue contained provisions usually found in leases, the tenant furnished all of the machinery and labor in the production of crops, and the tenant generally made decisions with a farm manager as to the day-to-day operations of the farm. The court concluded that the contracts as a whole clearly reflected the intention of the parties to create a landlord-tenant relationship, rather than a joint venture.

The IRS unsuccessfully contended that the charitable organization, by furnishing the seed and one half the cost of fertilizer, weed spray, and combining, had engaged in farming as a joint venturer. The court observed that these types of arrangements were not uncommon in share-crop leases and noted that the furnishing of these items ordinarily increased the crop yield and the net return of both the landlord and tenant substantially more than the amount invested by each for the items. The court also analyzed the effect on the landlord-tenant relationship of the hiring by the charity of a farm manager for the supervision of the tenant-farmer. The farm manager advised the tenant on topics such as crops, seed, weed spray, and fertilizer; decisions were made by mutual agreement of the tenant and the manager. The court concluded that the role of the farm manager did not mitigate against the overall conclusion that the arrangement was that of landlord and tenant.

In another illustration of this point, often a tax-exempt organization is endeavoring to characterize an item of income as a royalty, which is not taxable,[58] while the IRS is asserting that the exempt organization and other parties are actively participating in a joint venture, so that the income is taxable.[59]

On occasion, the IRS will invoke the joint venture rationale for the purpose of revoking or denying a tax exemption. For example, it is the view of the IRS that a tax-exempt hospital endangers its tax exemption, because of private inurement, as a result of its involvement in a joint venture with members of its medical staff, where the hospital has sold to the joint venture the net revenue stream of a hospital department for a stated period of time.[60] In this and similar situations, the application of the private inurement doctrine is triggered by the inherent structure of the joint venture (private inurement per se), irrespective of the reasonableness of the compensation.

Q 3:26   How do the unrelated business income rules apply in the joint venture context?

The unrelated business income rules apply in the joint venture context in the same way they do in the partnership setting (Q 3:21). That is, the *look-through rule* applies, so if there is unrelated business income generated by the joint venture, the exempt organization's share of it must be taken into account by the exempt organization in ascertaining its taxable income for the year.

   This is why, when the IRS sees an exempt organization characterizing income as excludable income (particularly as a royalty) and simultaneously actively participating in the undertaking that gives rise to the income, the IRS elects to impose a joint venture form on the arrangement, so as to cause the income to be taxable by application of the look-through rule (Q 3:6).

Q 3:27   How do these rules apply when the joint venture uses a limited liability company?

As noted (Q 3:24), a joint venture involving an exempt organization can be structured using the vehicle of the limited liability company. Essentially, the use of a limited liability company does not change the tax outcome, inasmuch as this type of company is treated as a partnership for tax purposes (Q 3:10).

   However, in 1998, the IRS issued a rare document in the exempt organizations setting: a revenue ruling. This document concerns the tax law ramifications of the whole-hospital joint venture. The ruling sketches two situations in which involvement by a hospital in one of these ventures does or does not jeopardize the hospital's tax-exempt status.[61] However, the implications of this ruling extend far beyond the realm of health care providers.

   This ruling is so significant that it deserves to be analyzed in some depth. First, here are the two fact situations:

Fact Situation 1

The first of these situations concerns a nonprofit corporation that owns and operates an acute care charitable hospital (H1), which has concluded that it could better serve its community if it obtained additional funding. A for-profit corporation (FP1), that owns and operates a number of hospitals, is interested in providing financing for the hospital if it can earn a reasonable rate of return. These two entities form a limited liability company (LLC1).

H1 contributes all of its operating assets, including the hospital, to LLC1. FP1 also contributes assets to LLC1. In return, H1 and FP1 receive ownership interests in LLC1 proportional and equal in value to their respective contributions.

LLC1's governing instruments provide that it is to be managed by a governing board consisting of three individuals selected by H1 and two individuals selected by FP1. H1 intends to appoint community leaders who have experience with hospital matters but who are not on the hospital staff and do not otherwise engage in business transactions with the hospital. These documents also provide that they may be amended only by the approval of both owners and that a majority of three board members must approve certain major decisions relating to the operation of LLC1 (such as the budget, distributions of earnings, and selection of key executives).

These governing documents further require that any LLC1-owned hospital be operated in a manner that advances charitable purposes by promoting health for a broad cross section of its community. They state that the board members' duty to adhere to this requirement overrides any obligation they may have to operate LLC1 for the financial benefit of its owners. Thus, the community benefit standard takes precedence over the consequences of maximizing profitability.

The governing documents provide that all returns of capital and distributions of earnings made to the owners of LLC1 must be proportional to their ownership interests in the venture. The terms of these instruments are legal, binding, and enforceable under state law.

LLC1 enters into an agreement with a management company (MC1) for the purpose of providing day-to-day management services to LLC1. MC1 is not related to H1 or FP1. This contract is for a five-year term and is renewable for additional five-year periods by mutual consent. MC1 will be paid a management fee based on the gross revenues of LLC1. The terms and conditions of the contract are reasonable and comparable to those that other management firms receive for comparable services for similarly situated hospitals. LLC1 may terminate this agreement for cause.

None of the directors, officers, or key employees of H1 who were involved in the decision to form LLC1 were promised employment or any other inducement by FP1 or LLC1 and their related entities if the transaction were approved. None of these individuals have any interest, directly or indirectly, in FP1 or any of its related entities.

H1 intends to use any distributions it receives from LLC1 to fund grants to support activities that promote the health of H1's community and to help the indigent obtain health care. Substantially all of H1's grant-making will be funded by distributions from LLC1. H1's projected grant-making program and its participation as an owner of LLC1 will constitute H1's only activities.

Fact Situation 2

The second of these situations concerns a nonprofit corporation that owns and operates an acute care charitable hospital (H2), which has concluded that it could better serve its community if it obtained additional funding. A for-profit corporation (FP2), which owns and operates a number of hospitals and provides management services to several other hospitals, is interested in providing financing for the hospital if it can earn a reasonable rate of return. These two entities form a limited liability company (LLC2).

H2 contributes all of its operating assets, including the hospital, to LLC2. FP2 also contributes assets to LLC2. In return, H2 and FP2 receive ownership interests in LLC2 proportional and equal in value to their respective contributions.

LLC2's governing instruments provide that it is to be managed by a governing board consisting of three individuals selected by H2 and three individuals selected by FP2. H2 intends to appoint community leaders who have experience with hospital matters but who are not on the hospital staff and do not otherwise engage in business transactions with the hospital. These documents also provide that they may be amended only by the approval of both owners and that a majority of board members must approve certain major decisions relating to the operation of LLC2 (such as the budget, distributions of earnings, and selection of key executives).

These governing documents further provide that LLC's purpose is to construct, develop, own, manage, operate, and take other action in connection with operating the health care facilities it owns and to engage in other health care-related activities. The documents also provide that all returns of capital and distributions of earnings made to LLC2's owners shall be proportional to their ownership interests in LLC2.

LLC2 enters into an agreement with a management company (MC2) for the purpose of providing day-to-day management services to LLC2. MC2 is a wholly owned subsidiary of FP2. This contract is for a five-year term and is renewable for additional five-year periods at the discretion of MC2. MC2 will be paid a management fee based on the gross revenues of LLC2. The terms and conditions of the contract, other than its renewal terms, are reasonable and comparable to those that other management firms receive for comparable services for similarly situated hospitals. LLC2 may terminate this agreement only for cause.

As part of the agreement to form LLC2, H2 agrees to approve the selection of two individuals to serve as MC2's chief executive officer and chief financial officer. These individuals have previously worked for FP2 in hospital management and have business expertise. They will work with MC2 to oversee the day-to-day management of LLC2. Their compensation will be comparable to that which like executives are paid at similarly situated hospitals.

H2 intends to use any distributions it receives from LLC2 to fund grants to support activities that promote the health of H2's community and to help the indigent obtain health care. Substantially all of H2's grant-making will be funded by distributions from LLC2. H2's projected grant-making program and its participation as an owner of LLC2 will constitute H2's only activities.

Here are two rules that are central to the findings in the ruling:

- A charitable organization may enter into a management contract with a private party, according that party authority to conduct activities on behalf of the organization and direct use of the organization's assets, as long as (1) the charity retains ultimate authority over the assets and activities being managed and (2) the terms and conditions of the contract (including compensation and the term) are reasonable.[62]
- If a private party is allowed to control or use the nonprofit organization's activities or assets for the benefit of the private party, and the benefit is not merely incidental, the organization will not qualify for tax exemption.[63]

In application of these principles, H1's tax exemption was preserved. H1's exempt functions consist of the health care services it will provide through LLC1 and its grant-making activities to be funded with income distributed by LLC1. H1's capital interest in LLC1 is equal in value to the assets it contributed to the venture. The returns from LLC1 to its owners will be proportional to their investments. The governing instruments of LLC1 clearly reflect exempt functions and purposes. The appointees of H1 will control the board of LLC1. The renewal feature of the contract is favorable to H1.

Under these facts, H1 can ensure that the assets it owns, and the activities it conducts, through LLC1 are used primarily to further exempt purposes. Thus, H1 can ensure that the benefit to FP1 and other private parties, such as MC1, will be incidental to the accomplishment of charitable ends.

It was stipulated that the terms and conditions of the management contract are reasonable, and that the grants by H1 are intended to support education and research and assist the indigent.

The IRS acknowledged that when H2 and FP2 form LLC2, and H2 contributes its assets to LLC2, H2 will—like H1—be engaged in activities that consist of the health care services to be provided through LLC2 and the grant-making activities it conducts using income distributed by LLC2. However, the IRS said that H2 will fail the primary purpose test because there is no binding obligation in LLC2's governing instruments for it to serve charitable purposes or otherwise benefit the community. Thus, LLC2 has the ability to deny care to segments of the community, such as the indigent.

The control element is significant in the second set of facts. H2 will share control of LLC2 with FP2. This means that H2 cannot initiate programs within LLC2 to serve new health needs within the community without the consent of at least one board member appointed by FP2. Inasmuch as FP2 is a for-profit entity, the IRS stated that it "will not necessarily give priority to the health needs of the community over the consequences for [FP2's] profits."

MC2 will have "broad discretion" over LLC2's activities and assets that may not always be under the supervision of LLC2's board. For example, MC2 can enter into all but "unusually large" contracts without board approval. Also, MC2 can unilaterally renew the management agreement.

The consequence of all of this for H2 is that FP2 will be receiving benefits resulting from the conduct of LLC2 that are private and not incidental. The operational test is failed by H2 when it participates in the formation of LLC2, contributes its operating assets to H2, and then serves as an owner of LLC2.

The fundamental flaw of the ruling lies in the starkness of the two extremes in the fact situation: a "pure" fact case and an "ugly" fact case. Exempt organizations are left, for the moment anyway, to divine what the law is as applied to the vast majority of "real life" situations that are in the middle.

There are many factors taken into account in this ruling—and the IRS subsequently said that others may be considered. What mix of factors will permit retention of exemption and what alchemy will result in its loss? The ruling seems to make it clear that the charitable-purposes language must be in the governing instruments of the joint venture entity (here, a limited liability company). It may be essential that the charitable participant at least share control over the joint venture. But, for example, how much discretion can a management company have?

(Surely, not every decision must be approved by the joint venture's governing board). Are the renewal terms in the contract between LLC2 and MC2 automatically fatal to H2's exemption? How critical is it that those who are employed by LLC2 have close ties to FP2?

The revenue ruling does not carry an effective date. Presumably, it can be applied retroactively with respect to existing arrangements.

Q 3:28   Does this ruling have any implications outside the health care setting?

This ruling has major implications outside the health care context. It should be noted, for example, that the term *joint venture* is not used in the revenue ruling. An exempt organization can, as noted (Q 3:6), find itself in a joint venture without realizing it; there does not have to be a formal document evidencing a joint venture or general partnership (essentially the same thing for these purposes).

What may seem, to an exempt organization, to be a management agreement or a lease, may in fact—by operation of law—be the basis for a finding of a joint venture. Once that label is placed on the arrangement, the focus quickly shifts to the matter of *control*. Does the exempt organization maintain *ultimate authority* over its assets and activities? That can be the basis for an opinion letter from a lawyer. Are the terms and conditions of the arrangement *reasonable*? That can be the basis for an opinion letter from a business consultant, such as an accounting firm. An exempt organization in this position should endeavor to be certain that some private party does not have "broad discretion," and that its board retains formal control, over the organization's assets and activities.

The intermediate sanctions rules are very much a part of the analysis. With respect to a charitable organization, the for-profit venturer, the joint venture itself, and/or the management company can be *disqualified persons* (Q 1:14). The compensation arrangement for the management company, based on the gross revenues of the limited liability company, may be a *revenue-sharing arrangement* (Q 1:10).

One aspect of this revenue ruling is certain: there will be many interpretations and expansions of it for the foreseeable future.

INFORMATION REPORTING

Q 3:29   How does an exempt organization know what income and the like to report from a partnership?

A partnership generally must furnish to each partner a statement reflecting the information about the partnership required to be shown on the partner's tax return or information return.[64] The statement must set forth the partner's distributive share of the partnership's income, gain, loss, deduction, or credit required to be shown on the partner's return, along with any additional information as provided by IRS forms or instructions that may be required to apply particular provisions of the federal tax law to the partner with respect to items related to the partnership.[65]

The instructions accompanying the statement for partners (Schedule K-1, Form 1065) require the partnership to state whether the partner is a tax-exempt organization. Moreover, the partnership must attach a statement furnishing any other information needed by the partner to file its return that is not shown elsewhere on the schedule.

In the case of a partnership regularly carrying on a business, the partnership must furnish to the partners the information necessary to enable each tax-exempt partner to compute its distributive share of partnership income or gain from the business.[66]

Partnerships of tax-exempt organizations, including those consisting wholly of exempt organizations, must annually file the federal information returns required of partnerships.[67]

CHAPTER 4

Acquiring Tax-Exempt Status

There is often much discussion about the substantive law of nonprofit and tax-exempt organizations—and little focus on the process by which tax-exempt status is acquired. A great myth is that the IRS grants tax-exempt status. This is not the case—and the correct concept, concerning recognition of exempt status, is frequently puzzling. The government's forms in this setting can appear daunting. Various and additional rules for charitable organizations can add to the perplexity. However, the procedure can be quite understandable, albeit sometimes with a little help.

Here are the questions most frequently asked by clients about acquisition of tax-exempt status—and the answers to them.

EXEMPTION APPLICATION BASICS

Q 4:1 How does a *nonprofit* organization become a *tax-exempt* organization?

Most organizations that are *nonprofit* entities have that status because they have qualified under state law (such as a nonprofit corporation or a charitable trust). However, that classification is only the beginning. Nonprofit status does not necessarily mean tax-exempt status.

For the most part, a reference to a tax-exempt organization is to an entity that is exempt from the federal income tax. There are other federal taxes from which nonprofit organizations are exempt, but the federal income tax exemption is certainly the principal one. There are state tax exemptions as well, including state income tax exemptions. Moreover, state law can provide exemptions from sales, use, tangible personal property, intangible property, real property, and other taxes. Frequently, the law providing exemption for nonprofit organizations from state income tax tracks the rules for exemption from federal income tax. Therefore, the federal rules are usually the place to start.

To qualify for tax-exempt status under the federal tax law, a nonprofit organization must meet the criteria of at least one provision in the Internal Revenue Code describing tax-exempt organizations. That is, in general, an organization that meets the appropriate statutory criteria qualifies—for that reason alone—as a tax-exempt organization.

NOTE: Most tax-exempt organizations under the federal tax law are those that are described in section 501(c)(1)-(27) of the Code. Other Code provisions that provide for income tax exemption are sections 521 and 526-529. Depending on how these provisions are parsed and the breadth of the term *tax-exempt organization* used, there are at least 63 categories of tax-exempt organizations provided for in the federal income tax law.[1]

Consequently, whether an organization is entitled to tax exemption, either on an initial or ongoing basis, is a matter of statutory law. It is Congress that, by statute, defines the categories of organization that are eligible for tax exemption, and it is Congress that determines whether a type of tax exemption should be continued.

OBSERVATION 1:   It should come as no surprise that this matter of eligibility for tax exemption has been litigated. However, the government always wins these cases—the courts repeatedly have held that Congress has great discretion in this area. For example, in creating a category of tax exemption for cooperative hospital service organizations,[2] Congress had the authority to exclude nonprofit laundry organizations.[3] Likewise, Congress is able to eliminate a category of tax exemption, such as when it denied tax exemption to certain organizations that provide commercial-type insurance[4] and to previously exempt trusts under qualified group legal services plans.[5]

OBSERVATION 2:   The Fifth Amendment guarantee of equal protection is not available here: Congress can make eligibility for tax
exemption pivot on the date the entity was created.[6] Examples:
exempt insurers of financial deposits must be organized before
September 1, 1957;[7] exempt funds underlying certain pension plans
must be created before June 25, 1959;[8] and certain exempt workers'
compensation reinsurance organizations must be established before June 1, 1996.[9] Indeed, one of the exemption categories for veterans' organizations requires that the entity be formed before
1880.[10]

Q 4:2   Is a nonprofit organization required to apply to the IRS for tax-exempt status?

There are two aspects of this answer. A very literal answer to the question is no. This is because the IRS does not grant tax-exempt status; that
is a tax feature of an organization that is available to it by operation of
law (Q 4:1).

What the IRS does is grant *recognition* of tax-exempt status. (This
role of the IRS in recognizing the exempt status of organizations
is part of its overall practice of evaluating the tax status of organizations.[11])

Q 4:3   What does *recognition* of tax exemption mean?

Eligibility for tax-exempt status is different from recognition of that status (Q 4:2). When the IRS *recognizes* the exempt status of an organization, it makes a written determination that the entity constitutes a
tax-exempt organization. When exercising this function, the IRS re-
views, analyzes, and interprets the law, and agrees with the organization that it is exempt. The process is almost always begun by the
organization's filing an application for recognition of tax-exempt status
with the IRS.

Q 4:4   Is an organization required to seek recognition of exempt status from the IRS?

As a general rule, an organization desiring tax-exempt status pursuant
to the federal tax law is not *required* to secure recognition of tax exemption from the IRS. Nonetheless, an organization *may,* on its own volition,
seek recognition of tax-exempt status.

OBSERVATION: Organizations frequently seek rulings and like determinations from the federal government, including the IRS. There are many factors to take into account in making this judgment, including the complexity of the facts and the available time. The advantages to be gained by obtaining recognition of exempt status include: the comfort of knowing that the IRS agrees that the organization qualifies, this status is a pathway to state tax exemption(s), and eligibility for various nonprofit mailing privileges.

However, there are two categories of organizations that are required by law to seek recognition of tax-exempt status from the IRS. Most charitable organizations[12] (Q 4:31) must seek this recognition.[13] Likewise, certain employee benefit organizations[14] must seek exemption recognition.[15] Moreover, an organization that wishes to be a central organization providing tax exemption on a group basis for subordinate organizations must first obtain recognition of its own tax-exempt status (Q 4:37).

Q 4:5   What is the procedure for seeking recognition of tax-exempt status?

The IRS has promulgated detailed rules by which a ruling as to recognition of exemption is to be sought.[16]

NOTE: A recognition of exemption by the IRS from an office outside Washington, D.C., is termed a *determination letter*.[17] This type of recognition from the IRS's National Office in Washington, D.C., is termed a *ruling*.[18] In practice, both of these types of determinations are often generically referred to as *rulings*—and that will frequently be the case in this discussion.

In almost all instances, the process is begun by the filing of an application for recognition of tax-exempt status. These applications are available as IRS forms. An organization seeking recognition of exemption as a charitable organization should file Form 1023. Nearly all other applicant organizations file Form 1024, although homeowners associations file Form 1120-H and farmers, fruit growers, and like associations file Form 1028. For a few categories of exempt organizations, there is no application form by which to seek recognition of tax exemption; in that case, the request is made by letter.

Q 4:6   Where are these applications filed?

Historically, applications for recognition of exemption were filed with the appropriate IRS key district director's office, determined in relation to the district in which the principal place of business of the organization was located. However, as part of a reorganization of the IRS, applications for recognition of exemption are filed with the IRS Service Center in Cincinnati, Ohio. Infrequently, there will be occasion to file the application with the National Office of the IRS.

Q 4:7   How long does it take the IRS to process an exemption application?

It is difficult to generalize as to the length of time required by the IRS to process an application for recognition of tax exemption. Three of the critical factors are the complexity and/or sensitivity of the case, the completeness of the application (and related documents), and the workload of the IRS representative who will be reviewing the file and preparing the ruling.

For rather straightforward filings, the organization should plan on an IRS processing period of about three months. The IRS may have questions, and this can lengthen the period. Once in a while, a case is referred to the IRS's National Office, and that development can have a bearing on the overall time period.

NOTE: It is very difficult to predict in individual filings how long it will take for a ruling (a favorable one) to be issued. An application virtually brimming with hearty exempt organization issues can sail through the process, without any IRS inquiries, and result in a ruling in a few weeks. Yet, a simple case, one lacking in any issues of substance, can be worried over by an IRS exempt organizations specialist for an agonizingly long period of time.

There is a process by which the applicant organization can request the IRS to expedite the processing of the application. For this to work, the organization must convince the IRS that there is a substantive reason as to why its application should be considered out of order (such as a large gift or grant that will be lost if recognition is not quickly extended). Understandably, out of overall fairness, the IRS is reluctant to grant expedited consideration of these applications, so the case for a quick processing must be a persuasive one.

TIP: The IRS has been known to formally decline to expedite consideration of an exemption application—and then process it speedily anyway.

Q 4:8   How long does an exemption ruling remain in effect?

These rulings are not accompanied by an expiration date. Generally, an organization whose tax-exempt status has been recognized by the IRS can rely on that determination as long as there are no substantial changes in its character, purposes, or methods of operation.[19] Of course, a change in the law can void a ruling or cause a reevaluation of it.

NOTE: Determining whether one of these changes is *substantial* is not always easy and can be a matter of considerable judgment. An applicant organization should endeavor to disclose as much information as is reasonably possible, to preclude a later contention that some material fact was omitted. Once the ruling is obtained, it is a recommended practice to periodically review the application, to see whether it reflects current programs and other practices. A ruling from the IRS is only as valid as the facts on which it is based—and a substantial change in purposes and the like could void or at least threaten the validity of the ruling.

Q 4:9   What happens if there is a substantial change in an organization's character, purposes, or methods of operation?

If there is a substantial change in an organization's character, purposes, or methods of operation, the rule of law is that the IRS is to be notified of the change or changes[20]—obviously so that the IRS can reevaluate the organization's exempt status. This notification is supposed to take place in proximity to the change.

However, in practice, this rule is rarely followed. As the years go by, organizations can evolve into and out of varying programs and purposes, and/or change management and methods of operation, and never give a thought to what was said in the exemption application (or, for that matter, in the articles of organization or bylaws). This is not a good practice; as noted, a periodic review in this regard is recommended (Q 11:29). There are organizations in operation today that have strayed so far from their original purposes and operations, and into nonexempt activities, that they would have their exempt status revoked were the IRS to learn the facts.

REMINDER: Even if these changes are not substantial, they are to be reported to the IRS as part of the filing of the annual information return (Q 11:29).

GENERAL PROCEDURES

Q 4:10   Will the IRS issue a ruling to an organization in advance of its operations?

In general, yes. The basic rule is this: A determination letter or ruling (Q 4:5) will be issued by the IRS to an organization, where its application for recognition of exemption and supporting documents establish that it meets the requirements of the category of exemption that it claimed.[21] Tax-exempt status for an organization will be recognized by the IRS in advance of operations where the entity's proposed activities are described in sufficient detail to permit a conclusion that the organization will clearly meet the pertinent statutory requirements.

TIP: The organization should not merely restate its purposes or state only that its proposed activities will be in furtherance of the organization's purposes. This approach does not satisfy the requirements and serves only to put the IRS on notice that the application has been prepared by those who lack experience with the rules.

The applicant organization is expected to fully describe the activities in which it expects to engage, including the standards, criteria, procedures, or other means adopted or planned for carrying out the activities, the anticipated sources of receipts, and the nature of contemplated expenditures.[22]

However, where an organization cannot demonstrate, to the satisfaction of the IRS (Q 5:11), that its proposed activities will qualify it for recognition of exemption, a record of actual operations may be required before a ruling is issued.[23]

Q 4:11   How much information must be provided to the IRS?

There is no precise standard in this regard. As noted, the IRS expects "sufficient details" and "full descriptions" (Q 4:10). Thus, an organization that took this issue to court lost in its bid to acquire recognition of exemption because it "failed to supply such information as would enable a conclusion that when operational, if ever, . . . [the organization] will conduct all of its activities in a manner which will accomplish its exempt purposes."[24] The entity was chided by the court for offering only "vague generalizations" about its ostensibly planned activities.[25]

Likewise, this court concluded that an organization could not be exempt, because it did not provide a "meaningful explanation" of its activities to the IRS.[26] In another instance, a court found that an organization's failure to respond "completely or candidly" to many of the inquiries of the IRS precluded it from receiving a determination as to its tax-exempt status.[27]

However, an organization is considered to have made the required "threshold showing" where it describes its activities in "sufficient detail" to permit a conclusion that the entity will meet the pertinent requirements,[28] particularly where it answered all of the questions propounded by the IRS.[29]

NOTE: This is essentially what this aspect of the process comes down to: the law "requires that the organization establish measurable standards and criteria for its operation as an exempt organization"; this standard does not necessitate "some sort of metaphysical proof of future events."[30]

TIP: This is not the time to hold back information; it is foolish for an organization to fail to be recognized as an exempt organization on the ground that it refused to submit suitable information. The organization should be willing to tell its story fully, treating the application as a business plan (Q 4:14). This document is, after all, a public one (Q 13:9), and its proper preparation should be regarded as a first step in presenting the organization's justification for existence and tax-exempt status.

This is, in essence, a burden-of-proof issue—with the burden on the would-be exempt organization. Moreover, there is a negative presumption: when the representatives of an organization fail to submit the appropriate factual information to the IRS, an inference arises that the facts involved would denigrate the organization's cause.[31]

Q 4:12   What happens if the IRS decides the application is incomplete?

If an application for recognition of tax exemption does not contain the requisite information, the IRS's procedures authorize it to return the application to the applicant organization without being considered on its merits.[32]

NOTE: As noted, the application will be returned to the organization—not to anyone on a power of attorney (such as a lawyer or accountant), with obvious implications. A competent representative of a nonprofit organization in this regard should have no experience with this rule.

The application for recognition of tax exemption as submitted by a would-be exempt organization will not be processed by the IRS until the application is at least *substantially completed.*

Q 4:13   What is a *substantially completed* application?

An application for recognition of exemption is a substantially completed one when it

1. Is signed by an authorized individual,
2. Includes an employer identification number or a completed application for the number (Form SS-4),
3. Includes information regarding any previously filed federal income tax and/or exempt organization information returns,
4. Includes a statement of receipts and expenditures and a balance sheet for the current year and the three preceding years (or the years the organization has been in existence, if less than four years), although if the organization has not yet commenced operations, or has not completed one full accounting period, a proposed budget for two full accounting periods, and a current statement of assets and liabilities is acceptable,
5. Includes a narrative statement of proposed activities and a narrative description of anticipated receipts and contemplated expenditures,
6. Includes a copy of the document by which the organization was established, signed by a principal officer or is accompanied by a written declaration signed by an authorized individual certifying

that the document is a complete and accurate copy of the
original or otherwise meets the requirement that it be a conformed copy,

7. If the organizing document is a set of articles of incorporation,
includes evidence that it was filed with and approved by an appropriate state official (such as a copy of the certificate of incorporation) or includes a copy of the articles of incorporation
accompanied by a written declaration signed by an authorized
individual that the copy is a complete and accurate copy of the
original document that was filed with and approved by the
state, and stating the date of filing with the state,

8. If the organization has adopted bylaws, includes a current copy
of that document, certified as being current by an authorized individual, and

9. Is accompanied by the correct user fee (Q 4:16).[33]

The application for recognition of exemption submitted by charitable organizations requests information concerning the composition
of the entity's governing body, any relationship with other organizations, the nature of its fund-raising program, and a variety of other
matters.

Q 4:14   Is the application for recognition of exemption an important document for an exempt organization?

Yes, this application is a very significant legal document for an exempt
organization, and it should be prepared and retained accordingly.

OBSERVATION: Thirty years of experience in this field suggests
that an unduly high proportion of exempt organizations cannot locate a
copy of their application for recognition of tax exemption.

The proper preparation of an application for recognition of tax
exemption involves far more than merely responding to the questions
on a government form. It is a process not unlike the preparation of a
prospectus for a business in conformity with the securities law requirements. Every statement made in the application should be carefully considered. Some of the questions may force the applicant
organization to focus on matters that solid management practices
should cause it to consider, even in the absence of the application re-

quirements. The application is a nicely constructed and factually sweeping document, and it should be approached and prepared with care and respect.

The prime objectives in this regard must be accuracy and completeness; it is essential that all material facts be correctly and fully stated (Q 4:9). Of course, the determination as to which facts are material and the marshaling of these facts requires judgment. Moreover, the manner in which the answers are phrased can be extremely significant; this exercise can be more one of art than of science.

The preparer or reviewer of the application should be able to anticipate the concerns the contents of the application may cause the IRS and to see that the application is properly prepared, while simultaneously minimizing the likelihood of conflict with the IRS. Organizations that are entitled to tax-exempt status have been denied recognition of exemption by the IRS, or have caused the process of gaining recognition to be more protracted, because of unartful phraseologies in the application that motivated the IRS to muster a case that the organization does not qualify for exemption.

Therefore, the application for recognition of tax exemption should be regarded as an important legal document and prepared accordingly. The fact that the application is available for public inspection (Q 13:9) only underscores the need for thoughtful preparation.

Q 4:15   How long does it take to prepare an application for recognition of tax exemption?

It is impossible to generalize on this point. The pertinent factors include the complexity of the organization, the extent to which the factual information and supporting documents are readily available, and the skill and expertise of those who prepare and review the document.

Nonetheless, apparently there is a way to produce some averages of time expenditures in this regard. Thus, in conjunction with Form 1023 (Q 4:23), it is the view of the IRS that the estimated average time required to keep records so as to be able to prepare the application (not including any schedules) is 55 hours and 29 minutes, to learn about the law in this regard is 4 hours and 37 minutes, and to prepare the application and send it to the IRS is 8 hours and 7 minutes.

NOTE: Perhaps the *Answer Books* can shorten one or more of these time estimates somewhat . . .

Q 4:16   Is there a charge for the processing of an application for recognition of exemption?

Yes, the IRS levies a user fee for processing an organization's application for recognition of exemption. This fee must be paid at the time of the filing of the application and must be accompanied by a completed user fee form (Form 8718).

Under the current schedule, the fee for the processing of one of these applications is $500, where the applicant has gross receipts that annually exceed $10,000. For smaller organizations, the fee is $150. A group exemption (Q 4:36) letter fee is $500.[34]

Q 4:17   Can an application for recognition of exemption be referred to the IRS's National Office?

Yes. The IRS representative considering the application must refer to the National Office of the IRS an application for recognition of tax exemption that (1) presents questions the answers to which are not specifically covered by the Internal Revenue Code, Department of Treasury regulations, an IRS revenue ruling, or court decision published in the IRS's *Internal Revenue Bulletin*, or (2) has been specifically reserved by an IRS revenue procedure and/or *Internal Revenue Manual* instructions for handling by the National Office for purposes of establishing uniformity or centralized control of designated categories of cases. In these instances, the National Office is to consider the application, issue a ruling directly to the organization, and send a copy of the ruling to the appropriate IRS office.[35]

NOTE: One of the purposes of the recent centralization efforts by the IRS in this context (Q 4:6) is to centralize the processing of exemption applications so as to consolidate expertise and increase the efficiency of the process.

Q 4:18   Can the applicant organization seek the assistance of the National Office?

Yes. If, during the course of consideration of an application for recognition of tax exemption, an applicant organization believes that its case involves an issue as to which there is no published precedent, the organization may ask the IRS to request *technical advice*[36] from the IRS's National Office.[37]

Q 4:19 Can an application for recognition of exemption be withdrawn?

Yes. An application for recognition of tax exemption filed with the IRS may be withdrawn, upon the written request of an authorized representative of the organization, at any time prior to the issuance of an initial adverse ruling. However, where an application is withdrawn, it and all supporting documents are retained by the IRS.[38]

Q 4:20 If an organization is denied recognition of exemption, may it later reapply?

Absolutely—the key is correction of the problem or problems that caused the denial in the first instance.

An organization may reapply for recognition of tax exemption if it was previously denied recognition, where the facts involved are materially changed so that the organization has come into compliance with the applicable requirements. For example, a charitable organization that was refused recognition of exemption because of excessive lobbying activities, by reason of the expenditure test,[39] may subsequently reapply for recognition of exemption for any tax year following the first tax year as to which the recognition was denied.[40] Essentially, the reapplication form must include information demonstrating that the organization was in compliance with the law during the full tax year immediately preceding the date of reapplication and that the organization will not knowingly operate in a manner that would disqualify it from exemption.

Q 4:21 What is the effective date of these rulings?

A determination letter or ruling recognizing tax exemption usually is effective as of the date of formation of the organization, where its purposes and activities during the period prior to the date of the determination letter or ruling were consistent with the requirements for tax exemption.[41]

CAUTION: There are special rules in this regard for charitable organizations (Q 4:29).

If the organization is required to alter its activities or to make substantive amendments to its enabling instrument, the determination letter or ruling recognizing its tax-exempt status is effective as of the date specified in the determination letter or ruling. If a nonsubstantive amendment is made, tax exemption ordinarily is recognized as of the date the entity was formed.[42]

Q 4:22   To what extent can the organization rely on its ruling?

In general, an organization can rely on a determination letter or ruling from the IRS recognizing its tax exemption. However, reliance is not available if there is a material change, inconsistent with tax exemption, in the character, purpose, or method of operation of the organization (Q 4:9).[43]

APPLICATION FORM

Q 4:23   What are the contents of the application?

As noted, there is more than one application form (Q 4:5). This answer will pertain to the application filed by charitable organizations (Form 1023), inasmuch as it is the most extensive one.

NOTE: The reader may wish to have a copy of Form 1023 (April 1996) handy while reviewing this portion of the chapter. The applications, part of a packet that includes general instructions as to their preparation, are available from the IRS and various commercial services and on the Internet.

Form 1023 consists of four parts. Each part will be reviewed separately.

Q 4:24   What is required in Part I of Form 1023?

Part I of Form 1023 requests basic information about the applicant organization and is relatively straightforward. Here, the organization supplies its name, address, employer identification number, date of formation, accounting period, and name and telephone number of a contact person. If the organization is being represented by a lawyer or accountant, that individual should be the contact person.

If the organization previously applied for recognition of tax exemption, that must be explained. There should also be an explanation for the filing of any annual information returns or income tax returns (Chapter 11).

Copies of articles of organization and any bylaws should be attached to the application. The articles for a corporation are its *articles of incorporation*, for an unincorporated association are its *constitution*, and for a trust are its *declaration of trust* or *trust agreement*.

TIPS: If the organization is a corporation, it should make certain that the date of formation is the date shown on the certificate of incorporation. If the organization is a charitable one, it should make certain that the facts concerning its accounting period are the same as those pertaining to its public support calculations (if applicable). The organization is expected to identify up to three *activity codes*; these codes are in the instructions and should be carefully selected.

Q 4:25   What is required in Part II of Form 1023?

Part II of Form 1023 is the most important portion. This is largely because here is where the organization describes its past, present, and planned activities (Q 4:10). These activities should be listed separately in order of importance.

NOTE: This is not the place to spare the language. The organization is not bound by the space made available on the form for the answer; some answers to this question are on an attachment numbering several pages (Q 4:14).

Other questions pertain to the organization's sources of financial support, its fund-raising program, the composition of and other information about the governing body, relationships with other organizations, its assets, its membership (if any), and its legislative and/or political campaign activities.

NOTE: In some instances throughout the application, it does not matter how the question is answered. For example, if there is no fund-raising program, an answer to that effect is all that is required.

TIP 1:   If the organization is a charitable one, it should be certain that its inventory of sources of financial support correlates with its public support schedule (if applicable) (Q 4:29).

TIP 2:   In answering the question about disqualified persons, the organization should use the definition of the term as provided in the private foundation context (Q 9:3), not the one used in the excess benefits transactions context (Q 1:14).

TIP 3:   As to the question concerning control, that term should be generously construed. This is a sensitive area, one where materiality of fact can be important (Q 4:8). Even if there is not formal control, there are questions as to "special relationships" and "financial accountability" to other organizations.

TIP 4:   There is a question about bond financing. This is a topic of great interest at the IRS these days. The organization should attach a statement about its plans in this area (if any) and should expect its bond financing plans to slow the processing of the application.

TIP 5:   There are questions about management contracts and leases. These arrangements should be carefully reviewed before the documents are submitted. For example, do these arrangements suggest a joint venture? (Q 3:6).

TIP 6:   There is a question about how the organization's charges for goods or services (if any) are determined. This question should be answered with some care. Whatever the response, the organization should not state that the charges are set to return a profit.

TIP 7:   The applicant organization being a charitable one, should answer the questions about lobbying and political campaign activities with the utmost caution.[44]

Q 4:26   What is required in Part III of Form 1023?

Part III of Form 1023 requests information about the timing of the filing of the application and the date the ruling is to take effect. These matters are discussed elsewhere (Q 4:21). This portion of the application also focuses on the public charity/private foundation status of the applicant organization.[45]

Q 4:27   What is required in Part IV of Form 1023?

Part IV of Form 1023 requests certain financial data, including revenue, expenses, assets, and liabilities. New applicant organizations may submit financial information by means of a budget.

Q 4:28   Are there any other portions of the application?

Yes. The other portions of the application are a series of schedules, as follows:

1. Schedule A, to be prepared by applicant organizations that are churches
2. Schedule B, to be prepared by applicant organizations that are schools, colleges, and universities
3. Schedule C, to be prepared by applicant organizations that are hospitals and medical research organizations
4. Schedule D, to be prepared by applicant organizations that are supporting organizations
5. Schedule E, to be prepared by applicant organizations that are private operating foundations
6. Schedule F, to be prepared by applicant organizations that are homes for the aged or the disabled
7. Schedule G, to be prepared by applicant organizations that are child care organizations
8. Schedule H, to be prepared by applicant organizations that provide scholarships and comparable benefits
9. Schedule I, to be prepared by applicant organizations that are successsors to for-profit organizations

The Form 1023 packet also contains the form that is used to extend the statute of limitations for the assessment of the private foundation net investment income tax (Q 9:39) for the years that constitute the advance ruling period (Q 4:29), should the entity become classified as a private foundation (Form 872-C).

SPECIAL REQUIREMENTS FOR CHARITABLE ORGANIZATIONS

Q 4:29   In the case of a charitable organization, when does the ruling take effect?

Assuming that the IRS ruling issued to a charitable organization is favorable, the date it takes effect depends on when the application for recognition of exemption was filed with the IRS. The optimum outcome is to have the IRS ruling effective as of the date the organization was formed.

NOTE: There are three aspects of this optimum outcome. When a charitable organization files a Form 1023 with the IRS, it is requesting as many as three rulings: that it is to be recognized as tax-exempt, that it is a public charity and not a private foundation (assuming that is the case), and that contributions to it be deductible. A charity is in the best position when all three of these rulings are effective from the organization's beginning.

Thus, an organization that desires recognition as a tax-exempt charitable organization *as of the date of its formation* generally must notify the IRS that it is applying for recognition of exemption on that basis, in conformity with a *threshold notice rule*. Thus, where the IRS recognizes the tax exemption of an organization that made a timely filing of this notice, the exemption is effective as of the date the organization was created.

NOTE: This requisite notice is given by the timely filing with the IRS of a properly completed and executed application for recognition of tax exemption (Form 1023).

Otherwise, the recognition of tax exemption as a charitable organization generally is effective only on a prospective basis.[46]

This *threshold notice rule* is of two parts. The general rule is that the notice to the IRS must be given within 15 months from the end of the month in which the organization was formed.[47] However, the IRS provided an automatic 12-month extension of time for this filing,[48] thereby converting it to a 27-month period.

If the organization files after the 27-month period, and if the organization has not been contacted by the IRS regarding its failure to file the notice within the 27-month period, the filing of the application constitutes a request for an extension of time to file (from the date the period ended until the date of filing) on the ground that the organization was acting reasonably and in good faith.[49]

If that does not work, the last resort is to appeal to the IRS, which has general discretionary authority, upon a showing of good cause, to grant a reasonable extension of time fixed by the tax regulations for making an election or application for relief in respect to the federal income tax law.[50] The IRS can exercise this discretionary authority to extend the time for filing of the notice/application, so that the resulting ruling has retroactive effect. The IRS outlined the information and representations that must be furnished and some factors that will be taken into consideration in determining whether an extension of this nature will be granted.[51]

Q 4:30   If the ruling is prospective only, is there anything that can be done to preserve tax exemption for the period preceding the effective date?

If a charitable organization is subject to the filing requirement (Q 4:31), has not satisfied the threshold notice requirement (Q 4:29), and has not convinced the IRS that it acted in good faith or otherwise that there was reasonable cause for the lack of timely filing, the favorable ruling will take effect as of the date the IRS received the application.

To preserve tax-exempt status for the period beginning on the date the organization was formed and ending as of the day before the charitable status took effect, the organization can be regarded as a social welfare organization (Chapter 6) during that initial period.[52]

NOTE: This works because social welfare organizations are not required to seek recognition of tax-exempt status and thus can voluntarily file at any time (Q 4:2).

TIP: Technically, the organization need not file anything to be regarded as a social welfare organization during its initial years. However, the IRS requests notice of this option and a completed page 1 of the application filed by social welfare organizations (Form 1024). The IRS should be accommodated in this regard.

However, this approach does nothing to salvage public charity or charitable donee status (Q 4:29).

Q 4:31 Are there any exceptions to this filing requirement for charitable organizations?

Yes, there are three exceptions. The following entities can be tax-exempt charitable organizations without having to file an application for recognition of exemption:

1. Churches, interchurch organizations of local units of a church, conventions or associations of churches, and integrated auxiliaries of churches[53]
2. Organizations whose gross receipts in each tax year are normally not more than $5,000 (as long as they are not private foundations)[54]
3. Subordinate organizations covered by a group exemption letter where the central organization has submitted to the IRS the requisite notice covering the subordinates (Q 4:39)

Q 4:32 What does the term *normally* mean?

The term *normally* embodies an averaging mechanism. That is, the gross receipts of an organization are normally not more than $5,000 if

1. During its first tax year, it received gross receipts of no more than $7,500,
2. During its first two tax years, it received gross receipts of no more than $12,000, and
3. In the case of an organization that has been in existence for three tax years, the gross receipts received by it during its immediately preceding two tax years plus the current year are not more than $15,000.[55]

Q 4:33 What happens when an initially small organization begins to receive greater amounts of income?

The exception for organizations with gross receipts that are normally no more than $5,000 can operate to relieve a small organization from the requirement of filing an application for recognition of tax exemption during the initial years of its operation (yet still be tax-exempt) but expire as the organization receives greater amounts of financial support. Once an organization fails to meet this exception, it is required to file the notice (application for recognition of exemption) within 90 days after the close of the year in which its gross receipts exceeded the amounts permitted under the exception.[56] Thus, this notice period is used in this circumstance instead of the general threshold notice rule.

NOTE: An organization in this circumstance can, therefore, be tax-exempt as a charitable entity from its inception—no matter how many years have passed—as long as it files the application on a timely basis (under the 90-day rule).

Q 4:34 How do the notice requirements work with respect to public charity status?

As noted, these notice rules apply with respect to public charity status as well as to tax-exempt status (Q 4:29). The requirement of notification to the IRS as to nonprivate foundation status does not apply to churches, conventions or associations of churches, or integrated auxiliaries of churches.[57]

A tax-exempt charitable organization (not exempt from the filing requirements) that is not a private foundation will (if the notice has been given) have its public charity status evidenced in either an advance ruling or a definitive ruling. Advance rulings are issued to newly formed publicly supported charities, and definitive rulings are issued to other types of public charities.[58]

Q 4:35 What happens when the requested ruling as to tax-exempt status is not granted?

The IRS has developed an extensive set of procedural rules to follow, should the requested ruling be adverse to the organization. These procedures, which are somewhat outdated as a result of the IRS's recent reorganization and consolidation (Q 4:6), are in many ways akin to the IRS practices and procedures in any instance in which there is a tax controversy beyond the level of the initial determination.

Thus, these procedures include the right of protest and appeal, conferences, the pursuit of technical advice from the National Office of the IRS, and occasionally consideration of the case by the National Office. Beyond that, there is access to the courts; an organization can take its case to the U.S. Tax Court (without a lawyer, if it chooses) or to a U.S. District Court or the U.S. Court of Federal Claims. Appeals can be taken to the appropriate U.S. Circuit Court of Appeals; on rare occasions, an exempt organization's case will be heard by the Supreme Court. For charitable organizations only, there is a declaratory judgment procedure by which issues as to tax-exempt status, private foundation/public charity status, and/or charitable donee status may be litigated.[59]

GROUP EXEMPTION

Q 4:36   What is the *group exemption* procedure?

The group exemption procedure[60] was devised by the IRS to eliminate the administrative burdens that would be caused by the pursuit of rulings by identical organizations, where there are many of them (perhaps hundreds) and they are related. This procedure is designed for entities such as chapters, locals, posts, or units that are affiliated with and subject to the general supervision or control of an organization, which is usually a national, regional, or state entity.

The supervisory organization is known as the *central organization*; the organizations that are affiliated with the central organization are *subordinate organizations*.

OBSERVATION: This an unfortunate choice of terminology, in that many organizations and those who manage them do not care to be regarded as *subordinates*. A preferable term would be *affiliates*. Aside from the psychology of the terminology, there are political aspects as well: the term *central organization* to some at the affiliate level stimulates fears of too much authority and control.

Tax exemption for subordinate organizations is recognized by the IRS by reason of their relationship with the central organization. This is known as tax exemption on a group basis.

These procedures contemplate a functioning of the central organization as an agent of the IRS, requiring that the organization responsibly and independently evaluate the qualification for tax-exempt status of the subordinate organizations from the standpoint of the organizational and operational tests applicable to them.[61]

Q 4:37   How is the group exemption initially established?

First, the entity intending to be a central organization must obtain recognition from the IRS of its own tax-exempt status. Then, the organization applies to the IRS for classification as a central organization.

This application (oddly, there is no IRS form for it) must establish that all of the subordinate organizations to be included in the group exemption letter are properly affiliated with the central organization (Q 4:38), are subject to its general supervision or control, have the identical tax-exempt status, are not private foundations, are not foreign organizations, have the same accounting period as the central organization if they are not to be included in group returns (Q 4:40), and, in the case of charitable entities, are formed within the 15-month period (Q 4:29) prior to the date of submission of the group exemption application.

A central organization must submit to the IRS the following information on behalf of the subordinate entities:

1. Information verifying the facts evidencing the aforementioned relationships and other requirements

2. A description of the principal purposes and activities of the subordinates, including financial information

3. A sample copy of a uniform or representative governing instrument adopted by the subordinates

4. An affirmation by a principal officer of the central organization that the subordinates are operating in accordance with their stated purposes

5. A statement that each subordinate has furnished the requisite written authorization

6. A list of subordinates to which the IRS has issued a determination letter or ruling recognizing exempt status,

7. If relevant, an affirmation that no subordinate organization is a private foundation

8. A list of the names, addresses, and employer identification numbers of the subordinates to be included in the group (or a satisfactory directory of them)

Certain additional information is required of a subordinate organization if it is claiming tax-exempt status as a school.

NOTE: There is only one court case involving the group exemption procedures. There, the IRS procedures were upheld, with an organization found to not be eligible for classification as a central organization because the requisite information was not provided.[62]

Q 4:38   What is required for organizations to be *affiliated?*

Interestingly, the term *affiliation* is not defined in this context. Usually, the requisite affiliation is found in the governance structure of the organizations involved, such as an association with chapters, a church denomination with many individual churches, or a veterans' or fraternal organization with lodges. Sometimes the affiliation is inherent in a relationship involving finances, such as dues-sharing. In general, the IRS will accept any reasonable interpretation of the word *affiliation* in this setting.

NOTE: This state of affairs is understandable, in that the group exemption is saving the IRS the task of processing thousands of applications for recognition of tax exemption.

Q 4:39   How is the group exemption maintained?

The group exemption is basically maintained by the central organization making an annual filing with the IRS. Certain information must be annually submitted to the IRS by the central organization (at least 90 days before the close of its annual accounting period) to sustain the group status.

This information consists of the following:

1. Information regarding any changes in the purposes, character, or method of operation of the subordinate organization

2. A list of subordinates that have changed their names or addresses during the year

3. A list of subordinates that are no longer part of the group

4. A list of organizations that were added to the group during the year

5. The information summarized previously concerning the subordinates that joined the group during the year

---

NOTE: Historically, these annual filings were made with the appropriate IRS service center. However, group exemption reports submitted on or after July 1, 1996, are filed with the IRS Service Center in Ogden, Utah.[63]

Q 4:40   How are the annual information return reporting requirements satisfied?

A central organization must, as a general rule, file an annual information return (Chapter 11). So too must each subordinate organization. However, many subordinate organizations are small and thus may be able to take advantage of the exception for organizations with annual gross receipts that normally do not exceed $25,000 (Q 11:3).

A subordinate organization has a choice in this regard. It can file its own annual information return (assuming no basis for an exception), or it can file with the central organization as part of a group annual return.[64]

NOTE: A central organization may exclude from its group return those subordinates the annual gross receipts of which are normally not in excess of $25,000 per year.[65]

Q 4:41   Do the central organization and the subordinate organizations have to have the same tax-exempt status?

No. These entities can have different tax-exempt organization classifications. For example, the central organization can be exempt as a business league (Chapter 5) and the subordinates can be exempt as charitable organizations. Alternatively, the central organization can be exempt as a charitable organization and the subordinates can be exempt as social welfare organizations (Chapter 6).

NOTE: As noted, the subordinate organizations in a group must have the same tax-exempt status. However, a central organization can have more than one group. For example, there can be a central organization that is a charitable entity with two groups: one comprised of charitable organizations and one comprised of social welfare organizations.

Q 4:42   Can the same organization be involved in more than one group?

Yes. For example, a state organization can be a central organization with respect to a group of subordinate entities throughout the state. Simultaneously, the state organization can be one of a number of state subordinate organizations in relation to a national central organization.

Q 4:43   When can the group exemption be terminated?

There are several instances when a group exemption may be terminated. One is when the central organization dissolves or otherwise ceases to exist. Other instances in which the group status can collapse are when the central organization ceases to qualify for tax-exempt status, fails to submit the requisite information, or fails to comply with the reporting requirements.

NOTE: Loss of tax exemption by some of the subordinate organizations in a group does not adversely affect the group exemption ruling for the other members of the group.[66]

Q 4:44   What are the advantages of the group exemption?

From the standpoint of the IRS, the group exemption procedure is advantageous because it relieves the agency of the processing of thousands of applications for recognition of tax exemption (Q 4:36).

The group exemption generally is very favorable for clusters of nonprofit organizations that are affiliated. This approach to tax exemption obviates the need for each member entity in the group to file a separate application for recognition of exemption, and this can result in savings of time, effort, and money. It is, then, a streamlined approach to the establishment of tax-exempt status for related organizations.

Q 4:45   Are there any disadvantages to the group exemption?

Yes—actually, there are several. One concerns the fact that the members of the group do not individually possess determination letters as to their tax exemption. In regard to charitable organizations, this can pose difficulties for donors and grantors. That is, a contributor of a major gift may want the security of a determination letter so as to have the requisite basis for relying on the organization's representation that it is a charitable entity. A private foundation grantor may desire similar assurance to be certain that the grant constitutes a qualifying distribution (Q 9:21), is not an expenditure responsibility grant (Q 9:36), and/or is not otherwise a taxable expenditure (Q 9:32).

Another disadvantage pertains to charitable subordinate organizations. By definition, the group exemption process does not entail any IRS review of these entities' public charity status. Sophisticated donors and grantors know this and thus know that they usually cannot assume that a particular subordinate entity is a public charity—which is the assurance they need. This dilemma is compounded by the practice of the IRS to automatically accord to the subordinate entities the same public charity status as that recognized for the central organization—and to do so on the basis of definitive rulings.

A third disadvantage pertains to state tax exemptions. Often, the state authorities will not recognize a state tax exemption unless the organization can produce a copy of a federal determination as to exemption under a comparable status. Obviously, with the group exemption, a subordinate organization does not have that evidence to produce, thereby often making the process of securing one or more state tax exemptions more difficult.

NOTE: At some point, if these burdens become too great, the subordinate organization may have to obtain recognition of tax-exempt status from the IRS and leave the group.

Finally, if a member of a group is found liable for damages, the existence of the group exemption may be used in an effort to assert "ascending" liability on the part of the central organization.

CHAPTER 5

Membership Associations

Associations represent a significant component of the nonprofit sector. They essentially can be classified as one of three types: trade associations, business associations, and professional associations (the latter often termed *societies*). Whatever the type, they usually have one fact in common: They operate to improve business conditions for their memberships. However, some associations (usually the societies) function more for the benefit of the public than for members.

There are many legal issues concerning associations. Those pertaining to nonprofit and tax status are reviewed in this chapter. However, the operations of associations involve other areas of the law, most notably, antitrust, postal services, labor, and employee benefits.

From a federal tax perspective, the principal areas of inquiry are eligibility for tax exemption, consequences of lobbying and political campaign activities, unrelated business income taxation, and use of related organizations.

Here are the questions most frequently asked by clients about the corporate and tax status of associations—and the answers to them.

BUSINESS LEAGUES IN GENERAL

Q 5:1   What is an *association*?

Dictionaries define the term *association* as an organization of persons having a common interest. From a legal standpoint, this definition is somewhat overstated, but it conveys the general idea. Terms that are synonymous with association are *league, society*, and, to some degree, *union*. Associations are the successors to medieval guilds, such as those controlled and operated by merchants. Thus, by definition, an association is a membership organization. From a federal tax law standpoint, an association is a form of *business league*.

Q 5:2   Does an association have to be incorporated?

No, there is no requirement that an association be incorporated, at least not for federal tax purposes. For other reasons, such as limitation on the liability of directors and officers, it may be a good idea to incorporate an association.[1]

Associations are formed under state law. They are one of two types of entities. One is a nonprofit membership corporation. This entity is created by the filing of *articles of incorporation*. It will usually have (and should have) a set of operating rules, termed its *bylaws*. The other type of entity in this context is the unincorporated association. This type of organization is formed by execution of a *constitution*. It, too, is likely to have bylaws.

Q 5:3   Is an association a tax-exempt organization?

Generally, under the federal income tax laws, yes.[2] However, there are associations that are nonprofit organizations, yet are taxable, and there are associations organized as for-profit organizations. But these latter instances are rare.

Nearly all associations are tax-exempt as business leagues. This means that they (assuming they otherwise qualify) are described in section 501(c)(6) of the Internal Revenue Code. Some associations qualify as educational, scientific, and/or charitable organizations; these are described in Code section 501(c)(3). An association may be organized as a social welfare organization (Code section 501(c)(4))[3] or a homeowners' association (Code section 528). There are other nonprofit, tax-exempt organizations that have a membership and certain other characteristics of an association, although they are not normally thought of as associations: unions and certain other membership organizations (Code section 501(c)(5)), social clubs (Code section 501(c)(7)),[4] fraternal groups (Code section 501(c)(8) and (10)), veterans' organizations (Code section 501(c)(19)), and farmers' cooperatives (Code section 521).

State law usually provides income tax exemption, and often other tax exemptions, for associations.

Q 5:4   What is a *business league*?

The term *business league* encompasses membership associations but has a broader range than that. On occasion, an organization that does not have a membership, but is closely associated with one that does, is able to be recognized as an exempt business league. Other organizations that look like business leagues, yet technically are not, are chambers of commerce, boards of trade, and real estate boards.

The federal statutory law concerning the tax-exempt status of business leagues (Code section 501(c)(6)) imposes only two requirements for exemption: These entities may not be organized for profit, and they may not allow their net earnings to inure to persons in their private capacity. The principal requirements for qualification for exempt status as a business league are found in the tax regulations.

TAX EXEMPTION CRITERIA

Q 5:5   What are the criteria for tax exemption as a business league?

Two of these criteria have been noted (Q 5:4). A business league may not be organized for profit (that is, it must be a nonprofit organization), and it must adhere to the private inurement doctrine.[5]

More specifically, a tax-exempt business league has two other general characteristics. First, it usually has a membership; it is what the tax regulations term an *association of persons*. Second, the persons who are associated must have *some common business interest.*[6]

Q 5:6   What does the term *business* mean in this context?

The term *business* in this setting is broadly construed. It includes nearly any activity carried on for the production of income.[7] It embraces trades and professions.[8] It may also include the activities of organizations, such as consumer cooperatives, that engage in business on a cooperative basis.[9] Activities that are hobbies do not qualify as businesses.[10]

An organization composed of individuals studying for a degree in a profession may qualify as a business league. This would occur even if the students are not presently engaged in a business, in that the purpose of the organization is to promote their common interests as future members of the profession.[11]

Q 5:7   What is the exempt purpose of a business league?

The exempt purpose of a business league is to promote the common business interest of its members. More technically, an exempt business league exists to improve the business conditions with respect to one or more lines of business. Therefore, to be tax-exempt, a business league must have as its primary purpose one or more ways of promoting the improvement of conditions as to at least one line of business.[12]

Q 5:8   What are some examples of tax-exempt business leagues?

Various IRS rulings offer illustrations of exempt business leagues. Here are some of them:

- A board was formed by members of the medical profession to improve the quality of medical care available to the public, and to establish and maintain high standards of excellence in a particular medical specialty. The board's activities included devising and administering written examinations and issuing certificates to successful candidates in the medical specialty. Listings of the certified physicians were made available by the board to various medical groups who in turn made the listings available to the public. The organization was held to promote the common business interest of the physicians.[13]

- An organization formed to stimulate the development and free interchange of information pertaining to systems and programming of electronic data processing equipment qualified. The membership was composed of representatives of diversified businesses that owned, rented, or leased one or more digital computers produced by various manufacturers. Semiannual conferences open to the general public were held, at which operational and technical problems were discussed. The common business interest of the members of the organization was their common business problems concerning the use of digital computers. The activities of this organization provided a forum for the exchange of information that would lead to the more efficient use of computers by members and other interested users, and thus improve the overall efficiency of the business operations of each.[14]

- An organization formed by members of a state medical association to operate peer review boards was held to be an exempt business league. Its primary purposes of establishing and maintaining standards for quality, quantity, and reasonableness of costs of medical services were seen as serving to maintain the professional standards, prestige, and independence of the medical profession and thereby further the common interest of the organization's members.[15]

- An organization formed to promote the commercial fishing industry in a state through the publication and dissemination of a newspaper containing news of events of interest to those engaged in fishing, and new techniques and advances in the commercial fishing industry, was held to qualify. The activities of the organization were directed toward the betterment of the conditions of those involved in commercial fishing. By operating in this manner, the organization was found to be promoting the common business interests of persons engaged in commercial fishing.[16]

- An organization formed as a membership entity of business and professional women that promoted the acceptance of women in business and the professions qualified. By sponsoring events devoted to the discussion and consideration of problems affecting women in business and the professions, the organization was held to be promoting a common business interest. To the extent that the organization achieved its goal of improving opportunities for and attitudes toward women, it was found to have improved conditions in each of the lines of business from which its members were drawn.[17]

- A trust established for the purpose of monitoring and coordinating business league activities of its member business leagues, and collecting, administering, and disbursing funds to the member business leagues for business league purposes, was itself ruled to be a business league. The trust was created pursuant to collective bargaining agreements between a labor union and several business leagues, which promote the home building industry in a particular geographic area.[18]

Q 5:9   What are some examples of organizations that do not qualify as exempt business leagues?

Here are some illustrations of organizations that did not achieve tax-exempt status as business leagues:

- An organization composed of individuals, firms, associations, and corporations, each representing a different trade, business, occupation, or profession, the purpose of which was to exchange information on business prospects, was ruled not to have a common business interest other than a mutual desire to increase their individual sales. The activities were held to not be directed to the improvement of one or more lines of business, but rather to the promotion of the private interests of the members.[19]

- A national association composed of individual automobile owners and affiliated automobile clubs was held not to qualify. Notwithstanding its broad purposes of improving highway traffic safety and educating the public in traffic safety, its principal activities were determined to consist of securing benefits and performing particular services for members (Q 5:17).[20]

Q 5:10   What is a *line of business*?

Basically, a *line of business* is an industry or a subpart of an industry. It is any trade or occupation, into which entry is not restricted in some manner, such as by patent or trademark, that allows private parties to restrict the right to engage in the business.[21]

A line of business may be envisioned as a horizontal line; the line basically may be as thin as wished but it cannot be broken (intersected) by a vertical line. The line represents an industry (or a trade or profession); the exempt business league must represent all persons in that field, so that they share a common business interest, and membership must be open to all in that field. The industry can be as broad or as narrow (even esoteric) as wanted.

EXAMPLE: A bar association is a business league, with the profession of the law being the requisite industry. There can be an association of lawyers who confine their practice to the representation of nonprofit organizations; there can be an exempt association of lawyers who represent only tax-exempt organizations. The industry involved can be further narrowed to encompass only lawyers who represent business leagues, or professional societies, or trade groups.

This issue went to the Supreme Court. In dispute was the tax status of an organization that confined its membership to muffler dealers franchised by the Midas International Corporation. The Court ruled that this organization could not qualify as an exempt business league because of the composition of its membership, which was confined to muffler dealers franchised by only one manufacturer, so that the association was not engaged in the improvement of business conditions of a line of business.[22] This was an example of an impermissible vertical breaking of the horizontal line: there can be a tax-exempt association of muffler dealers, but there cannot be a tax-exempt association of Midas Muffler dealers.

Another illustration is the computer users group. These entities cannot qualify as an exempt business league. By definition, the membership of these organizations is concerned with and relates only to the hardware and software manufactured by one company. Thus, tax exemption as a business league is not available for organizations that endeavor to improve business conditions in only a *segment* of a line of business.[23]

Two other examples. An association of licensed dealers in a certain type of patented product was ruled not to qualify as an exempt business league where the association owned the controlling interest in a corporation holding the patent, because it was engaged mainly in furthering the business interests of its member-dealers and did not benefit persons who manufacture competing products of the same type covered by the patent.[24] An association of dealers selling a particular make of automobile that engaged in financing general advertising campaigns to promote the sale of that make could not achieve tax exemption because it did not promote the automobile industry as a whole.[25]

COMMENT: One aspect of the line of business requirement is that direct competitors are represented by the same association. Stated another way, an exempt business league is not supposed to be available to aid one group in competition with another within an industry. Thus, just as the antitrust laws endeavor to minimize contacts between competing businesses, the tax laws operate to link and otherwise enhance those relationships.

It was said earlier that the horizontal line reflecting an industry cannot be vertically broken in defining the membership of an exempt business league. That was somewhat of an overstatement: the membership can be restricted by geography. Thus, for example, there can be an exempt association representing all components of an industry within a multistate region, a state, or a city.[26]

Q 5:11   How does a business league accomplish its requirement of promoting a common business interest?

Basically, an association or other type of business league engages in this requirement as to promotion by providing services to or for the benefit of its members. Generally, these services include one or more publications, sponsorship of one or more conferences or seminars, lobbying, certification, presentation of information to government agencies, subsidization of litigation, maintenance of a library, maintenance of a members' code of ethics, and engaging in public awareness and information dissemination efforts.

These matters can be quite fact-specific (Q 5:8–5:9). Thus, an association of insurance companies created pursuant to a state's no-fault insurance statute to provide personal injury protection for residents of the state who sustain injury and are not covered by any insurance was held to qualify as a tax-exempt business league because its activities "promote[d] the common business interests of its members by fulfilling an obligation that the state has imposed upon the insurance industry as a prerequisite for doing business within the state and by enhancing the image of the industry."[27] An organization that operated a "plan room" and published a news bulletin that contained information about plans available at the room, bid results, and activities of concern to persons in the industry was ruled to be an exempt business league.[28]

NOTE: Activities of this nature should be contrasted with those that amount to the performance of particular services for individuals. These services can cause loss or denial of exempt status or be deemed unrelated businesses (Q 5:17).

Q 5:12   Can an association qualify as an educational, scientific, or charitable organization?

Generally, no. However, this all depends on the primary purpose of the organization. When the IRS or a court considers a membership organization, there is almost a presumption that its tax exemption will be predicated on its status as a business league. This determination is made, in part, on the nature of the organization's membership, that is, whether it is composed of individuals, businesses, and nonprofit organizations or a blend of these entities (Q 5:13).

This presumption arises out of the belief that the activities of an association are directed primarily at the promotion of the particular industry and that they are principally operated to further the common business purpose of its members. Advancement of a charitable, educational, or scientific purpose is usually viewed as a secondary objective, if it is recognized at all.

For example, a medical society may undertake the following activities: meetings concerned with the promotion and protection of the practice of medicine, operation of a legislative committee, conduct of a public relations program, provision of a patient referral service, and maintenance of a grievance committee. It may also engage in the following charitable and educational activities: conferences where technical papers are presented, maintenance of a library, publication of a journal, provision of lecturers and counseling services at medical schools, and the support of public health programs. In almost every instance, the former activities will be considered by the IRS and the courts as the primary ones, so that medical societies are generally considered business leagues, not charitable organizations.[29]

A bar association may engage in such charitable and educational endeavors as law institutes, publication of a journal, sponsorship of a moot court program and speakers' panels, and the provision of legal assistance to indigents. Yet, the following activities will almost always be seen to predominate: preparation of studies on the economics of law office administration, programs directed at ways of making the practice of law more profitable, enforcement of standards of conduct, and sponsorship of social events (such as travel and sporting events). Thus, a bar association will almost certainly be considered a business league.[30]

There can be a dispute as to the purpose, and thus classification, of a particular program activity. A contemporary illustration of this is *certification*. It has become common practice for associations of individuals to certify their members in accordance with particular criteria; these individuals display the certification (usually, a set of initials) in a variety of professional contexts.

NOTE: One of the first of these designations came out of the accounting field, which recognizes certified public accountant (CPA), as used, for example, on business cards and letterhead (e.g., Mary F. Smith, CPA). More recent illustrations are Peter F. Jones, CFRE (certified fund raising executive), Ann P. Black, CAE (certified association executive), and Robert E. White, CSCM (certified shopping center manager).

One view of certification programs is that they exist primarily for the benefit of the general public, in that they are an integral component of an educational process designed to provide important information to the purchasers of services. The other view is that certification programs are primarily beneficial to those who are certified, in that their professional standing and the prospects of their employment are enhanced. It is the judgment of the IRS that the primary purpose of certification is to improve the reputation and business interests of the members of the certifying organization and the profession of which they form a part. In one instance, the IRS stated that the certification program "is designed and operated to achieve professional standing for [the profession involved] and to enhance the respectability of those who have been certified."[31] Therefore, at least in the eyes of the IRS, certification is a proper function for a business league but not for a charitable organization.

Nonetheless, there have been a few instances in which a membership association has been held by the IRS or a court to be a charitable or educational organization.

Q 5:13 What is the significance of the nature of an organization's members?

The nature of an organization's membership can be determinative of its tax-exempt status. Generally, there are three types of members: commercial businesses, tax-exempt organizations, and individuals.

The typical association of commercial businesses (a *business association*) is a business league. An association of individuals is likely to be a business league (perhaps as a *trade association*), although if the primary purpose of the organization is the advancement of charitable, educational, or scientific ends, it may be exempt as a charitable organization (a *professional society*).

An association of tax-exempt organizations (or of individuals who are employed by exempt organizations) may well have the same tax status as its members. Thus, associations of exempt organizations such as schools, colleges, and universities are often exempt as charitable entities. The same is the case with respect to associations of entities such as churches and private foundations. An association of associations is likely a business league.

Some associations have a blend of these memberships. These entities tend to be business leagues. For example, an association of both nonprofit and for-profit hospitals is almost certain to be a business league.

NOTE: The purpose for having differing categories of members can also have consequences in the realm of unrelated business income (Q 5:28).

Q 5:14   Are there limitations on the amount of lobbying a business league can engage in?

From the standpoint of exempt organizations law as such, the answer is no. That is, an association can lobby as much as it wishes and its status as a business league will not be adversely affected. However, lobbying by a business league can cause some or all of the dues paid to the association to not be deductible as a business expense.[32]

Q 5:15   Are there limitations on the amount of political campaign activity a business league can engage in?

Again, from the standpoint of exempt organizations law as such, the answer is no. In fact, there is little law on the point. However, because of election law considerations and partially because of the tax law, most business leagues form and utilize related political organizations for this purpose (Chapter 8). Moreover, political campaign activity by a business league can cause some or all of the dues paid to the association to not be deductible as a business expense.[33]

Q 5:16   What are the principal reasons for loss of tax exemption as a business league?

As the foregoing discussion reflects (Q 5:5–Q 5:15), there are several bases on which tax-exempt status as a business league may be lost (or denied). One is violation of the doctrine of private inurement. Thus, an association that issued shares of stock carrying the right to dividends was denied tax exemption as a business league.[34] Other instances involving private inurement include an organization that used its funds to provide financial assistance and welfare benefits for its members,[35] an organization that paid its members for expenses they incurred in defending malpractice suits and paying judgments rendered in the suits,[36] and an association of wholesale grocers that owned a copyright on certain grocery labels and that distributed royalties to its members.[37] (However, a provision in an organization's charter, providing for the distribution of assets to its members in the event of dissolution, will not in itself preclude exemption as a business league.[38])

The inurement proscription precludes a business league from furnishing benefits for some members at special rates, at the expense of the other members. Nevertheless, an exempt business league may generally make cash distributions to its members without loss of exemption where the distributions represent no more than a reduction in dues or contributions previously paid to the league to support its activities.

However, if the refund of the dues is not made in the same proportion as the dues are paid, inurement may result.[39]

In one instance, cash rebates were made by an exempt business association to member and nonmember exhibitors who participated in the association's annual industry trade show. The rebates represented a portion of an advance floor deposit paid by each exhibitor to ensure the show against financial loss, were made to all exhibitors on the same basis, did not exceed the amount of the deposit, and thus did not adversely affect the association's tax-exempt status.[40]

A second basis is the prohibition on business activities for profit. In large part, this is a matter of unrelated business income taxation. However, it can relate to tax exemption as well. This often implicates the commerciality doctrine (Chapter 2). For example, an association of insurance companies that accepted for reinsurance high-risk customers who would ordinarily be turned down by its member companies was ruled to not qualify as a tax-exempt business league, because reinsurance is a business ordinarily carried on by commercial insurance companies for a profit.[41]

A third basis for loss or denial of tax exemption as a business league is failure to be structured along particular business or industry lines (Q 5:10).

The fourth basis on which tax exemption as a business league may be lost or denied is a finding that the organization is performing particular services for its members, or for some of them, as distinguished from the improvement of business conditions in the particular business or industry. For example, an association sold its local chapters and members various supplies, charts, books, shop emblems, and association jewelry. A court concluded that the association was undertaking activities that "serve as a convenience or economy to . . . [its] members in the operation of their businesses" and was not promoting a common business interest.[42]

In another illustration, an association of insurance companies in a state that provided medical malpractice insurance to health care providers where the insurance was not available from for-profit insurers, was held to be "performing particular services for its member companies and policyholders" because its "method of operation involves it in its member companies' insurance business, and since the organization's insurance activities serve as an economy or convenience in providing necessary protection to its policyholders engaged in providing health care."[43] This rationale was also applied to the activities of an association of insurance companies that accepted for reinsurance high-risk customers who would ordinarily be turned down by its member companies.[44] Likewise, an engineering society that provided food and beverage service to its individual members was found to be providing a service for individual persons, and thus was deprived of qualification for tax-exempt status as a business league.[45]

A telling factor in this regard is signalled when the economics are outside the usual model of members paying dues and receiving services of equivalent value. If separate payment is required for services, they are likely to be regarded as *particular* services. Thus, a court held that a major factor in determining whether services are particular is whether they are supported by fees and assessments in approximate proportion to the benefits received.[46]

Advertising that carries the names of members generally constitutes the performance of particular services for the members. Thus, an association of the merchants in a particular shopping center, whose advertising material contained the names of the individual merchants, was denied recognition of tax-exempt status.[47] So too was an association created to attract tourists to a local area, where its principal activity was the publication of a yearbook consisting largely of paid advertisements by its members.[48] In another case, tax exemption was denied to an association that published catalogs that listed only products manufactured by the members.[49]

NOTE: An organization formed to promote the business of an industry and that conducts a general advertising campaign to encourage the use of products and services of the industry as a whole is tax-exempt, notwithstanding that the advertising to a minor extent constitutes the performance of particular services for its members.[50] Thus, an association of apple growers that engaged in promotion of the sale of apples grown in a state was held to be exempt, since its purpose was to promote the industry as a whole and not the members of the organization.[51]

However, despite this express prohibition as to particular services, it is the long-standing position of the IRS that a tax-exempt business league will be deprived of its exemption because it performs particular services for individual members only where the services are a principal or sole undertaking of the organization. Where these services are less than a primary function of a business league, the IRS will characterize them as a business of a kind ordinarily carried on for profit and treat the business as an unrelated activity. For example, the IRS concluded that an executive referral service conducted by an exempt professional association constituted the performance of particular services for individual persons, but inasmuch as other activities were the association's primary ones, the IRS ruled that the referral service was an unrelated business.[52]

Q 5:17 Isn't it difficult to distinguish between the performance of particular services and activities directed to the improvement of business conditions?

Yes, that is often the case. One court concluded that an activity of a business league was an exempt function where the undertaking benefited its membership as a group, rather than in their individual capacities. The benefit to the group occurred where the business league provided a product or service to its members for a fee, with the benefit not directly proportional to the fees (such as seminars and legislative activities). This court wrote that "[s]ervices which render benefits according to the fee that is paid for them are taxable business activities, not tax exempt services."[53] The court added: "Therefore, the activities that serve the interests of individual . . . [members] according to what they pay produce individual benefits insufficient to fulfill the substantial relationship test, since those activities generally do not generate inherent group benefits that inure to the advantage of its members as members."[54]

Subsequently, the IRS grappled with these distinctions, differentiating between "an industry-wide benefit or a particular service to members." The IRS held that activities that provide an industry-wide benefit "usually possess certain characteristics," such as being an "activity for which individual members could not be expected to bear the expense and thus lends itself to cooperative effort" and the fact that the "benefits are intangible and only indirectly related to the individual business." Activities constituting particular services "can usually be characterized as either a 'means of bringing buyers and sellers together' or a 'convenience or economy' to members in conducting their business," wrote the IRS, which also cautioned that "[f]ull participation by industry components does not guarantee that the activity provides an industry-wide benefit."[55]

In one case, an organization of contractors operated a plan room, containing information about plans available, bid results, and activities of concern to persons in the industry. The IRS ruled that the organization was a tax-exempt business league because its activities improved the business conditions of the line of business served, inasmuch as it made the information on construction projects freely available to the entire construction industry.[56]

COMMENT: In this case, the plan room was clearly an "economy or convenience" for the member contractors. However, the IRS devised a form of doctrine of redundancy in minimizing the legal effect of this activity: the information on file at the plan room was said to duplicate the information already available to the members. This function, having been thus dismissed, was ruled to not preclude the organization from achieving exempt business league status.

Here are some other examples of situations in which tax exemption was denied because of the performance of particular services for individual persons:

1. An organization formed to sell advertising in its members' publications.[57]

2. An organization that promoted the publication of its members' writings.[58]

3. Organizations that facilitated the purchase of supplies and equipment, or supplied management services, for their members.[59]

4. A traffic bureau that arranged shipments and billings for a fee.[60]

5. An organization of florists to promote the exchange of orders by wire among its members.[61]

6. An organization formed to give financial assistance to individuals entering a particular profession.[62]

7. A bureau that operated a credit information service for its members.[63]

8. An organization that operated a telephone answering service for member physicians.[64]

9. An organization of commercial banks that provided and promoted a credit card plan for member banks.[65]

10. An organization that published and distributed to its members' customers and potential customers a directory containing members' names and addresses.[66]

In contrast, here are some instances where an activity carried on by a business league was found to benefit a common business interest, even though there was also an incidental benefit to individual members which, standing alone, might have appeared to be a particular service to individuals:

1. An organization of employers in an industry that negotiated terms of a uniform labor contract for the entire industry, mediated and settled labor disputes affecting the industry, and interpreted contracts.[67]

2. An association of insurance companies formed to investigate criminal aspects of claims against its members.[68]

3. An organization of financial institutions that offered rewards for information leading to the arrest and conviction of individuals committing crimes against its members.[69]

4. An organization formed to regulate the sale of a specific agricultural commodity to ensure equal treatment of producers, warehousers, and buyers.[70]

5. An organization of advertising agencies that verified the advertising claims of publications selling advertising space and made reports available to members of the advertising industry generally.[71]

The IRS held that the operation, by an exempt association of members in the trucking industry, of an alcohol and drug testing program for members and nonmembers was a particular service (as opposed to an incident of membership), notwithstanding the fact that the prevention of alcohol and drug abuse is a "legitimate goal" of trucking companies.[72]

This discussion of these distinctions can be ended with this contrast. An association of plywood manufacturers owned a trademark that was licensed for use only by its members. Advertising sponsored by the association did not contain the names of individual manufacturers, but did refer to the trademark. A court found that the trademark was analogous to the industry-wide advertising approved in another case[73] and that the trademark was only an incidental part of the advertising, which extolled the virtues of plywood in general, so that tax exemption was preserved.[74] Thereafter, the IRS held that a nonprofit association of manufacturers, the principal activity of which was the promotion of its members' products under the association's required trademark, did not qualify as a tax-exempt business league.[75]

Q 5:18   Is there potential confusion between business league status and classification as another type of exempt organization?

Yes. There has already been discussion of the considerations in distinguishing between an exempt business league and an exempt charitable organization (Q 5:12).

In addition, business leagues should be contrasted with organizations operating to better the conditions of persons engaged in agriculture or to improve the grade of their products. These organizations may qualify for tax exemption as labor, agricultural, or horticultural organizations, rather than as business leagues.[76] However, if an organization is promoting the common business interests of persons in an industry related to agricultural pursuits, tax-exempt business league designation would be appropriate—assuming the organization otherwise qualifies.[77]

A nonprofit trust created by an agreement between a labor union and a business league, the activities of which were considered appropriate for a business league, was considered an association of persons having a common business interest and thus an exempt business league.[78]

Moreover, there can be interplay between the rules describing a qualified business league and those defining an exempt social club. In one instance, the IRS attempted to classify a professional society as a social club, claiming it was regularly engaged in substantial restaurant, beverage, and other social operations. Although this approach was rejected in litigation, with the social and like functions considered incidental, a court determined that the society did not constitute an exempt business league, albeit on other grounds.[79]

Q 5:19   Are business leagues involved with the intermediate sanctions rules?

No. The intermediate sanctions rules involve only *applicable tax-exempt organizations*.[80] These are public charities and social welfare organizations (Q 1:15).

COMMENT: There is talk from time to time about including tax-exempt business leagues within the scope of the applicable tax-exempt organization (Q 1:5). However, to date, there has not been any attempt to amend the law in this regard.

CAUTION: A membership association can, nonetheless, be a disqualified person with respect to an applicable tax-exempt organization (Q 1:14).

Q 5:20   Are business leagues required to file annual returns with the IRS?

Generally, yes. Business leagues are among the types of exempt organizations that are required to file annual information returns with the IRS (Q 11:1).[81] These are usually on Form 990.

If a business league has, in a year, gross receipts of less than $100,000 and total assets of less than $250,000, it may file a simpler (two-page) version of the return (Q 11:7). This is Form 990-EZ.

If a business league normally receives $25,000 or less in gross receipts annually, it is excused from this filing requirement (Q 11:3).[82]

Q 5:21   Are business leagues required to apply to the IRS for recognition of tax-exempt status?

No. If an organization satisfies the legal requirements as to business league status, it is exempt by operation of law (Q 4:4). There is no need, as a matter of law, to file an application with the IRS for a ruling recognizing the tax exemption.

However, a business league *may* seek a determination as to its tax-exempt status with the IRS. This is done by filing a completed Form 1024. It is often a good practice to obtain a determination letter, so that the business league has the protection that the document affords (Q 4:4).

CAUTION: The IRS encourages the filing of exemption applications by business leagues. Thus, there can be complications when a business league that does not have a determination letter from the IRS files annual information returns with the agency. When a return is received, the government's computer will be confused, inasmuch as there is no independent record of the organization's existence.

NOTE: A business league that does not seek an IRS determination letter is nonetheless required to obtain an employer identification number. This is secured by filing Form SS-4.

Q 5:22   What happens when a business league elects to give up its tax-exempt status?

First, there is no procedure by which a tax-exempt organization abandons its exempt status.[83] Technically, all it can do is violate one or more rules on which its exempt status is predicated and then either claim that the exemption is gone by operation of law or induce the IRS into an inquiry and formal revocation of exemption.

However, irrespective of how it is accomplished, a membership association should be very careful in foregoing tax-exempt status. This is because there are special rules pertaining to nonexempt membership organizations.[84]

When a tax-exempt business league—or, for that matter, any other type of exempt organization—decides to give up its exempt status, it almost certainly is for one of two reasons. First, the leadership or management of the organization is expecting to escape one or more forms of governmental regulation that are applicable only to exempt entities. Second, those advocating this approach assume that tax exemption is not very important, because the organization's total income and expenses are about the same. As to the latter, the thought is that there will not be any net income to be taxed (or very little), because all expenses can be offset against income.

The tax law envisions a tax-exempt organization as a bundle of activities. As is the case with the unrelated business income rules, the IRS is empowered to fragment the organization into its component parts for purpose of analysis, with each discrete activity analyzed in isolation for tax purposes.[85] Generally, each activity generates some income and some expenses. Usually, some activities produce net income and some net losses. Where all income and expenses are lumped together, as is the case with respect to most exempt organizations, there often is no net income. This is because the net losses of some activities are allowed to be subtracted from the net income of other activities.

However, these special rules for nonexempt membership organizations in effect bar the practice of using the expenses from one activity to offset income from another activity. They allow expenses to be deductible only in relation to income from the same activity. For many organizations, this leaves a considerable number of expenses that end up being nondeductible. This, in turn, means that there can be far more income than realized that is subject to taxation.

Thus, the cost of "giving up" tax-exempt status for business leagues can be high. This aspect of the matter should be fully explored before any such conversion is implemented.

Of course, should exempt status be abandoned, the organization would become a taxable one, although it could remain a nonprofit organization.

Q 5:23   Are entities such as chambers of commerce and boards of trade considered business leagues?

No. Organizations of this nature do not qualify as business leagues because they do not represent the common business interests of persons in a line of business (Q 5:10).

A chamber of commerce or board of trade is an organization that promotes the common economic interests of all commercial enterprises in a particular community. Membership in these organizations is generally open to all business and professional persons in the community. Nonetheless, these organizations are tax-exempt, by reason of the same statute exempting business leagues.[86]

UNRELATED BUSINESS ACTIVITIES

Q 5:24   Are membership associations subject to the unrelated business rules?

Absolutely. In fact, membership associations and other forms of business leagues are generating many issues in the unrelated business area.

Q 5:25   What are the principal unrelated business issues being raised by membership associations?

One of these issues is reflected in the preceding discussion. That is, the provision of particular services for individual members can be regarded as an unrelated business (Q 5:17). Associations derive unrelated income from a variety of involvements in insurance programs. Another issue concerns the matter of associate member dues.

Q 5:26   What are some of the instances in which services provided by associations are unrelated businesses?

Illustrations of IRS rulings in this area include the sale of legal forms by an exempt bar association to its members,[87] the sale of equipment by an exempt association to its members,[88] the management of health and welfare plans for a fee by an exempt business league,[89] the provision of insurance for the members of an exempt association,[90] the operation of an executive referral service,[91] and the publication of commercial advertising for products and services used by lawyers in an exempt bar association's journal.[92]

In one instance, the IRS examined seven activities of a tax-exempt trade association and found each one of them to be an unrelated business. These activities were the sale of vehicle signs to members, the sale to members of embossed tags for inventory control purposes, the sale to members of supplies and forms, the sale to members of kits to enable them to retain sales tax information, the sale of price guides, the administration of a group insurance program, and the sale of commercial advertising in the association's publications.[93]

However, the IRS is not always successful in this context. For example, a court concluded that the sales of preprinted lease forms and landlord's manuals by a tax-exempt association of apartment owners and managers was a related activity.[94]

Q 5:27   What are some of the instances in which insurance programs of associations are unrelated businesses?

Nearly any involvement by a membership association with insurance is likely to give rise to some unrelated business activity. An association may directly participate in the management of an insurance plan, such as by endorsing and advertising it, providing information as to coverage, or processing claims. That type of involvement is almost certain to be unrelated business.[95]

In contrast, an association may have little relationship to an insurance offering, other than a licensing of its name and logo to, and/or making its membership records available to, an insurer or broker. Although some early court opinions held this type of activity to be passive in nature and thus not taxable, the current view is that promotional and administrative fees received by associations from insurance companies and brokers for the sponsorship of insurance programs for the benefit of their memberships are taxable as unrelated business income. These activities are generally considered businesses because they are entered into with an intent to earn a profit.[96]

However, in rare instances, an association may be able to demonstrate that the activity does not rise to the level of a business,[97] that the income from an insurance activity is a royalty (and thus not taxable),[98] or that the insurance activity is an exempt function.[99]

Q 5:28   What are the instances in which associate member dues paid to associations are taxed as unrelated business income?

Taxation of associate member dues is a relatively new phenomenon. Nonetheless, this aspect of the law has a tortuous history.

It is common for an association to have *associate* members. These members are to be distinguished from what are generally termed *regular* members. A regular member is a person who is directly involved in the industry (or, more technically, line of business) that the association serves (Q 5:10). A regular member usually has a vote in association matters, can serve on the board of directors and as an officer, can be a member of committees, and the like. An associate member, traditionally, has been thought of as a person interested in the affairs of the association but who is ineligible to be a regular member.

For decades, there was no issue about the taxation of these dues. Like dues paid by regular members, dues paid by associate members was regarded as exempt function revenue (or related business income). Then the IRS discovered two practices in this regard that it thought warranted taxation of associate member dues.

One of these practices was sale by an association of a good or service only to its members. Members of the public, desirous of purchasing the good or service, were joining such an association solely for that purpose. That is, in many instances, those joining as associate members had no interest in the programs or objectives of the association.

COMMENT: The principal case on this point concerned the National League of Postmasters. The organization maintains an attractive health plan; however, it is available only to its members. Individuals were joining the League as associate members, not because of an abiding interest in the lives and times of the nation's postmasters, but because they wanted to participate in the health plan. The IRS was successful in court in its contention that dues of this nature are taxable.[100]

The other practice involved persons joining an the association as associate members solely to gain access to the regular members for the purpose of selling a good or service to them.

NOTE: As to this latter practice, the IRS recharacterizes these dues as *access fees*. To date, there is no decided case on the point.

In both of these instances, the IRS regards the associate member activity to be an unrelated business. This is because the category of members has been formed or availed of for the purpose of producing unrelated business income.[101]

However, in 1996, Congress legislated a rule that associate member dues paid to tax-exempt agricultural and horticultural organizations are not taxable as unrelated business income where the annual amount does not exceed $100.[102] Thus, this exception became available to certain organizations described in Internal Revenue Code section 501(c)(5) but was not extended to the principal recipients of associate member dues, namely, associations and other forms of business leagues.

Thereafter, the IRS announced that it would administratively apply the terms of the statutory exception to business leagues. Thus, the current policy of the IRS is not to tax the associate member dues of associations where the principal purpose for joining as an associate member is to further the tax-exempt purposes of the association.[103]

RELATED ENTITIES

Q 5:29   Can membership associations have related entities, such as foundations, for-profit subsidiaries, title-holding companies, and political action committees?

Absolutely. In fact, it is very common for associations to utilize one or more related entities of this nature. These are sometimes referred to as *in-tandem* relationships.

Q 5:30   What is the underlying reason for this use of related entities?

Usually, membership associations utilize related entities because the practice is forced on them by reason of the law. Often, this is called *bifurcation*: two organizations are, by necessity, used instead of one. Were the law different, one organization would probably suffice, but because the law is as it is, the organization must be divided. The reasons for doing this in specific instances are discussed in response to the following questions.

Q 5:31   What is the relationship between the entities? Are they always subsidiaries of the association?

In these in-tandem arrangements, there is not always a requirement that the relationship be that of parent and subsidiary. However, it is usually best if that is the case.

The parent-subsidiary relationship is established and is continued where the parent entity—here, the association—*controls* the entity that is the subsidiary (Q 5:32).

A related political action committee (PAC) is, almost by definition, a subsidiary of the association.

NOTE: The federal election law recognizes a free-standing political action organization—that is, one not affiliated in any formal way with another organization—but these are rare. This is particularly true in the association arena, where those solicited for contributions by the PAC are exclusively members of the association.[104]

Most title-holding companies are subsidiaries of one tax-exempt organization, although it is possible to have a title-holding company serving two or more unrelated tax-exempt organizations. A for-profit subsidiary is, of course, by definition, a subsidiary, although an association may have occasion to own less than a majority interest in a corporation.

The trickiest aspect of all of this is the matter of the related foundation. If all works out, the foundation will accumulate assets and have income to expend in support of the association. The association will have expended considerable effort, including time and money, in launching and maintaining the foundation. The association presumably will not want to see this effort wasted should the foundation shift its focus of support elsewhere. To prevent this, the foundation should be a subsidiary of the association.

COMMENT: There are a surprising number of associations who are of the belief, because of incorrect legal advice or otherwise, that a foundation cannot be controlled by an association. That clearly is not true. Moreover, there are situations in which an association is of the view that it controls a foundation when, as a matter of law, it does not.

Where the relationship between the organizations is not that of parent and subsidiary, it may be termed an *affiliation*. This is all that is required, for example, in connection with the group exemption (Q 4:36).

Q 5:32   How is the relationship of parent and subsidiary established?

There are many models, and blends of these models, that may be followed. Basically, the control mechanisms are interlocking directorates, memberships, and stock.

Where the subsidiary is a for-profit enterprise, the parent-subsidiary relationship is established by means of stock. There may also be a manifestation of control by means of overlapping boards of directors. Here, for the control element to be present, the parent exempt organization must own, directly or indirectly, more than 50 percent of the subsidiary's stock. (Prior to 1997, the ownership standard for certain tax purposes (Q 5:35) was 80 percent and an indirect control test did not exist.)

Where both the parent and the subsidiary are tax-exempt organizations, the most common method of control is the *interlocking directorate*, otherwise known as *overlapping boards*. In some instances, the parent entity is the sole member of the subsidiary entity. The rarest control mechanism in this context is stock; there are still a few states in which nonprofit organizations can issue stock.

Q 5:33 Why would an association establish a foundation?

This is a classic example of the reason for bifurcation. Associations that are business leagues are generally not eligible to receive grants from charities and deductible charitable contributions.

NOTE: The word "generally" is used here because it is possible to establish a charitable "fund" within a business league, to which deductible contributions may be made.[105] However, these funds are of limited utility; they can be suitable for activities such as scholarship or research grants. But, particularly where there is active program and/or fund-raising activity, a separate organization is usually far preferable.

Thus, if an association wants to receive gifts and grants, it must create a separate *foundation*. The foundation, then, becomes a vehicle for the receipt of contributions and grants that are used for support of appropriate association programs.

This foundation must have purposes that are charitable, educational, or scientific.[106]

NOTE: There are other ways to be *charitable*, such as engaging in religious activities or preventing cruelty to children, but it is not likely that these charitable ends would be suitable for an association-related foundation.

These charitable endeavors can be programs in existence, conducted by the association, or programs that are devised under the auspices of the foundation. One of two models is usually followed in this regard, although there may be a blend of them. The association-related foundation may operate its own programs, the association itself can conduct the charitable programs, with the association-related foundation providing the funding for them. Almost always, the foundation is a fund-raising vehicle, generating gifts and grants in support of charitable programs. Moreover, the foundation can generate exempt function revenue by means such as seminar admission fees and payments for publications.

TIP: Where the second of these two models is selected, the foundation is a grantmaking entity, with the grantee being the association or a person directed by the association to receive the funds. Because the foundation should not be used to provide general support to the association, the paperwork surrounding these grants should be clear that the grant funds are restricted for charitable purposes.

Programs that are typical for association-related foundations include seminars, other forms of training, publications, research, library maintenance, scholarships, fellowships, and awards.

It is important for a charitable organization to avoid private foundation status if it can. For an association-related foundation, there are two basic alternatives in this regard. One is to be a publicly supported charity. If the foundation is to operate its own programs, it may be a *service provider* publicly supported organization.[107] Otherwise, it can be a *donative* type of publicly supported organization.[108] The second of these alternatives is to be a *supporting organization.*[109]

NOTE: An organization may be a supporting organization with respect to certain types of tax-exempt organizations that are not charitable in nature, including associations.

Q 5:34   Why would an association establish a related political organization?

Again, the basic reason for this type of bifurcation is dictated by law. This involves both federal tax and election law. Much political activity by associations is taxed or prohibited by both bodies of law. Yet this activity is an appropriate or exempt function for political organizations.[110] This is a subject that has been discussed previously.[111]

Q 5:35 Why would an association establish a for-profit subsidiary?

The principal reason that an association—or any other type of tax-exempt organization—utilizes a for-profit subsidiary is to have a place to house one or more unrelated business activities. In this fashion, the association can indirectly engage in far more unrelated business than it could directly, that is, within the association.

On occasion, the unrelated activity is conducted in a for-profit subsidiary to avoid the charge of unfair competition. That is, by operating the unrelated business in a corporation that is taxable, the for-profit competitors with this business are less likely to feel that the competition is unfair, inasmuch as taxes are taken into account as a cost of doing business (Q 2:1). Sometimes a for-profit subsidiary is created to be a partner in a partnership, rather than have the exempt organization be a (or the) partner.

There is a fourth reason for use of a for-profit subsidiary. This is to try to convert some or all of what might be taxable unrelated business income into non-taxable unrelated business income, by structuring the nature of the income received by the exempt organization so that it is one of the sheltered forms, such as interest or rent.

These are matters that have been reviewed previously.[112] However, there has been a change in the law in regards to these issues. One is that, as discussed, the definition of a controlled subsidiary has been revised (Q 5:32). A second is that a popular tax planning technique essentially has been obliterated. This technique involves the *second-tier subsidiary*.

The usual relationship between a tax-exempt organization and a for-profit subsidiary has the latter being a *first-tier subsidiary*. This means that the subsidiary, being directly controlled by the parent entity, is directly below the parent exempt organization. By contrast, the second-tier subsidiary is two levels below the exempt organization; it is a subsidiary of a first-tier subsidiary. Thus, a tax-exempt association might have a for-profit subsidiary and that subsidiary might have a for-profit subsidiary.

If this association leased property or lent money to the first-tier subsidiary, the resulting rent or interest would be taxable. However, for a time, the law was that if this association leased property or lent money to the second-tier subsidiary, the resulting rent or interest would not be taxable, because that revenue would be sheltered by the passive income rules.[113] The rationale underlying this state of the law was that the association did not control the second-tier subsidiary; only the first-tier subsidiary had that control. That is, the rule was that the association did not indirectly control the second-tier subsidiary.

The law in this regard was revised in 1997. Now, for purposes of determining control, certain constructive ownership rules are applied.[114] This causes indirect ownership arrangements to be taken into account, including the use of second-tier subsidiaries. Today, an association receiving interest, an annuity, royalties, or rent from a second-tier (or third-tier or more) subsidiary is almost certain to have that revenue taxed as unrelated business income.

Q 5:36   Why would an association establish a title-holding company?

Once again, the answer lies in the concept of bifurcation. Here we are concerned with management principles and the prospect of liability.

The purpose of a title-holding company[115] is to hold title to property. That is considered a *passive* function. The title-holding entity is not supposed to be in the active business of operating the property; it is to hold the title, collect any income from use of the property, and remit any net proceeds to the parent organization.

There may be one or more reasons that the property ought not to be held in the name of the tax-exempt organization, such as an association. The property might, for example, carry with it the likelihood of legal liability. By placing the property in a title-holding company, the hope is that any actual liability will be confined to the title-holding entity, that is, the liability will not ascend to the parent entity.

NOTE: Whether this form of planning will actually work is a matter of state law. The issue basically is whether a court would respect the separateness of the two legal entities or, because of the control element, regard the two as one for this purpose.

TIP: A growing practice is to utilize a supporting organization rather than a title-holding corporation. This approach works, of course, only where the parent entity is able to have a supporting organization, as is the case with associations, and where holding title to a property is a bona fide charitable and benefiting activity. When a supporting entity is used, there is no need to be concerned as to whether the subsidiary's activities are active or passive.

CHAPTER 6

Social Welfare Organizations

Social welfare organizations are one of the most misunderstood types of tax-exempt entities. Often, they look like charities—but they are not. Some types of health care entities are social welfare organizations, symbolizing—if not adding to—this confusion. The perplexity deepens as Congress creates new categories of exempt organizations, causing some nonprofit organizations to depart the social welfare fold.

Although social welfare and charitable organizations are different in many fundamental respects, Congress persists in treating them alike in important ways. In 1996 alone, the private inurement doctrine was added to the criteria for qualification as a social welfare organization, and these entities became caught up in the intermediate sanctions penalties.

Here are the questions most frequently asked by clients about the corporate and tax status of social welfare organizations—and the answers to them.

SOCIAL WELFARE ORGANIZATIONS IN GENERAL

Q 6:1   What is a *social welfare organization*?

Federal tax law is skimpy when it comes to defining the term *social welfare organization*. The Internal Revenue Code blandly references, in section 501(c)(4), "[c]ivic leagues or organizations not organized for profit but operated exclusively for the promotion of social welfare." As will be discussed, there are many varieties of social welfare organizations, principally advocacy groups and health care entities (Q 6:9).

Q 6:2   Does a social welfare organization have to be incorporated?

No, there is no requirement that a social welfare organization be incorporated, at least not for federal tax purposes. For other reasons, however, such as limitation on the liability of directors and officers, it may be a good idea to incorporate a social welfare organization.[1]

Q 6:3   Is a social welfare organization a tax-exempt organization?

Generally, under the federal income tax laws, yes.[2] These entities (assuming they otherwise qualify) are described in section 501(c)(4) of the Internal Revenue Code.

State law usually provides income tax exemption, and often other tax exemptions, for social welfare organizations.

Q 6:4   Are contributions to social welfare organizations deductible?

No. However, a social welfare organization may establish a related charitable entity (Q 6:28), and contributions to it would be deductible.[3]

TAX EXEMPTION CRITERIA

Q 6:5   What are the criteria for tax exemption as a social welfare organization?

The two basic criteria have been noted (Q 6:1). These elements are embellished somewhat by the tax regulations. For example, the tax regulations state that the promotion of social welfare does not include activities that primarily constitute "carrying on a business with the general public in a manner similar to organizations which are operated for profit."[4]

NOTE: This rule essentially is a formulation of the commerciality doctrine (Chapter 2).

These regulations also contain a prohibition on political campaign activity[5] and state that an organization is not operated primarily for the promotion of social welfare "if its primary activity is operating a social club for the benefit, pleasure, or recreation of its members."[6]

Q 6:6   What does the term *social welfare* mean in this context?

The tax regulations are rather vague on this point. They provide that *social welfare* is commensurate with the "common good and general welfare" and "civic betterments and social improvements."[7]

Q 6:7   What is the exempt purpose of a social welfare organization?

To be tax-exempt, a social welfare organization must (in addition to meeting the other criteria (Q 6:5)) function primarily to promote social welfare. The key principle in this regard is that for an entity to qualify as an exempt social welfare organization, its activities must be those that will benefit the community as a whole, rather than benefit merely the organization's membership or another select group of individuals or organizations.

Q 6:8   What is a *community* for this purpose?

As the previous answer indicates, the requisite *community* must be more than a *select group* of entities. For example, a trust formed to provide group life insurance only for members of an association was held to not qualify as an exempt social welfare organization.[8] Similarly, a resort operated for a school's faculty and students was held to not be an exempt social welfare entity.[9]

A community clearly includes the general public or a large segment of it. Thus, a court wrote that the "exemption granted to social welfare . . . organizations is made in recognition of the benefit which the public derives from their social welfare activities."[10] Three examples follow:

1. A consumer credit counseling service, which assisted individuals and families with financial problems, was held to be an exempt social welfare organization because its objectives and activities "contribute[d] to the betterment of the community as a whole" by checking the rising incidence of personal bankruptcy in the community.[11]

2. Tax-exempt social welfare organization status was accorded to an entity that processed consumer complaints concerning products and services provided by businesses, met with the parties involved to encourage resolution of problems, and recommended appropriate solutions, and (where the solutions were

not accepted) informed the parties about administrative or judicial remedies available to resolve disputes.[12]

3. An organization created to maintain a system for the storage and distribution of water to raise the underground water level in a community was ruled to be a tax-exempt social welfare organization because of the benefits to those whose wells were thereby supplied.[13]

Nonetheless, it has proved to be difficult to quantify the meaning of the term *community*. In one context, the IRS became so exercised over the issue that a separate Internal Revenue Code provision had to be created. This involved the matter of homeowners and like associations.[14]

COMMENT: There are many varieties of these associations. Some are created by the real estate developer and later turned over to the residents. Others are created directly by the owners (sometimes including tenants). Their functions are manifold, such as owning and maintaining common areas (e.g., sidewalks, parks) for all residents, administration and enforcement of architectural covenants, and/or participation in the formulation of public policies having an impact on the community (such as those addressing development of nearby lands, expansion of nearby roads, and encroaching commercialization).

As will be noted, the IRS came to the opinion that a community, at least in this context, is akin to a governmental unit or political subdivision.

As far back as 1972, the IRS was finding homeowners' associations to be tax-exempt social welfare organizations. In one instance, a typical homeowners' association was found to be "serving the common good and the general welfare of the people of the entire development," with the IRS noting that a "neighborhood, precinct, subdivision, or housing development" may constitute a community.[15] The core issue was private benefit to the developer or the members, with the IRS finding these benefits to be incidental. (The existence of the association may have aided the developer in selling units, and the organization may have served to protect property values.)

Soon thereafter, however, from the IRS's standpoint, events began to spin out of control, largely because of the reference in the 1972 ruling to "subdivisions" and "housing developments." A mere two years later, the IRS abruptly shifted course. It ruled that these associations are *presumed* to be primarily operated for the benefit of their members and, accordingly, are not tax-exempt social welfare organizations.[16]

In this 1974 ruling, the IRS said that the term *community* "has traditionally been construed as having reference to a geographical unit bearing a reasonably recognizable relationship to an area ordinarily identified as a governmental subdivision or a unit or district thereof."[17] The IRS went on to state that a community is "not simply an aggregation of homeowners bound together in a structured unit formed as an integral part of a plan for the development of a real estate subdivision and the sale and purchase of homes therein." This ruling also addressed the matter of property maintenance, with the IRS stating that exempt social welfare objectives are being advanced only where the areas maintained are those "traditionally recognized and accepted as being of direct governmental concern in the exercise of the powers and duties entrusted to governments to regulate community health, safety, and welfare." Thus, the IRS's "approval" was extended in this context only to ownership and maintenance by a homeowners' association of areas such as "roadways and parklands, sidewalks and street lights, access to, or the use and enjoyment of which is extended to members of the general public, as distinguished from controlled use or access restricted to the members of the homeowners' association."[18]

This matter then became even more confused when the IRS began issuing inconsistent rulings. In 1975, the IRS ruled that an organization with membership limited to the residents and business operators within a city block, and formed to preserve and beautify the public areas in the block, could qualify as an exempt social welfare organization because it benefited the community as a whole (albeit also enhancing the members' property rights).[19] Later that year the IRS issued a ruling that, assuming the presence of a community, accorded tax-exempt social welfare organization status to an organization formed to provide the community with security protection, improved public services, recreational and holiday activities, and a community newspaper.[20] Five years later, the IRS held that tax exemption as a social welfare organization was not available to a homeowners' association because it did not represent a community and restricted the use of its facilities (such as those for parking and recreation) to its members.[21]

Not surprisingly, all of this led to litigation. In many instances, the basic approach of the IRS was upheld.[22] There were some instances, however, where the courts rebuffed the IRS's position.[23]

Matters worsened with the expanded use of condominiums and cooperatives. Condominium management corporations and cooperative housing corporations sought tax-exempt status as social welfare organizations. The IRS resisted this, refusing the assertion that those who reside in a condominium or a cooperative constitute a community. Indeed, the view of the IRS is that entities of this nature do not qualify for exemption as social welfare organizations, because they operate for the private benefit of their members.[24] Ultimately, this issue was largely resolved when Congress intervened in 1976 in an effort to clarify the law as to tax exemption for homeowners' associations.[25]

There has not been much in the way of subsequent developments updating the thinking of the IRS or the courts as to the composition of a community. Indeed, there is somewhat of an impasse in this regard, as illustrated by a case involving a business corporation that maintained a vacation home for "working girls and women of proper character."[26] All of the trustees were required to be employees of a particular business corporation; the use of the farm's facilities was by invitation only to a select and limited number of women who were predominantly (80 percent) employees of the same corporation. The IRS asserted—unsuccessfully—that this vacation home did not benefit the community as a whole, by virtue of the predominance of the employees of a single business and the invitational process. However, a court concluded that the organization was an "institution which has served a broad community need in the sense that Congress intended, that is, that when one segment or slice of the community, in this case thousands of working women . . . , are [sic] served, then the community as a whole benefits."[27]

NOTE: The IRS refuses to follow this decision. The view of the IRS is that an organization providing recreational facilities to the employees of selected corporations cannot qualify as a tax-exempt social welfare organization.[28]

Q 6:9   What are some examples of tax-exempt social welfare organizations?

Some examples have been provided in the discussion of the requisite community (Q 6:8). As will be noted, certain types of health maintenance organizations qualify as social welfare entities (Q 6:15). Here are some other examples of qualifying exempt social welfare organizations:

1. An organization that provided a community with supervised facilities for the teaching of the safe handling and proper care of firearms.[29]
2. One that encouraged industrial development to relieve unemployment in an economically depressed area.[30]
3. One that helped to secure accident insurance for the students and employees in a school district.[31]

NOTE: An entity of this type might not be able to qualify for tax exemption as a social welfare organization today (Q 6:1).

---

4. One that provided bus transportation between a community and the major employment centers in a metropolitan area during rush hours when the regular bus service was inadequate.[32]

5. One that conducted a community art show for the purpose of encouraging interest in painting, sculpture, and other art forms.[33]

6. One that established and maintained a roller-skating rink for residents of a county.[34]

COMMENT: Organizations of this nature also illustrate how difficult it can be to draw a distinction between a social welfare organization and a charitable one.

---

7. Junior chambers of commerce.[35]

8. An organization that promotes sports. In one instance, an organization that sponsored programs to stimulate the interest of youth in organized sports, by furnishing youths virtually free admission and encouraging their attendance at sporting events, was ruled to be an exempt social welfare organization because it provided "wholesome entertainment for the social improvement and welfare of the youths of the community."[36]

NOTE: It was in this context that the commerciality doctrine[37] made a rare appearance as applied to social welfare organizations. An organization that provided facilities for training men and horses for use in emergencies was recognized as an exempt social welfare organization. However, this exemption was lost when it evolved into a commercial riding stable. Wrote a court: "[T]he few persons eligible to use . . . [the organization's] facilities as members or on any basis other than by paying a regular commercial fee for such use causes . . . [the] operation (no matter how laudable) to be such as not to come within the meaning of 'social welfare.' "[38]

Q 6:10   What are the reasons causing organizations to not qualify as exempt social welfare organizations?

There are several reasons. Some of them are reflected in the foregoing discussion. Thus, one way an organization can fail to be a tax-exempt social welfare organization is to not sufficiently engage in programs that constitute the promotion of *social welfare*, by failing to operate for the common good and general welfare (Q 6:6). The *public policy doctrine*, normally associated with charitable organizations,[39] can apply in this setting. Thus, the IRS refused to recognize tax exemption for an antiwar protest organization that urged demonstrators to commit violations of local ordinances and breaches of public order. Said the IRS: "Illegal activities, which violate the minimum standards of acceptable conduct necessary to the preservation of an orderly society, . . . are not a permissible means of promoting social welfare."[40]

Another reason is failure to serve a *community* (Q 6:8). A third reason is an organization's undertaking activities that primarily constitute the carrying on of business in a commercial manner (Q 6:26). Here are some additional examples of organizations that failed to be exempt social welfare organizations because of this third reason:

1. An organization that provided managerial, developmental, and consultation services for low- and moderate-income housing projects, for a fee, on behalf of tax-exempt organizations.[41]

2. One that provided security services for residents and property owners of a community, on a regular basis in return for compensation.[42]

3. One that promoted public dances for profit, the proceeds from which were used for speculative real estate dealings.[43]

NOTE: Here, too, it can be difficult to distinguish between carrying on a commercial business with the public and serving a community. The IRS granted exempt status as a social welfare organization to an entity that operated an airport used by the public. Exemption was achieved, despite this seemingly commercial activity, because the airport served a rural area without any other airport facilities, was supervised by a city council, and received government grants.[44]

COMMENT: Earlier it was noted that the IRS refuses to follow a court decision according social welfare status to an organization providing recreational facilities to a select group of employees (Q 6:8). In the airport ruling, however, most of the airplanes berthed at the airport were owned by key local businesses that were deemed essential to the area's economy; the airport was used predominantly by executives, employees, and clients of the companies.

A fourth reason is an organization's substantially functioning as a social club (Chapter 7). A fifth reason is transgression of the private inurement doctrine.[45]

NOTE: The is the most recent of reasons for an entity's not qualifying as an exempt social welfare organization. This proscription on private inurement was added to the Internal Revenue Code in 1996.[46] It is generally effective with respect to inurement occurring on or after September 14, 1995.

TIP: This private inurement ban is not applicable to inurement occurring before January 1, 1997, pursuant to a written contract that was binding on September 13, 1995, and at all times thereafter before the inurement occurred.[47]

A sixth reason for loss or denial of exemption is operation of an organization primarily for the economic benefit or convenience of its members. Here are some examples:

1. An organization that purchased and sold unimproved land, invested proceeds received from the sales, and distributed profits to its members.[48]

2. A consumer and producer cooperative, which rebated a percentage of net income to its members as patronage dividends.[49]

3. A mutual assistance association established by a church in furtherance of its "mutual aid" practices, which practices benefited only a "select few" (its members).[50]

4. An association of police officers primarily engaged in providing retirement benefits to members and death benefits to beneficiaries of members.[51]

5. An automobile club.[52]

6. An organization that operated a dining room and bar for the exclusive use of its members.[53]

7. A national sorority controlled by a business corporation that furnished the member chapters with supplies and services.[54]

8. An organization formed to purchase groceries for its membership at the lowest possible prices on a cooperative basis.[55]

9. A cooperative organization providing home maintenance services to its members.[56]

However, the rendering of services to members does not necessarily lead to denial or loss of status as an exempt social welfare organization. The following are examples of exempt entities:

1. A memorial association that developed methods of achieving simplicity and dignity in funeral services and maintained a registry for the wishes of its members in regard to funeral arrangements.[57]

2. An organization engaged in rehabilitation and job placement of its members.[58]

3. One that promoted the legal rights of all tenants in a community and occasionally initiated litigation to contest the validity of legislation adversely affecting tenants.[59]

NOTE: Once again, these distinctions can be close. Thus, a tenants' rights group was denied tax-exempt social welfare organization status because its activities were directed primarily toward benefiting only tenants who are its members.[60]

Furthermore, qualification as a tax-exempt social welfare organization will not be precluded where an organization's services are equally available to members and nonmembers. For example, the IRS accorded tax-exempt social welfare classification to an organization formed to prevent oil and other liquid spills in a city's port area and to contain and clean up any spills that occur.[61] The organization's membership included business firms, primarily oil and chemical companies, that stored or shipped liquids in the port area. Because the organization cleaned up spills of both members and nonmembers, the IRS concluded that it was acting to prevent deterioration of the port community and not merely to prevent damage to the facilities of its members; any benefits to the members were considered incidental.

NOTE: Had this organization confined its repairs to property damaged by its members, tax exemption would not have been available.[62]

A seventh reason an entity may not qualify as an exempt social welfare organization is that it engages in an undue amount of political campaign activity (Q 6:17). (There is not, however, any limitation with respect to legislative activities (Q 6:16).)

An eighth reason that an organization cannot qualify as an exempt social welfare entity is that a substantial part of its activities consists of the provision of *commercial-type insurance*.[63] This is a body of law that was enacted in 1986 and significantly amended in 1996 (Q 6:11).

NOTE: This body of law is also applicable with respect to charitable organizations.[64]

COMMENT: An organization does not escape these rules where the provision of commercial-type insurance is not a *substantial* part of its activities. In this instance, the insurance activity is treated as the conduct of an unrelated business[65] and taxed under the rules pertaining to for-profit insurance companies.[66]

Q 6:11   What is *commercial-type insurance*?

The term *commercial-type insurance* generally means any insurance of a type provided by commercial insurance companies.[67]

COMMENT: This, then, is an element of the commerciality doctrine.[68] However, it is the only aspect of the doctrine that, at least for charitable organizations, is stated in the Internal Revenue Code (Q 2:14). As noted, this doctrine is generally reflected in the Code in respect to social welfare organizations (Q 6:5).

This rule was enacted essentially to preclude tax-exempt status for prepaid health care plans, principally those administered by Blue Cross and Blue Shield organizations.[69] However, it is significant to note that the term *commercial-type insurance* is not confined to *health* insurance.

As one court stated, the term encompasses "every type of insurance that can be purchased in the commercial market."[70] Thus, there is the basic requirement that the risk of liability be shifted to at least one third party (the insurer) and that the risk be shared and distributed across a group of persons.[71]

Moreover, for these purposes the issuance of annuity contracts is generally considered the provision of insurance.[72]

Q 6:12 Are there any exceptions to this meaning of the term *commercial-type insurance*?

Yes. The term does not include (1) insurance provided at substantially below cost to a class of charitable recipients, (2) incidental health insurance provided by a health maintenance organization of a kind customarily provided by these organizations, (3) property or casualty insurance provided (directly or through a qualified employer) by a church or convention or association of churches for the church or convention or association of churches, and (4) retirement and/or welfare benefits provided by a church or a convention or association of churches (directly or through a qualified organization) for the employees of the church or convention or association of churches or the beneficiaries of these employees.[73]

NOTE: As to the first of these exceptions, the phrase *substantially below cost* apparently means a subsidy of at least 85 percent.[74]

Furthermore, despite the fact that an annuity contract can generally constitute insurance (Q 6:11), the commercial-type insurance rules do not apply to a charitable gift annuity. This is an annuity whereby (1) a portion of the amount paid in connection with the issuance of the annuity is allowable as a charitable deduction for federal income or estate tax purposes and (2) the annuity is described in a special rule for annuities in the unrelated debt-financed income rules[75] (determined as if any amount paid in cash in connection with the issuance were property).[76]

Q 6:13 Still, isn't the concept of commercial-type insurance very broad?

It certainly is. Congress clearly overdid it. For example, a nonprofit organization established to administer a group self-insurance pool for the benefit of charitable organizations that were social service paratransit providers was held not to be exempt because of this rule. These organizations, which could not afford or could not obtain insurance for the vehicles they used in their charitable programs, utilized the risk pool to acquire the necessary financing for comprehensive automobile liability, risk management, and related services. A court observed that the insurance offered by the pool organization was "basic automobile liability insurance, a type of insurance provided by a number of commercial insurance carriers."[77]

Another case concerned an organization that administered a group self-insurance risk pool for a membership of nearly 500 charitable organizations that operate to fund or provide health or human services. It was formed to provide its membership with affordable insurance; these entities had endured periods of large premium increases, coverage reductions, and cancellations. As to insurance coverage, the organization provided commercial general liability, automobile liability, employer's non-owned and hired automobile liability, and miscellaneous professional liability. Observing that the organization "exist[ed] solely for the purpose of selling insurance to nonprofit exempt organizations at the lowest possible cost on a continued, stable basis," a court wrote that "[s]elling insurance undeniably [was] an inherently commercial activity ordinarily carried on by a commercial for-profit company."[78] The court said that despite the fact that the insurance was provided on a low-cost basis and that loss control and risk management services were provided without charge, the "nature and operation" of the organization were commercial in nature.

A third case extended the commercial-type insurance rules to self-insurance funds established by charitable organizations. A court observed that the funds involved (which included, for hospitals, coverage for professional liability and workers' compensation claims) provided "actuarial, accounting, underwriting, claims payment, and similar services" that were "essential to the administration of the insurance programs." It added that there "is no dispute that hospital professional liability and workers' compensation insurance are normally offered by commercial insurers."[79]

These outcomes were not intended by Congress when it acted in 1986 in its zeal to end tax exemption for Blue Cross and Blue Shield plans (Q 6:11). This fact was recognized by Congress 10 years later. There was an attempt to remedy the matter, at least in regard to these court cases, by legislation enacted in 1996. This law accords tax-exempt status to *qualified charitable risk pools*.[80]

A qualified charitable risk pool is an entity that is organized and operated solely to pool insurable risks (other than in the realm of medical malpractice) of its members and to provide information to its members with respect to loss control and risk management. Only charitable organizations can be members of these pools. Among the additional criteria for exemption are requirements that the organization obtain at least $1 million in start-up capital from nonmember charitable organizations and be controlled by a board of directors elected by its members.[81] An exempt charitable risk pool must also satisfy the rules for tax exemption as a charitable organization.[82]

NOTE: The various Internal Revenue Code citations are provided in the notes at the end of this book, but it is irresistible to point out here that to be exempt, a charitable risk pool must sidestep Code section 501(m) by meeting the rules of Code section 501(n) and also satisfy the criteria of Code section 501 (c)(3). Such are the intricacies of the federal tax law.

Q 6:14   Can a social welfare organization have members?

Yes. As indicated by several of the foregoing answers, a social welfare organization can have members. However, there is no requirement that there be members.

Q 6:15   How does a social welfare organization differ from a charitable organization?

The two types of organizations differ in many material ways, although sometimes the distinctions are not very clear. The principal difficulty in this regard lies in the fact that *promotion of social welfare* is a way to be charitable.[83] There can be confusion about the term *social welfare* as used in the context of social welfare organizations and as used with respect to charitable organizations. The mystery can deepen when it is remembered that a social welfare organization must serve a community (Q 6:8), whereas a charitable organization often must serve a charitable class[84]; the concepts of a community and a charitable class can often overlap.

For a social welfare organization, the ways to promote social welfare are generally unlimited. As noted, the tax regulations state that an organization of this type must promote social welfare "in some way" (Q 6:6). For a charitable organization, however, it is not sufficient to promote social welfare in some amorphous fashion. Rather, in the case of a charitable organization that is exempt under this rationale, the social welfare that must be promoted must be directly associated with at least one of the following ends:

1. Relief of the poor and distressed or of the underprivileged
2. Advancement of religion
3. Advancement of education or science
4. Erection or maintenance of public buildings, monuments, or works
5. Lessening of the burdens of government
6. Lessening of neighborhood tensions
7. Elimination of prejudice and discrimination
8. Defense of human and civil rights secured by law
9. Combating of community deterioration and juvenile delinquency[85]

Here are some examples of programs of organizations deemed to be charitable because they promote social welfare:

1. Furnishing of housing to low-income groups[86]
2. Relieving unemployment by area development[87]
3. Rehabilitating the elderly unemployed[88]
4. Inducing industry to locate in a community[89]

These distinctions were well illustrated in the health care context as the consequence of litigation over the tax-exempt status of health maintenance organizations (HMOs). It is possible for an HMO to be an exempt charitable organization. The characteristics of this type of HMO are that it provides health care services (rather than simply arranging for others to provide them to subscribers), it provides services to both subscribers and the general public, and it treats emergency patients (subscribers or not) regardless of ability to pay. One court stated:

> The most important feature of the Association's [an HMO] [subscribership] form of organization is that the class of persons eligible for [subscribership], and hence eligible to benefit from the Association's activities, is practically unlimited. The class of possible [subscribers] of the Association is, for all practical purposes, the class of members of the community itself. The major barrier to [subscribership] is lack of money, but a subsidized dues program demonstrates that even this barrier is not intended to be absolute. . . . It is safe to say that the class of persons potentially benefitted [sic] by the Association is not so small that its relief is of no benefit to the community.[90]

In contrast, other types of HMOs can qualify for tax exemption only as social welfare organizations. This is what a court had to say about an HMO that tried to shift from social welfare to charitable status:

> GHP [the HMO] cannot say that it provides any health care services itself. Nor does it ensure that people who are not GHP subscribers have access to health care or information about health care. According to the record, it neither conducts research nor offers educational programs, much less educational programs open to the public. It benefits no one but its subscribers.[91]

Thereafter, the court wrote: "An HMO must primarily benefit the community [i.e., a charitable class], not its subscribers plus a few people, in order to qualify for tax-exempt status under section 501(c)(3)."[92]

There are some identical characteristics in respect to social welfare organizations and charitable organizations. Both are nonprofit organizations.[93] Both are subject to the private inurement doctrine.[94] Both are governed by the unrelated business income rules (Q 6:26). Neither type of organization may engage in a substantial amount of political campaign activities (Q 6:17). Indeed, an organization may simultaneously qualify under both categories of tax exemption.[95] However, contributions to social welfare organizations are not tax deductible (Q 6:4).

The remaining distinctions concern permissible lobbying activities (Q 6:16) and permissible political campaign activities (Q 6:17).

Q 6:16 Are there limitations on the amount of lobbying a social welfare organization can engage in?

Not really. The only limitation is that the lobbying must be in furtherance of the social welfare organization's purposes, but that is almost certain to be the case as a matter of course. Otherwise, a social welfare organization can engage in as much lobbying as it wishes without concern as to its exempt status. Lobbying can be all it does.[96]

The IRS noted that "seeking of legislation germane to [a social welfare] organization's program is recognized by the regulations . . . as [a] permissible means of attaining social welfare purposes."[97] Offering a rationale for allowing a tax-exempt social welfare organization to engage in legislative activities, the IRS stated: "The education of the public on [controversial subjects] is deemed beneficial to the community because society benefits from an informed citizenry."[98]

In some instances, a social welfare organization serves as a lobbying arm of a public charity (Q 6:28).

Q 6:17   Are there limitations on the amount of political campaign activity a social welfare organization can engage in?

Yes. A social welfare organization may not participate or intervene in a political campaign on behalf of or in opposition to a candidate for public office where that activity would be a primary portion of its activities.[99] Thus, a social welfare organization is permitted to engage in political campaign activities as long as they are incidental to its other activities.[100]

NOTE: However, campaign activities of this nature are likely to cause the social welfare organization to become subject to the tax on political activities expenditures (Q 8:12).

Social welfare organizations may use related political organizations for this purpose (Q 6:28).

Q 6:18   What are the principal reasons for loss of tax exemption as a social welfare organization?

As the foregoing discussion reflects, there are several bases on which tax-exempt status as a social welfare organization may be lost (or denied). One basis is failing to promote social welfare in some fashion (Q 6:6). Another is failing to serve a community (Q 6:8). A third reason is violation of the commerciality doctrine (Q 6:11). A fourth reason is violation of the doctrine of private inurement (Q 6:20) A fifth reason is engaging in excess political campaign activities (Q 6:17). A sixth is primarily operating as a social club (Q 6:19).

Q 6:19   Is there potential confusion between social welfare organization status and classification as another type of exempt organization?

There can be. The greatest potential for confusion is between social welfare organization and charitable organization status (Q 6:6). Homeowners' organizations can look like (and may even be) social welfare organizations (Q 6:9).

Occasionally, an organization that cannot qualify as a social welfare organization can be a tax-exempt social club. This is the case, for example, in the instance of an organization that has as its primary purpose the operation of facilities, such as a swimming pool, for the benefit of homeowners in a community.[101] A membership organization consisting of buyers of ready-to-wear apparel and accessories was found not to be an exempt social welfare organization, in part because its functions were largely social.[102]

NOTE: A big disadvantage with social club classification is that social clubs must pay tax on their investment income (Q 7:27).

It is possible that there may be uncertainty as to whether an organization, with a membership, qualifies as an exempt social welfare organization or as an exempt business league. Again, a social welfare organization can have as its members persons from the general public, whereas a business league's membership must be confined to that of a line of business (Q 5:10).

A veterans' organization may qualify as a social welfare organization.[103] However, there is a separate category of tax exemption for veterans' groups.[104]

Q 6:20 Does the private inurement doctrine apply to social welfare organizations?

Yes. However, this is a relatively recent development.

The private inurement proscription[105] is applicable to tax-exempt social welfare organizations, generally effective with respect to inurement occurring on or after September 14, 1995.[106]

TIP: This private inurement proscription is not applicable to inurement occurring before January 1, 1997, pursuant to a written contract that was binding on September 13, 1995, and at all times thereafter before the inurement occurred.[107]

Nonetheless, even before the adoption of the private inurement rule, there was a general prohibition on social welfare organizations as to private gain. Part of this prohibition came out of the ban on commerciality (Q 6:5), and part was derived from the rule forbidding these organizations from operating primarily for the economic benefit or convenience of their members (Q 6:5).

Q 6:21 Are social welfare organizations involved with the intermediate sanctions rules?

Very much so. A social welfare organization is a type of *applicable tax-exempt organization*.[108] Thus, the provision of an economic benefit by a social welfare organization to a disqualified person with respect to the organization may entail an excess benefit transaction.

Q 6:22 Are social welfare organizations required to file annual returns with the IRS?

Generally, yes. Social welfare organizations are among the types of exempt organizations that are required to file annual information returns with the IRS (Q 11:1).[109] These are usually on Form 990.

If a social welfare organization has, in a year, gross receipts of less than $100,000 and total assets of less than $250,000, it may file a simpler (two-page) version of the return (Q 11:7). This is Form 990-EZ.

If a social welfare organization normally receives $25,000 or less in gross receipts annually, it is excused from this filing requirement (Q 11:3).[110]

CAUTION: The key word in this last rule is *normally*. This nonfiling threshold is not a year-to-year test. Rather, it is based on the average of receipts over the most recent four-year period. This averaging mechanism is what the word *normally* connotes.[111]

Q 6:23 Are social welfare organizations required to apply to the IRS for recognition of tax-exempt status?

No. If an organization satisfies the legal requirements as to social welfare organization status, it is exempt by operation of law (Q 4:2). There is no need, as a matter of law, to file an application with the IRS for a ruling recognizing the tax exemption.

However, a social welfare organization *may* seek a determination as to its tax-exempt status with the IRS. This is done by filing a completed Form 1024. It is often a good practice to obtain a determination letter, so that the social welfare organization has the protection that the document affords (Q 4:4, Q 5:21).

TIP: If an organization seeking to be recognized as a tax-exempt charitable organization files the application for recognition of tax exemption after the close of the 27-month period, so that the recognition of charitable status will not become effective until the date the IRS received the application, the organzation can be tax-exempt as a social welfare organization from the date of its inception until the date the charitable status kicks in.[112]

Q 6:24   What disclosure rules apply to social welfare organizations?

There is a fund-raising disclosure rule that is applicable (Q 13:17). This rule is reflective of the fact that a social welfare organization can look like a charitable one. This can be a problem particularly in the realm of fund-raising, inasmuch as contributions to social welfare organizations are not tax deductible (Q 6:4). Although this rule is potentially applicable with respect to nearly all categories of tax-exempt organizations, it is targeted at social welfare entities.

The law requires each *fundraising solicitation* by, or on behalf of, a noncharitable tax-exempt organization to "contain an express statement (in a conspicuous and easily recognizable format)" that gifts to it are not deductible for federal income tax purposes.[113] This term means any solicitation of gifts made in written or printed form, or by means of television, radio, or telephone.

TIP: The IRS had occasion to promulgate similar rules in 1988 concerning fund-raising solicitations.[114] These rules concern the format of the disclosure statement in instances of use of print media, telephone, television, and radio. The IRS follows these 1988 rules in applying the requirements as to *fundraising solicitations.*

A *fundraising solicitation* does not include a solicitation of contributions in the form of letters or telephone calls that are not part of a "coordinated fundraising campaign soliciting more than 10 persons during the calendar year."

Generally, this rule applies to any organization to which contributions are not deductible as charitable gifts and that (1) is tax-exempt,[115] (2) is a political organization,[116] (3) was either type of organization at any time during the five-year period ending on the date of the fund-raising solicitation, or (4) is a successor to this type of organization at any time during this five-year period. However, this body of law is not applicable to any organization that has annual gross receipts that are normally no more than $100,000. Moreover, where all of the parties being solicited are tax-exempt organizations, the solicitation need not include the disclosure statement (inasmuch as these grantors do not utilize a charitable contribution deduction).[117]

Further exempt from this disclosure rule is the billing of those who advertise in an organization's publications, billings by social clubs for food and beverages, billing of attendees at a conference, billing for insurance premiums of an insurance program operated or sponsored by an organization, billing of members of a community association for mandatory payments for police and fire (and similar) protection, or billing for payments to a voluntary employees' beneficiary association, as well as similar payments to a trust for pension and/or health insurance.[118]

CAUTION: The IRS is of the view that the fund-raising solicitation rules apply to the solicitation of dues by tax-exempt organizations, including social welfare organizations, trade and business associations, and social clubs.[119] This is the case even though these payments are not *gifts* to begin with.

The IRS is accorded the authority to treat any group of two or more organizations as one entity for these purposes where "necessary or appropriate" to prevent the avoidance of these rules through the use of multiple organizations.

Failure to satisfy this disclosure requirement can result in imposition of penalties.[120] The basic penalty is $1,000 per day (maximum of $10,000 per year), albeit with an exception for instances of reasonable cause. In the case of an *intentional disregard* of these rules, the penalty for the day on which the offense occurred is the greater of $1,000 or 50 percent of the aggregate cost of the solicitation that took place on that day, and the $10,000 limitation is not applicable. For these purposes, the days involved are those on which the solicitation was telecast, broadcast, mailed, otherwise distributed, or telephoned.

NOTE: This disclosure rule applies to solicitations made after January 31, 1988. At the time of its enactment, Congress, in making it not applicable to charitable organizations, noted that these entities may not have been disclosing the nondeductibility of payments, or portions of payments, to them. Organizations representing the charitable community

---

were exhorted to "further educate their members as to the applicable tax rules and provide guidance as to how charities can provide appropriate information to their supporters in this regard."[121] This was not accomplished to Congress's satisfaction, and disclosure rules of this nature applicable to charitable organizations were enacted in 1993.[122]

There are also disclosure rules concerning the annual information returns filed by social welfare organizations (Q 13:1).

Q 6:25   What happens when a social welfare organization elects to give up its tax-exempt status?

Basically, once a social welfare organization is no longer tax-exempt, the entity becomes a taxable one, although it remains a nonprofit organization. However, if the social welfare organization is a membership entity, special rules apply, which could increase the extent of its tax liability. These special rules have been discussed previously (Q 5:23).

UNRELATED BUSINESS ACTIVITIES

Q 6:26   Are social welfare organizations subject to the unrelated business rules?

Yes. However, there are not as many current unrelated business income issues being raised by social welfare organizations as is the case with other types of exempt organizations, such as business leagues (Q 5:25).

Q 6:27   What are the principal unrelated business issues being raised by social welfare organizations?

There is very little law on the subject of unrelated business activity by social welfare organizations. Usually, the matter is one of all or nothing: whether or not the organization can be tax-exempt.

The principal unrelated business issue in this context is a component of the rule that the provision of commercial-type insurance is not an exempt function (Q 6:10). Where that activity is a substantial part of what the organization does, the entity cannot be tax-exempt. However, where the provision of commercial-type insurance is less than a substantial activity, it becomes an unrelated business.[123] This business activity is not taxed in accordance with the general unrelated business taxation rules;[124] rather, it is taxed by application of the special tax rules applicable to the taxation of insurance companies.[125]

RELATED ENTITIES

Q 6:28   Can social welfare organizations have related entities, such as foundations, for-profit subsidiaries, title-holding companies, and political action committees?

Absolutely. In fact, it is quite common for social welfare organizations to utilize one or more related entities of this nature.

Q 6:29   What is the underlying reason for this use of related entities?

This is discussed elsewhere (Q 5:30). Again, this use of related entities is required as a matter of compliance with the law.

Q 6:30   What is the relationship between the entities? Are they always subsidiaries of the social welfare organization?

This subject is discussed in the context of membership associations (Q 5:31). The answer given there is the same for social welfare organizations.

Q 6:31   How is the relationship of parent and subsidiary established?

This too is discussed in the setting of membership associations (Q 5:32). Again, the answer given there is the same for social welfare organizations.

Q 6:32   Why would a social welfare organization establish a foundation?

Basically, a social welfare organization would establish a related foundation as the entity to engage in charitable, educational, and like activities.[126] In this way, these activities could be funded by grants and deductible contributions. This subject is discussed in the context of membership associations (Q 5:33), and the various considerations summarized there are applicable here.

As noted, there can be considerable program overlaps in regard to social welfare and charitable organizations. This use of a related foundation enables the social welfare organization to engage in activities that a charitable entity cannot (usually substantial lobbying) and yet have many of the activities it would otherwise engage in be operated through a charitable vehicle.

Q 6:33 Why would a social welfare organization establish a related political organization?

This matter is briefly referenced in the discussion of membership associations (Q 5:34). Similarly, much political activity by social welfare organizations is prohibited by the federal election law or taxed by the federal tax law. Yet this activity is an appropriate exempt function for political organizations. For one thing, this use of a political organization can eliminate imposition of the political activities tax on social welfare organizations (Q 8:17). This is a subject that is discussed elsewhere.[127]

However, there has been a development worth mentioning since that previous discussion. This matter is reflected in two IRS private letter rulings.[128] A social welfare organization can establish a related political organization to engage in election year voter education activities. In this way, the social welfare entity can raise public consciousness about issues of concern to it and can focus on the positions of public officials and candidates on these issues. This is done, in part, by addressing past legislative decisions through paying for the distribution of incumbents' voting records. These distributions are targeted to particular locations and are timed to coincide with elections. The political organizations will also pay for grass roots lobbying messages, again targeted by location and timed in relation to campaigns. The political funds will pay for voter guides, targeted and timed for political reasons, and distribute handouts in door-to-door canvassing.

To a substantial extent, these activities are forms of *lobbying*. If that was all they were, the social welfare organization could engage in these activities itself (Q 6:16). However, the IRS said that the "content, timing, and targeting" of the lobbying also has a "political purpose," in that voters are likely to take the issue-oriented information into account in making judgments about the candidates. The IRS saw a "link" between the issues involved and the candidates, with the link "reinforced" through the voting records and the voter guides. Thus, this type of grass-roots lobbying was also found to be *political campaign activity*, necessitating the deployment of a related political organization.

NOTE: This is the first time that the IRS has ruled that a form of lobbying—here, grass roots lobbying—is also a form of political campaign activity. The IRS characterized the activity as having a "dual character."

Q 6:34   Why would a social welfare organization establish a for-profit subsidiary?

This is a manifestation of the concept of bifurcation that is discussed in the membership association setting (Q 5:35). The reasons that an association would establish a for-profit subsidiary are the same for social welfare organizations.

Q 6:35   Why would a social welfare organization establish a title-holding company?

Once again, this matter is discussed in the realm of membership associations (Q 5:36). The reasons that an association would establish a title-holding company are the same for social welfare organizations.

CHAPTER 7

Social Clubs

In the previous chapter, it was observed that social welfare organizations are often misunderstood. However, social clubs are among the least understood of tax-exempt organizations. Most exempt entities have as their purpose an objective that is beneficial to the general public or some large segment of it. Social clubs, however, do not lay claim to such a lofty rationale: they are exempt because they provide private benefits to their close circle of members in the form of social and recreational services and events (Code section 501(c)(7)). The very justification for their exemption is unusual in the sense that it is one of the few pure tax rationales.

Social clubs present ample opportunities for competition with for-profit entities, such as athletic clubs, restaurants, bars, and night clubs. This raises several unrelated business income issues and, sometimes, disputes as to eligibility for tax-exempt status. Moreover, social clubs are not as tax-exempt as most other nonprofit organizations.

Here are the questions most frequently asked by clients about the corporate and tax status of social clubs—and the answers to them.

SOCIAL CLUBS IN GENERAL

Q 7:1   What is a *social club*?

A *social club* is a nonprofit organization that has a singular purpose: the provision of recreation and other forms of pleasure to its members.

Q 7:2   Does a social club have to be incorporated?

No, there is no requirement that a social club be incorporated, at least not for federal tax purposes. For other reasons, however, such as limitation on the liability of directors and officers, it may be a good idea to incorporate a social club.[1]

Q 7:3   Is a social club a tax-exempt organization?

Generally, under the federal tax laws, yes.[2] These entities (assuming they otherwise qualify) are described in section 501(c)(7) of the Internal Revenue Code. However, unlike most tax-exempt organizations, social clubs are only semi-tax-exempt.

Q 7:4   What does it mean to be *semi-tax-exempt*?

Usually, when an organization is only *semi-tax-exempt*, it means that its investment income is subject to tax.[3]

As a general proposition, a nonprofit organization can receive only three categories of revenue. One is income from related activities (including gifts and grants).[4] The second is investment income. The third is income from unrelated business activities.

Most tax-exempt organizations are taxable only on their net unrelated business income, if any. That is, their related business income and investment income are not taxed. In contrast, organizations like social clubs are tax-exempt only with respect to income from related activities; they are required to pay tax on their net unrelated business income *and* their investment income.

NOTE: This aspect of the tax treatment of social clubs is not widely understood or even realized. This is a big audit issue for social clubs, and representatives of the IRS, from time to time, in speeches remind the exempt organizations community of this rule of tax law.

Q 7:5   Is there any way to avoid this tax on investment income?

Yes, there is one lawful way. The law provides that a social club can set aside some or all of its investment income for charitable[5] purposes. When that is properly done, the income is not taxable.[6] Thus, a social club may transfer funds to an existing charitable organization and sidestep the tax, or it can create a charitable entity and transfer the funds to it with the same result (Q 7:30). A common illustration of this is a fraternity or sorority (Q 7:10) that has a related foundation, which is funded in whole or in part by investment income granted to it by the fraternity or sorority.

Q 7:6   How is a set-aside accomplished?

The law is quite vague on this point. Essentially, the matter turns on the requisite documentation, showing that the funds have in fact been transferred from one account to the other. One court, in what is perceived as the classic opinion on the subject of set-asides, wrote that the tax consequences depend "upon who is ultimately entitled to the property constituting [the] income."[7]

The case law views this as a matter of the establishment of a trust, although not in a formal sense. Thus, it is sufficient to meet the criteria of a constructive trust, an implied trust, or a resulting trust. In one instance, a court, having found in the facts a "reasonable certainty as to the property, the objects and the beneficiaries," held that funds transferred to an organization for the purpose of carrying out certain objectives "were impressed with a trust upon their receipt."[8] "No express words of trust were used, but none are necessary," wrote this court, in concluding that the recipient organization "was merely a designated fiduciary."[9] The court stated the essential criteria for what is also known as a set-aside: The organization's "books showed the total amount of such fees it received and the unexpended balance thereof at all times."[10] A commingling of the funds with other receipts was held to "not destroy their identity as a trust fund."[11]

TIP: It is important for a social club that is attempting to utilize a set-aside in this fashion to be certain that the funds set aside are in fact utilized for charitable *purposes.* In one instance, a set-aside failed to immuninize net investment income from taxation because the activity funded by the income—publication of a magazine—was found by a court to not be *educational.*[12]

TAX EXEMPTION CRITERIA

Q 7:7   What are the criteria for tax exemption as a social club?

Basically, there are three requirements. One is that the club must be organized primarily for the pleasure and recreation of its members (Q 7:8).

The second requirement is that substantially all of its activities must be devoted to that end. Third, the club must not contravene the private inurement doctrine.[13]

NOTE: It may seem odd that the private inurement doctrine is applicable to social clubs, inasmuch as private benefit is what a social club is all about. However, the type of private benefit that a social club provides (services and facilities) is different from that encompassed by the private inurement doctrine. Thus, for example, a social club may not pay unreasonable compensation to key employees or engage in unreasonable business dealings with board members.

COMMENT: There is not much law on the subject of the application of the private inurement doctrine to social clubs. In one instance, the IRS found private inurement in a dual membership class structure, where both classes enjoyed the same rights and privileges, yet one paid lower dues; private inurement occurred because the members of the class paying lower dues were being subsidized by the members of the other class.[14] In contrast, the IRS ruled that private inurement did not take place where a club paid a fee to each member who brought a new member into the club, inasmuch as the payments were reasonable compensation for the performance of a necessary administrative service.[15]

Q 7:8   What is the exempt purpose of a social club?

The exempt purpose of a social club is to provide services and facilities to its members so as to accord them pleasure in the form of recreation and like social opportunities. This criterion is paramount to qualification of a club for tax exemption. For example, a club can be tax-exempt when it provides its members with the opportunity to gamble—even where the gambling is illegal—as long as the source of the gambling revenue is the club's members and their guests.[16]

There is a related tax law provision that denies a business expense or other tax deduction for amounts paid or incurred for membership in a social club.[17] For this purpose, a *club* is a membership organization where "a principal purpose of the organization is to conduct entertainment activities for members of the organization or their guests or to provide members or their guests with access to entertainment facilities."[18]

Q 7:9   Apparently, a social club must have a membership.

Absolutely. This requirement is inherent in the notion of a *club*. Moreover, the membership must be of individuals with ample means for personal contacts and fellowship.[19] Indeed, one of the critical requirements is that there be a *commingling* of the members.[20] There should be conditions of membership and members must actively share interests or goals.[21]

CAUTION: It is not enough for the members of an organization to have a common interest or objective. This is one of the reasons that nonprofit automobile clubs cannot qualify as exempt social clubs.[22] The commingling requirement is essential.

Q 7:10   What are some examples of tax-exempt social clubs?

The most common forms of exempt social clubs include country clubs, golf and tennis clubs, swim clubs, and luncheon and dinner clubs.[23] Other types of social clubs include garden clubs,[24] pet clubs,[25] and college and university fraternities and sororities.[26] Gem and mineral clubs or federations of such clubs may qualify as exempt social clubs.[27]

A flying club qualified for tax exemption, as its members were interested in flying as a hobby, commingled in informal meetings, maintained and repaired aircraft owned by the club, and flew together in small group.[28]

NOTE: A club operated primarily to provide flying facilities suitable for its members' individual business or personal use cannot qualify as an exempt social club.[29]

Social club status was accorded an organization composed solely of individuals who were members of a political party and those interested in party affairs,[30] and to an entity consisting of members of a family to bring them into closer communication through social, family history, and newsletter activities.[31]

Q 7:11   What are some examples of organizations that do not qualify as exempt social clubs?

Some organizations do not qualify as exempt social clubs for reasons discussed previously. They may not be exempt because they are not nonprofit entities. That is, there can be for-profit clubs, such as those maintained by airlines in airports. Another reason for nonqualification is violation of the private inurement doctrine (Q 7:7). Still another reason is an absence of commingling by the membership (Q 7:9).

Of course, a club cannot be tax-exempt where its primary purpose is something other than the provision of pleasure to its members (Q 7:7). This can happen where a club makes its facilities available to the general public (Q 7:13). Nor can a club be an exempt club if it has certain types of discriminatory policies (Q 7:19).

Q 7:12   Why are social clubs only semi-tax-exempt?

The answer to this question first requires an understanding of why social clubs are exempt to any extent. The rationale for this exemption is a pure tax rationale: These entities are not taxable because they are not appropriate subjects of taxation to begin with, in that there is no shifting of income from one person to another. In a club, individuals are simply doing collectively what they could do individually without taxation.

A famous summary of this rationale is the following:

> Congress has determined that in a situation where individuals have banded together to provide recreational facilities on a mutual basis, it would be conceptually erroneous to impose a tax on the organization as a separate entity. The funds exempted are received only from the members and any "profit" which results from overcharging for the use of the facilities still belongs to the same members. No income of the sort usually taxed has been generated; the money has simply been shifted from one pocket to another, both within the same pair of pants.[32]

Thus, this tax exemption is extended to social and recreational clubs that are supported primarily by membership dues, fees, and assessments.[33]

The Treasury Department once summarized this rationale as follows:

> [T]he tax exemption for social clubs is designed to allow individuals to join together to provide recreational or social facilities on a mutual basis, without further tax consequences . . . [where] the sources of income of the organization are limited to receipts from the membership. . . . [T]he individual [member] is in substantially the same position as if he [or she] had spent his [or her] income on pleasure or recreation without the intervening separate organization.[34]

The Supreme Court reviewed this rationale, and restated and somewhat extended it, albeit in more elegant terms. The Court observed that, as already noted (Q 7:8), the federal tax exemption for social clubs "has a justification fundamentally different from that which underlies the grant of tax exemption to other nonprofit entities."[35] That is, although for most nonprofit organizations, "exemption from federal income tax is intended to encourage the provision of services that are deemed socially beneficial . . . [s]ocial clubs are exempted from tax not as a means of conferring tax *advantages*, but as a means of ensuring that the members are not subject to tax *disadvantages* as a consequence of their decision to pool their resources for the purpose of social or recreational services."[36] The Court restated this rationale by observing that the "statutory scheme for the taxation of social clubs was intended to achieve tax *neutrality*, not to provide these clubs a tax advantage: even the exemption for income derived from members' payments was designed to ensure that members are not disadvantaged as compared with persons who pursue recreation through private purchases rather than through the medium of an organization."[37]

However, this rationale is appropriate only where the sources of income of the organization are limited to receipts from the membership. If revenue flows to the club from other sources, such as investments, the rationale breaks down, in that the members are receiving an unwarranted tax-free subsidization of their recreational pursuits. When these distinctions were first noted, the courts disregarded them, finding the investment activity incidental. The most well known of these situations involved country clubs that allowed oil drilling on their golf courses, which generated substantial income.[38]

The extension of the unrelated business income tax to the investment income of social clubs—the conversion of clubs to semi-tax-exempt status—was done to eliminate the economic subsidies that members of some clubs were deriving. This law change took place in 1969. The legislative history explains why the law was revised:

[W]here the organization receives income from sources outside the membership, . . . upon which no tax is paid, the membership receives a benefit not contemplated by the exemption in that untaxed dollars can be used by the organization to provide pleasure or recreation (or other benefits) to its membership. . . . In such a case, the exemption is no longer simply allowing individuals to join together for recreation or pleasure without tax consequences. Rather, it is bestowing a substantial additional advantage to the members of the club by allowing tax-free dollars to be used for their personal recreational or pleasure purposes. The extension of the exemption to such investment income is, therefore, a distortion of its purpose.[39]

Thus, social clubs became semi-tax-exempt organizations to correct this "distortion" of the rationale for their basic exemption.

Q 7:13   Are there limitations on the extent to which social clubs can provide services or facilities to the general public?

Yes. Here again, there is a variation of application of the commerciality doctrine,[40] triggered because of the obvious fact that social clubs compete with restaurants, night clubs, health and fitness clubs, and the like. Extensive utilization of club facilities by the general public is thus inconsistent with the rationale for exempt status (Q 7:12). Even solicitation of the general public to utilize club facilities will disqualify a social club for tax exemption.[41]

The IRS promulgated guidelines for determining the effect on a social club's tax exemption of gross receipts derived from nonmember use of the club's facilities.[42] The concern is not with the situation in which a club member occasionally entertains a few guests at his or her club, but when a club's facilities are made available to the general public on a regular and recurring basis.[43] Infrequent use of a tax-exempt social club by the public would not jeopardize its exempt status because that would be an incidental use.[44]

The IRS guidelines make it clear that use of a tax-exempt social club's facilities by the general public may indicate the existence of a nonexempt purpose (which could endanger its exemption) or raise unrelated business income issues.[45] These guidelines establish a basic set of assumptions—which are also utilized for audit purposes—regarding member-sponsored income and a complex recordkeeping system to substantiate them. Detailed records are also required to determine under what circumstances and to what extent the social club makes its facilities available to nonmembers.

Essentially, the guideline assumptions are as follows:

1. Where a group of up to eight individuals, at least one of whom is a member of the club, uses club facilities, it is assumed that the nonmembers are the guests of the member, as long as payment for the club use is received by the club directly from the member or his or her employer.
2. Where at least 75 percent of a group using club facilities are members, a similar assumption is made.

> **NOTE:** This test was rejected by a court as being "unreasonable," with the court opining that "revenue from member-sponsored occasions involving attendance of nonmembers should not be considered as outsider transactions with respect to their impact on exempt status if it would be reasonable and normal, in the ordinary course of the activities usually pursued by social clubs, to utilize club premises or services for such occasions."[46]

3. Payment by a member's employer is assumed to be for a use that serves a direct business objective of the employee-member. A corporation may pay for individual club memberships without jeopardizing the club's tax exemption,[47] although an organization the membership of which was entirely in the name of corporations would not qualify for tax exemption.[48] However, to the extent a tax-exempt social club has corporate members, the individuals who use the club's facilities under the memberships are treated as part of the general public for purposes of the guidelines.[49]

4. In all other situations, a host-guest relationship is not assumed but must be substantiated. As to these occasions, the social club must maintain books and records containing specific information (as stated in the guidelines) about each use and the income derived from the uses. However, even as to the first and second of these items, adequate records must be maintained.

> **NOTE:** It is the position of the IRS that amounts paid to a tax-exempt social club by visiting members of another exempt social club are forms of nonmember income, even if paid pursuant to a reciprocal arrangement.[50]

These guidelines mandate that, where a group using a tax-exempt social club includes no more than eight individuals, the club must maintain records that substantiate that fact, that at least one of them was a member, and that payment was received from the member or his or her employer. Where 75 percent or more of the group are members of the club, records must be maintained that substantiate this fact and that payment was received directly from members or members' employers.

On all other occasions involving nonmembers, the tax-exempt social club must maintain records showing each use and the income derived from the use, even though a member initially pays for the use. The club's records must also include the following: the date, the total number in the party, the number of nonmembers in the party, the total charges, the charges attributable to nonmembers, and the charges paid by nonmembers. If a member pays all or part of the charges, there must be a statement signed by the member as to whether he or she has been or will be reimbursed, and to what extent, by the nonmembers.

Further, where a member's employer reimburses the member or pays the social club directly for nonmember charges, there must be a statement indicating the name of the employer, the amount attributable to nonmember use, the nonmember's name and business or other relationship to the member, and the business, personal, or social purpose of the member served by the nonmember use. If a nonmember (other than a member's employer) makes payment to the club or reimburses a member and claims the amount was paid gratuitously, the member must sign a statement indicating the donor's name, relationship to the member, and information demonstrating the gratuitous nature of the payment.

COMMENT: It is apparent that the requirements for recordkeeping under these IRS guidelines are extensive. Moreover, the penalty for failing to maintain adequate records is severe. If these records are not maintained, the IRS will not apply the audit assumptions and all income will be treated as unrelated business income. Therefore, tax-exempt social clubs must maintain adequate records for the purpose of labeling income from members as *exempt function income* (Q 7:27).

One of the statutory requirements for tax exemption of social clubs is that they be organized and operated so that substantially all of their activities are for exempt purposes. This *substantially all* standard allows an exempt social club to receive some outside income (including investment income) and some income from nonmembers using its facilities and services without losing its tax-exempt status.

The intent of Congress in this regard is that an exempt social club can receive up to 35 percent of its gross receipts (other than unusual amounts) from investment income and receipts from nonmembers, as long as the nonmember receipts do not exceed 15 percent of total receipts.[51]

Q 7:14   How do clubs handle the revenue from tournaments attended by the general public?

In computing this 35 percent threshold (Q 7:13), a tax-exempt social club does not need to take into consideration "unusual amounts of income." This rule was generally intended to cover receipts from the sale of a clubhouse or similar facility. Presumably, the rule is also applicable to receipts from a major sporting event, such as a golf or tennis tournament, that is open to the public but is held by the club on an irregular basis. This interpretation would be in conformance with prior case law.[52]

However, some clubs hold tournaments on a regularly recurring basis (such as annually). In this situation, the exclusion for unusual amounts is presumably unavailable. Thus, the tax exemption of a social club in this circumstance would be adversely affected if the 15 percent limitation was exceeded,[53] but even if the level of receipts did not trigger revocation of tax exemption, the return from the tournament would nonetheless be subject to taxation as income other than exempt function income (Q 7:27).

It is clear that a tax-exempt social club that makes its facilities available to the general public in hosting an athletic tournament generates receipts from nonmember use of the facilities, with these receipts subject to the 15 percent test. For example, the IRS ruled that an association of professional tournament golfers that maintained a championship course may make the course available to the general public when the tournament is not being held, without disturbing its tax-exempt status, but with the income from the use subject to taxation as unrelated business income.[54]

There is a related rule of law concerning the derivation of revenue from the conduct of an activity that does not advance social club exempt purposes. It is the view of the IRS that this type of revenue is not sheltered by the 35 percent test, although exempt status is not to be lost where the amount of income involved is incidental. These activities are known as *nontraditional* ones. In one instance, lawyers at the IRS considered the tax status of a social club that rented rooms as temporary principal residences, rented offices, operated a barber shop, provided a take-out food service, operated a service station and parking garage, and maintained in its lobby a commercial travel agency, a flower and gift shop, and a liquor store. The sale of petroleum products and services, and of take-out food, were classified as nontraditional activities; the rental of rooms, operation of the barber shop and parking garage, and maintenance of the travel agency were termed "questionable."[55]

Q 7:15 Are there limitations on the amount of lobbying a social club can engage in?

There is no law on the point. This undoubtedly is because social clubs rarely engage in lobbying. (When they do, it is usually through an association of social clubs (Chapter 5).)

However, there are no restrictions in this regard, so an exempt social club can engage in as much lobbying as it wishes—as long as, of course, the lobbying is in advancement of exempt purposes (which it most likely always would be).

Dues paid to social clubs are not deductible as business expenses, so the rules by which the deductibility of dues paid to membership organizations is limited (Q 5:14) are not applicable with respect to social clubs.

Q 7:16 Are there limitations on the amount of political campaign activity a social club can engage in?

No. Again (Q 7:15), this is because there is no law on the point. It is rare for a social club to be involved in political campaign activities. Undertakings of this nature are more likely to be conducted by political action committees affiliated with associations of social clubs (Chapter 8).

Q 7:17 What are the principal reasons for loss of tax exemption as a social club?

The reasons for loss of tax exemption as a social club are reflected in the foregoing discussion. They are failure to engage in exempt functions (Q 7:7),[56] transgression of the private inurement doctrine (Q 7:7), engaging in substantial business operations (Q 7:18), insufficient commingling of the members (Q 7:7), and undue public use of club facilities and services (Q 7:13). Discriminatory practices can also lead to loss of tax-exempt status (Q 7:19).

Q 7:18 What are the rules concerning business activities?

An exempt social club is not supposed to engage in nonmember activities, except to a limited extent as permitted by the unrelated business income rules (Q 7:27). For example, a social club was denied tax exemption because it regularly sold liquor to its members for consumption off the club premises.[57] Likewise, a club that leased building lots to its members in addition to providing them recreation facilities was deemed not entitled to tax exemption.[58]

In a somewhat comparable set of circumstances, the IRS ruled nonexempt a club operating a cocktail lounge and cafe as an integral part of a motel and restaurant business; about one fourth of the club's "membership" was composed of individuals temporarily staying at the motel.[59]

Q 7:19   What are the rules concerning discriminatory practices?

Tax exemption as a social club is barred where the club has a written policy of discrimination on account of race, color, or religion.[60] This proscription on discriminatory practices does not extend to tax-exempt social clubs that limit membership on the basis of ethnic or national origin.[61]

Q 7:20   Is there potential confusion between social club status and classification as another type of exempt organization?

Yes. Sometimes it is difficult to differentiate between a business league (Chapter 5) and a social club. For example, an organization operated to assist its members in their business endeavors through study and discussion of problems and similar activities at weekly luncheon meetings; it was denied tax exemption as a social club on the ground that any social activities at the meetings were incidental to the business purpose of the organization.[62]

There can also be confusion as between a social club and a social welfare organization. This subject was reviewed in the discussion of social welfare organizations (Q 6:18).

Q 7:21   Are social clubs involved with the intermediate sanctions rules?

Not really. A social club is not an *applicable tax-exempt organization*.[63] It is possible for a social club to be a *disqualified person* with respect to an applicable tax-exempt organization,[64] but that is unlikely.

Q 7:22   Are social clubs required to file annual returns with the IRS?

Generally, yes. Social clubs are among the types of exempt organizations that are required to file annual information returns with the IRS (Q 11:1).[65] These are usually on Form 990.

If a social club has, in a year, gross receipts of less than $100,000 and total assets of less than $250,000, it may file a simpler (two-page) version of the return (Q 11:7). This is Form 990-EZ.

If a social club normally receives $25,000 or less in gross receipts annually, it is excused from this filing requirement (Q 11:3).[66]

Q 7:23   Are social clubs required to apply to the IRS for recognition of tax-exempt status?

No. If an organization satisfies the legal requirements as to social club status, it is exempt by operation of law (Q 4:2). There is no need, as a matter of law, to file an application with the IRS for a ruling recognizing the tax exemption.

However, a social club may seek a determination as to its tax-exempt status with the IRS. This is done by filing a completed Form 1024. It is often a good practice to obtain a determination letter, so that the social club has the protection that the document affords (Q 4:4, Q 5:21).

Q 7:24   What disclosure rules apply to social clubs?

There are two sets of disclosure rules that are applicable to social clubs. One of these sets of rules pertains to *fundraising solicitations*. This is because, in this setting, the solicitation of member dues is considered a fund-raising solicitation.[67] These rules, which are discussed elsewhere (Q 6:24, Q 13:17), require the solicitation to contain an express statement, in a conspicuous and easily recognizable format, that gifts and like payments to the organization are not deductible for federal income tax purposes.[68]

Q 7:25   What happens when a social club elects to give up its tax-exempt status?

Basically, once a social club is no longer tax-exempt, the entity becomes a taxable one, although it remains a nonprofit organization. As noted (Q 5:23), however, special rules apply in the case of taxable membership organizations, which can operate to increase the extent of tax liability.

NOTE 1:   Loss of tax-exempt status by a social club is not usually quite as devastating as can be the case with other exempt entities, in that a social club's investment income is subject to tax even while the club is "tax-exempt" (Q 7:4).

CAUTION: Loss of exemption by a social club can, in a unique set of circumstances, trigger a tax hit far worse than that in other exempt organization contexts—because of the personal holding company rules. For example, a tax-exempt social club had as its membership the lineal descendants of two individuals. It had its exempt status re-

---

voked. The issue arose as to whether the club should be treated as a personal holding company (PHC). One of the tests for a PHC is that, at any time during the last half of the tax year, more than 50 percent in value of its stock is owned by or for no more than five individuals.[69] The IRS treated the club's members as shareholders for this purpose, found that the stock ownership test was met, and held that the club was a PHC.[70] The result: payment of the regular corporate tax, plus a tax of 39.6 percent on the undistributed personal holding company income.

NOTE 2:   A tax-exempt organization cannot be a PHC.[71]

Q 7:26   Are contributions to social clubs deductible?

The general answer to this question must be no, inasmuch as social clubs are not on the list of organizations that are eligible donees for charitable deduction purposes.[72] However, it is not uncommon for a payment by a third party to be made to one organization, with some or all of the payment destined for another organization. The tax treatment accorded some or all of a payment of this nature (such as deductibility as a charitable contribution) can depend on whether the payment is deemed made to the initial payee or whether it or a portion of it is deemed made to another, sometimes related, organization that is the transferee of the initial payee. In many of these instances, the organization that initially received the payment is regarded as the *agent* of the organization that is the ultimate recipient of the payment, so that the payor is considered, for tax purposes, to have made the payment directly to the ultimate transferee, notwithstanding the flow of the payment through one or more intermediate organizations functioning as *conduit* entities.

In one instance reflecting these principles, contributions to an exempt social club were held to be deductible as charitable gifts, where the club functioned as an authorized agent for one or more charitable organizations, enabling the members of the club, when purchasing tickets for a social event, to direct that the amount of their total payment in excess of the price of the tickets be transferred to charitable organizations and to deduct, as charitable gifts, that portion of the payment to the club that was paid over to the charitable organizations.[73] Here, the club was considered the mere conduit of some of the payments, and thus the federal tax consequences of the payment were determined as if these payments were made directly to the charities.

UNRELATED BUSINESS ACTIVITIES

Q 7:27   Are social clubs subject to the unrelated business rules?

Yes. In fact, they are conceptually more exposed to the unrelated business rules than most exempt organizations, as explained next.

Q 7:28   What are the principal unrelated business issues being raised by social clubs?

The principal unrelated business issue being raised these days by social clubs derives from the fact that their net investment income is subject to unrelated business income taxation.

Conceptually, a tax-exempt organization can receive three types of income: related business income, investment income, and unrelated business income. Most exempt organizations are taxable only on net revenue derived from unrelated business.[74] However, social clubs are taxed not only on conventional unrelated business income but also on investment income.[75]

NOTE: An example of the application of this rule is that the interest earned by an exempt social club on deposits required for its charter flights was held to be taxable.[76]

TIP: There is a useful exception to this rule of taxation, which is that investment funds set aside for charitable purposes are generally not taxed.[77] This is one reason that an exempt social club may wish to create and operate a related charitable organization (Q 7:29).

Another issue generated by social clubs in the unrelated business context is the tax treatment of revenue received from nonmembers. Most frequently, this is a matter of controversy that can adversely affect a club's tax exemption (Q 7:13). However, it can arise in the unrelated business setting.

NOTE: This tax can arise in peculiar ways. In one case, an exempt social club had as its principal activity the annual staging of a mock pirate invasion and a parade. A court ruled that the club incurred taxable

---

income from the sale of refreshments along the parade route, souvenirs, and advertising, inasmuch as the concession and other income was derived from dealings with nonmembers.[78]

A third issue that originated with social clubs—and that has now spread to nearly all categories of exempt organizations—is the extent to which losses incurred in connection with sales to nonmembers can be used to offset investment income. After much thrashing around of this issue in the lower courts, the Supreme Court held that that can be done only when the sales were motivated by an intent to generate a profit.[79] This has led to the larger principle that, to be a *business* for unrelated business tax purposes, the activity must be conducted with the requisite profit motive.[80]

An "issue" that receives much less attention is the sale of club assets, such as real estate. Where the purpose of the sale is not profit but rather to facilitate relocation or a comparable end, there is no taxation of the gain but, instead, a nonrecognition of gain and a carryover of basis. In contrast, where the sale of an exempt social club's assets occurs more frequently, the IRS is likely to resist application of this special rule.[81]

RELATED ENTITIES

Q 7:29   Can social clubs have related entities, such as foundations, for-profit subsidiaries, title-holding companies, and political action committees?

Yes, but it is not common for a social club to have one of these types of in-tandem relationships. For example, it is highly unlikely that a social club would maintain a political action committee, although it is legally possible. Furthermore, a typical social club would not often operate a related charitable organization, if only because the charity would probably be a private foundation, with all of the attendant regulatory difficulties.[82]

Q 7:30   What is the underlying reason for this use of related entities?

The underlying reason for use of a related entity by a social club is the same reason this practice is engaged in by other types of exempt organizations: what has been elsewhere termed *bifurcation* (Q 5:30). Here, two organizations are used instead of one, usually because this duality is forced into existence by the nature of the tax law. The reasons for doing this in specific instances are discussed in answers to the following questions.

Q 7:31   What is the relationship between the entities? Are they always subsidiaries of the club?

In these in-tandem arrangements, there is not always a requirement that the relationship be that of parent and subsidiary. However, it is usually best if that is the case.

The parent-subsidiary relationship is established and is continued where the parent entity—here, the social club—*controls* the entity that is the subsidiary (Q 5:31).

Q 7:32   How is the relationship of parent and subsidiary established?

The mechanics by which a parent-subsidiary relationship is established are discussed elsewhere (Q 5:32). Most frequently, however, particularly in the club setting, the method of control is the *interlocking directorate*, where the club controls the other entity by means of *overlapping boards*.

Q 7:33   Why would a social club establish a related charitable organization?

The usual reason that a social club would establish a charitable organization is to create a vehicle that advances the charitable, educational, or like program with which the social club would like to be associated, and then use that related entity to receive grants from charities and deductible charitable contributions. To this end, the related charity would function much like one affiliated with a membership association (Q 5:30).

Another reason for this in-tandem use of a charitable organization is to maintain a vehicle that can be the subject of a set-aside grant (Q 7:6). A classic example is a college or university fraternity or sorority—regarded as a social club for tax purposes—that has a related "foundation." Such an organization may engage in a variety of programs of benefit to the education and maturity of the club's student members—and be a source of funding by means of the set-aside: the transfer of investment funds from the fraternity or sorority to the charitable organization.

The difficulty inherent in this approach is that the related charity is likely to be a private foundation, particularly those that are established in relation to local clubs. These entities may not be able to qualify as publicly supported charities,[83] and the club cannot be eligible to be a supported organization.[84] Of course, for national organizations, such as national collegiate fraternities and sororities, the alumni and alumnae membership base will be sufficiently large to enable them to constitute publicly supported organizations.

Q 7:34 Why would a social club establish a for-profit subsidiary?

In the unlikely event that an exempt social club utilizes a for-profit subsidiary, it would be—as is usually the case with any other type of exempt organization—to house one or more unrelated business activities. However, because the principal purpose of a social club is to service its members (Q 7:7), it is not likely that it would operate an unrelated business that presumably would serve the general public.

Moreover, many tax-exempt organizations are able to receive dividends from corporations that are not taxable.[85] In contrast, however, even if they are not otherwise taxable (such as because the payor corporation is not a subsidiary[86]), dividends paid to social clubs are always taxable because of the special tax rule discussed earlier (Q 7:4), unless a set-aside is utilized.

Q 7:35 Why would a social club establish a title-holding company?

A social club might establish a title-holding company—again, an example of bifurcation (Q 5:30)—because of principles of management and concern in respect to liability. The use of title-holding companies by social clubs is infrequent, however.

The purpose of a title-holding company[87] is to hold title to property. This is, in the law, a *passive* function. The title-holding entity is not supposed to be in an active business of operating the property; it is to hold the title, collect any income from use of the property, and remit any net proceeds to the parent organization.

There may be one or more reasons that a property ought not to be held in the name of a tax-exempt organization. The property may, for example, carry with it the likelihood of legal liability. By placing the property in a title-holding company, the hope is that any actual liability will be confined to the title-holding entity, that is, that the liability will not ascend to the parent entity.

NOTE: In some other exempt organization contexts, a supporting organization can be used instead of a title-holding company, the former being in many respects more flexible in use than the latter (Q 5:33, Q 6:32). However, because a social club is not a qualified supported organization,[88] this option is not available to these clubs.

Social clubs often own real estate—the usual asset of a title-holding company. These properties include country clubs, golf and tennis clubs, swim clubs, and urban athletic clubs. However, such a property is not likely to be placed in a title-holding entity because it is used in a related business—in this instance, one or more exempt functions of a social club.

CHAPTER 8

Political Organizations

The prior two chapters discuss tax-exempt organizations that are among the least understood. Political organizations are, for the most part, even less fathomed; they are often mysteries. The idea of nonprofit organizations having political activity as their primary exempt function is a concept that, for some, is contrary to their knowledge of the law of tax-exempt organizations—particularly public charities. The mystery stems partly from the origins of the law in this field, which basically started in 1974. At that time the IRS issued some rulings finding political campaign committees to be taxable. Congress was not enamored of the IRS's handiwork and responded with a statute, enacted later that year.

Here are the questions most frequently asked by clients about political organizations—and the answers to them.

POLITICAL ORGANIZATIONS BASICS

Q 8:1   What is a *political organization*?

The federal tax law definition of a *political organization* is that it is a party, committee, association, fund, or other organization (whether or not incorporated) that is organized and operated primarily for the purpose of directly or indirectly accepting contributions or making expenditures for an exempt function.[1]

Q 8:2   What are *contributions* for these purposes?

The term *contribution* includes a gift, subscription, loan, advance, deposit of money, or anything of value, which includes a contract, promise, or agreement to make a contribution, whether or not legally enforceable.[2]

Q 8:3   What are *expenditures* for these purposes?

The term *expenditures* means a payment, distribution, loan, advance, deposit, gift of money, or anything of value, which includes a contract, promise, or agreement to make an expenditure, whether or not legally enforceable.[3]

NOTE: Obviously, the terms *contributions* (Q 8:2) and *expenditures* are sweepingly defined in this context. For example, a tax-exempt organization can usually make an interest-bearing loan to an entity, purely as an investment, that is, without the use of the loan proceeds traced back to it for ongoing exemption qualification purposes. However, in this setting, a loan is a *political expenditure*—inclusion of that term in the definition of *expenditures* overrides the general treatment of a loan.[4]

Q 8:4   What is an *exempt function*?

The concept of an *exempt function* embodies three definitions.[5] The first and most common one is the activity of influencing or attempting to influence the selection, nomination, election, or appointment of any individual to any federal, state, or local public office. The second is the activity of influencing or attempting to influence the selection, nomination, election, or appointment of any individual to any office in a political organization.

NOTE: One of the significant aspects of the term *exempt function* is that it is broader than the concept of *political campaign activities* that are normally thought of in the public charity setting, where they are prohibited.[6] An exempt function can include efforts to support or oppose *nominees* for an office, where there is no *campaign* (at least not in the conventional sense). This aspect of the law is discussed later (Q 8:8).

The third type of *exempt function* is the influencing or attempting to influence the election of presidential or vice-presidential electors, whether or not the electors are selected, nominated, elected, or appointed.

Q 8:5   What is a *public office*?

The term *public office,* as used in the political organizations setting, is defined in the same manner as in the private foundation context, where it is used in determining when an individual is a *government official* as part of the process of ascertaining whether the individual is a *disqualified person* (Q 9:12).[7]

Q 8:6   What are some examples of political organizations?

Political organizations include national, state, and local political parties. They include political action committees (PACs), campaign committees for individual candidates (including the principal campaign committees designated by candidates for Congress[8]), many other vehicles used to collect political campaign contributions and make political campaign expenditures, and newsletter funds of political officeholders.[9]

Q 8:7   What is a *newsletter fund*?

A *newsletter fund* is a fund established and maintained by an individual who holds, has been elected to, or is a candidate for nomination or election to any federal, state, or local elective public office for use by the individual exclusively for the preparation and circulation of the individual's newsletter.[10] The exempt function of a newsletter fund is limited to the preparation and distribution of the newsletter, including secretarial services, printing, addressing, and mailing.[11]

NOTE: In this setting only, the term *candidate* means an individual who publicly announces that he or she is a candidate for nomination or election to office and meets the legal qualifications for that position.[12] Thus, this term is narrower than the term *candidate* used in other contexts.[13]

Q 8:8   Do these rules require the involvement of a *candidate*?

Not at all. As noted (Q 8:4), the individuals supported or opposed can be nominees or appointees. Even where there is a conventional campaign, the individual for whom expenditures are made does not have to be an announced candidate, nor is it critical that the individual ever actually become a candidate for an office.[14] Even activities engaged in "between elections" can be exempt function activities, as long as they are directly related to the process of selection, nomination, or election of an individual in the next applicable political campaign.[15]

Q 8:9   What are some examples of exempt function expenditures?

Oddly, there are not many published examples. The chief type of exempt function in this context is, as noted, to collect money and spend it to cause someone to be elected to a public office or to oppose someone's election. Here are some other illustrations of this type of exempt function:

1. Disbursements for the distribution of voter guides and incumbents' voting records.[16]
2. Amounts expended for voter research, public opinion polls, and voter canvasses on behalf of an elected legislator who was a candidate for another office.[17]
3. Cash awards to campaign workers after the election.[18]
4. Expenses for parties or other celebrations given on election night by a candidate's campaign committee for the candidate's campaign workers.[19]
5. Payments of salary to a candidate who took a leave of absence from his employment to campaign on a full-time basis.[20]

OBSERVATION: One of the most interesting of these examples is expenditures for grass roots lobbying.[21] Normally, lobbying is not an exempt function. However, in this instance, the targeting of the distributions of the lobbying literature and the timing of the distributions in relation to elections was seen by the IRS as creating a "link" between the issues and the candidates. Indeed, for the first and only time, the IRS ruled that lobbying was of a "dual character": it was simultaneously an attempt to influence legislation and a political organization exempt function.[22]

The IRS looks at all of the pertinent facts and circumstances in determining whether an expenditure constitutes an exempt function. For example, a proper exempt function expenditure included expenses for "voice and speech lessons to improve [a candidate's] skills," but does not include expenses of an incumbent for "periodicals of general circulation in order to keep himself informed on national and local issues."[23]

Moreover, as discussed (Q 8:4), the concept of an *exempt function* extends to influencing or attempting to influence nominations of individuals to public offices. Thus, for example, when the president appoints an individual to serve on the Supreme Court, efforts in support of or opposition to the nomination are exempt functions.

Q 8:10   How much exempt function activity does a political organization have to engage in to be tax-exempt?

Like nearly all exempt organizations, political organizations are subject to a *primary purpose test.*[24] Thus, a political organization is not required to engage *exclusively* in exempt function activities.[25] For example, a political organization may sponsor nonpartisan educational workshops, carry on social activities unrelated to an exempt function, support the enactment or defeat of a ballot proposition, or pay an incumbent's office expenses, as long as these are not the organization's primary activities.[26]

CAUTION 1:   As a general rule, legislative activities[27] are differentiated from political activities, so lobbying is not an exempt function in this setting.[28] However, lobbying can qualify as an exempt function in instances where it has a "dual character" (Q 6:33, Q 8:9).

CAUTION 2:   In some situations, expenditures by a political organization are treated as gross income to the individual beneficiary, such as payment of an incumbent's office expenses[29] or payment of a candidate's tax liability.[30]

Q 8:11   Are contributions to political organizations subject to the gift tax?

No. Usually, the only exempt organizations that can attract gifts without concern over gift taxation are charitable organizations. However, by virtue of a special tax law, contributions to political organizations are not subject to the gift tax.[31] There is no comparable gift tax exclusion in other exempt organization settings, such as for gifts to social welfare organizations (see Chapter 6).

TAXATION OF POLITICAL ORGANIZATIONS

Q 8:12   Are political organizations tax-exempt?

A political organization is considered a tax-exempt organization for purpose of legal references to exempt organizations.[32] Although they are tax-exempt organizations, they are not as exempt as most other types of exempt organizations. This is because they are taxed, not only on unrelated business income, but also on investment income.[33]

NOTE: In this regard, political organizations are taxed much the same as social clubs (Q 7:4).

Technically, the income tax falls on a political organization's *political organization taxable income*.[34]

Q 8:13   What is *political organization taxable income*?

A political organization's *political organization taxable income* is its gross income, less *exempt function income* and less allowable deductions directly connected with the production of gross income (other than exempt function income).[35] There is a specific deduction of $100,[36] although that deduction is not available to newsletter funds (Q 8:7).[37]

Q 8:14   What is *exempt function income*?

A political organization's *exempt function revenue* is any amount received as (1) contributions of money or other property, (2) membership dues, fees, or assessments from members, (3) proceeds from a political fund-raising or entertainment event, (4) proceeds from the sale of political campaign materials, and (5) proceeds from the conduct of bingo games, as long as these amounts are segregated for use only for the exempt function of the political organization.[38]

CAUTION: As to the fourth category of exempt function income, it is necessary to distinguish this type of revenue from that received in the ordinary course of conduct of a business (which is taxable). As a general rule, proceeds from casual, sporadic fund-raising or entertainment events are not considered the regular conduct of a business.[39] In con-

---

trast, for example, proceeds received by a political organization from the sales of art reproductions were ruled to be derived from the ordinary course of conducting a business.[40]

NOTE: As in charitable fund-raising, there are many ways to generate gifts for political organizations. An intriguing one is the "charity-PAC" matching programs established by businesses. These programs allow employees of a business to designate a charitable organization to be the recipient of a contribution from the corporate employer. The contribution made by the corporation is an amount equal to the sum of the contributions made by the employees to the corporation's political action committee during the previous year. It is the position of the IRS, however, that the corporation's gift to the charity is not eligible for a charitable deduction, on the ground that the corporation received a quid pro quo for the payment to the charity, in the form of the contributions to the PAC.[41]

In an instance of a political organization that limits its activities to exempt functions, only its investment income is subject to taxation.

Q 8:15   What is the tax consequence of excess funds in a political organization following a campaign?

Excess funds controlled by a political organization or other person after a campaign or election are treated as expended for the personal use of the individual having control over the ultimate use of the funds, with two exceptions.[42] One exception is available where the funds are held in reasonable anticipation of use by the political organization for future exempt functions.[43] The other exception arises where the amounts are transferred to another exempt political organization, a publicly supported charity, or a government.[44]

OBSERVATION: There is a curious "stretching" of the law in this area. The Internal Revenue Code provides for this exception for transfers to these public charities.[45] However, the IRS has allowed this exception to operate where the amounts are paid over to private foundations, as long as the foundation's governing instruments confine its grant-making to these charities. Here the private foundation is cast as a "trust," with the funds transferred "for the use of" these public charities.[46]

Q 8:16   What is the tax rate imposed on political organization taxable income?

Political organization taxable income is taxed at the highest rate of corporate tax.[47] At the present, that rate is 35 percent.[48]

TAXATION OF OTHER EXEMPT ORGANIZATIONS

Q 8:17   What happens when another type of tax-exempt organization expends funds for an exempt function?

That question pertains to two of the great secrets in the law of tax-exempt organizations. One is that an exempt organization can be taxed for making an expenditure (as opposed to generating a form of income). The other is that the tax imposed on political organizations can be imposed on other types of exempt organizations.

Here is the rule: If a tax-exempt organization (other than a political one) expends an amount during a tax year for what would be a political organization exempt function, it must include in its gross income for the year an amount equal to the lesser of (1) its net investment income[49] for the year or (2) the aggregate amount expended during the year for the exempt function.[50]

NOTE: Items taken into account for purposes of unrelated business income taxation[51] are not taken into account in calculating net investment income.[52] This adjustment is provided to avoid double taxation.

CAUTION: In this context as well, the rate of tax is the highest corporate rate (Q 8:16).

Q 8:18   How does this rule relate to the rules applicable to political campaign activities by other exempt organizations?

It does not change those other rules, which often pertain to an organization's ongoing eligibility for tax-exempt status.[53] For example, a social welfare organization (see Chapter 6) may, without adversely affecting its exempt status, participate in political campaign activities as long as it is primarily engaged in social welfare functions, although the amounts expended for the political activities are likely to be treated as political organization taxable income.[54]

CAUTION: This allowance of political campaign activity by social welfare organizations is applicable only from a tax law perspective. Such activities may be prohibited by the federal and/or state campaign finance laws.[55]

This matter is more complex when considered in the realm of public charities, which are flatly prohibited from participating or intervening in political campaign activities.[56] A public charity that engages in a political campaign activity faces one or more tax consequences: loss of tax-exempt status, imposition of a special tax because of the political campaign activity,[57] and/or imposition of the tax for undertaking a political organization exempt function.[58]

However, the concept of political organization exempt function is broader than the concept of political campaign activity applicable to public charities—largely because attempts to influence nominations are included in the former (Q 8:4). Thus, a public charity could make expenditures in an effort to secure Senate confirmation of a Supreme Court nominee. The result would be a levying of the political organization exempt function tax, but the charity would not lose its exempt status nor would it have to face the tax for political campaign activity.

USE OF POLITICAL ORGANIZATIONS BY OTHER EXEMPT ORGANIZATIONS

Q 8:19   Can a tax-exempt organization establish a related political organization?

The general answer to this question is yes. Usually, this type of political organization is a PAC. The tax-exempt organizations that are most likely to establish a PAC are membership associations (see Chapter 5), labor organizations,[59] and social welfare organizations (see Chapter 6).

OBSERVATION: Illustrating this point, social welfare organizations established political organizations to engage in election-year issue consciousness-raising efforts. Through this technique, the social welfare organizations were able to enhance the public debate on issues of concern to them and to focus on the positions of public officials and candidates on these issues—and do so without tax exposure.[60] Moreover, contributions to the political organizations were excluded from gift taxation (Q 8:11); the same gifts to the social welfare organizations would have been subject to federal gift taxation.

Under certain circumstances, a public charity can have a PAC (Q 8:21).

Q 8:20   Why would an exempt organization want to establish a political organization?

There are two basic reasons motivating a tax-exempt organization to establish a related PAC. Both of these are based on the fundamental principle of *bifurcation*: a splitting into two organizations of what would probably otherwise be one, were it not for legal requirements.[61] One reason relates to taxes: by placing political organization exempt functions in a PAC, rather than conducting them itself, the parent exempt organization can sidestep the political organization exempt function tax—and perhaps avoid loss of tax-exempt status. In parallel fashion, and the other reason for use of a related PAC, is that it significantly reduces the likelihood that the parent organization will commit an election law transgression.

NOTE: In the parlance of the federal election law rules, a political action committee is a *separate segregated fund.*

This type of political entity that is maintained by a tax-exempt organization is treated as an entity separate from the parent organization for purposes of the rules pertaining to political organizations.[62] Thus, a tax-exempt organization that engages in a political organization exempt function as a relatively small part of its operations may have much or all of its net investment income taxed, whereas an exempt organization that maintains a separate political organization can segregate contributions for use in an exempt function, with the result that only the net investment income of the fund is subject to tax.

Q 8:21   Can a public charity operate a related political organization without adverse tax consequences?

The general answer is no—a public charity cannot establish and maintain a related PAC, inasmuch as the PAC's activities would be attributed to it, and thus the charity would be in violation of the prohibition on political campaign involvement. However, a charitable organization may establish and use a PAC if the purpose of the PAC is to engage in political activities (political organization exempt functions) that are not political campaign activities.[63] For example, if a public charity intended to make a regular practice of supporting and/or opposing nominations to the Supreme Court, it would be well advised to transfer that function to a related PAC.

Q 8:22   Can a parent exempt organization pay the expenses of its related political organization?

It depends on the nature of the expenses. The parent exempt organization can pay the expenses of establishing and maintaining the political entity (such as legal and accounting fees). (These are sometimes referred to as *soft-dollar expenditures*.) These expenditures generally are not considered an exempt function outlay and thus would not subject the parent exempt organization to the political organization exempt function tax. However, the parent organization's monies should not be used for political purposes. (Such expenses are sometimes referred to as *hard-dollar expenditures*.)

Organizations in this position should keep good records, differentiating between soft-dollar expenditures and hard-dollar expenditures. The IRS may endeavor to tax some or all of the expenditures of a tax-exempt organization where the records do not clearly distinguish between the two types of outlays.[64]

Q 8:23   Can a parent exempt organization collect funds from its members for its related political organization?

Yes, but the practice should be engaged in with care. The exempt organization will not have difficulties in this regard (that is, be taxed) where it merely receives contributions from its members for political action and promptly and directly transfers the funds to the political organization that solicited them.[65] In this regard, the parent organization is considered a conduit of the political contributions, rather than a contributor of them. For example, an exempt membership association can send notices to its members seeking the annual dues payments and include a request for contributions to the related PAC; the members can make the dues payments and political contributions by means of a single check (or other charge) payable to the association. When these rules are properly followed, the political contributions paid over by the association are regarded for tax purposes as having been made directly to the PAC by the individual members.

A transfer is considered *promptly and directly* made if the organization's procedures satisfy requirements of applicable federal or state campaign laws, the organization maintains adequate records to demonstrate that the amounts transferred are in fact political contributions (rather than investment income), and the political contributions transferred are not used to earn investment income for the organization.[66]

NOTE: The same principle operates with respect to charitable gifts. For example, an association can seek dues from its members, along with a solicitation for gifts to its related foundation. Although both are paid to the association in a single payment, the gifts are treated as if made by the individual members—and are deductible as such.

Q 8:24 Does the IRS recognize the *independent* political organization?

There is no word to date from the IRS as to independent political organizations. This type of political organization has, however, been addressed by the Federal Election Commission (FEC).

It is possible for the managers of a charitable organization (and/or other tax-exempt organizations), acting in their individual capacity, to establish and maintain an *independent* political action committee, even if the PAC has the function of supporting or opposing a candidate's political campaign. The virtue of this type of entity—if it works for tax purposes—is that the political campaign activities of the PAC are not attributed to the charitable organization.

Although the IRS has yet to rule on this point, the FEC published an advisory opinion sanctioning the concept of what the federal campaign law implicitly recognizes as a "non-connected political committee."[67] According to the FEC, a non-connected political committee has the following characteristics:

1. It is established by the members of the governing board of the charitable organization, acting in their individual capacities.

2. The committee operates and is governed independently of the charitable organization.

3. The committee is not financially supported by the charitable organization.

4. The committee appropriately reimburses the charitable organization for expenses incurred on behalf of the committee.

5. The committee pays a fair rent to the charitable organization for the use of any office space and/or facilities.

6. The committee pays a "commercially reasonable" consideration for the services of individuals who are employees or agents of the charitable organization.

7. The charitable organization does not engage in conduct that favors or appears to favor the solicitation activity of the committee.

8. Neither the charitable organization nor the committee asserts a proprietary interest in or control over use of the name of the political committee.

CHAPTER 9

Private Foundation Rules

One of the most complex bodies of statutory law in the tax-exempt organizations setting is the battery of rules applicable to private foundations. Created 30 years ago, the private foundation rules are the subject of hundreds of IRS private determinations (and a few court opinions), and this process is unabated. New issues continue to arise. This body of law is onerous and, because of a myriad of penalty excise taxes, can be costly. If a charitable organization can avoid being a private foundation, it is well advised to do so. However, if private foundation status is unavoidable, these rules must be faced. Life as a private foundation is by no means impossible, but the organization's management and its advisors should proceed with caution.

Here are the questions most frequently asked by clients about the private foundation rules—and the answers to them.

PRIVATE FOUNDATION BASICS

Q 9:1 What is a *private foundation*?

There is no affirmative definition of a *private foundation*. Technically, a private foundation is a charitable organization[1] that is not a public charity.[2]

Generically, a private foundation has three characteristics: (1) it is a charitable organization that is initially funded from one source (usually, an individual, a married couple, a family, or a business), (2) its ongoing income derives from investments (in the nature of an endowment fund), and (3) it makes grants to other charitable organizations rather than operate its own program. The nature of its funding and, sometimes, the nature of its governance (such as a closed, family-oriented board of trustees[3]) are the characteristics that make this type of charitable organization *private*.

Q 9:2   What is a *public charity*?

There are several types of public charities. One category includes churches, integrated auxiliaries of churches, associations and conventions of churches, universities, colleges, schools, hospitals, medical research organizations, and certain governmental entities.[4]

Another category of public charity is the publicly supported charity. There are two basic types of publicly supported charity: the *donative* type (principally supported by gifts and grants)[5] and the *service provider* type (principally supported by exempt function revenue, gifts, and/or grants).[6]

The third category of public charity is the *supporting organization*.[7]

NOTE: The various types of public charities are discussed in Chapter 6 of *The Legal Answer Book for Nonprofit Organizations.*[8]

In applying these definitions of the term *public charity*, and in deciphering the private foundation rules, it is often critical that the charitable organization know which persons are disqualified persons with respect to it.

DISQUALIFIED PERSONS

Q 9:3   What is a *disqualified person*?

A basic concept of the tax laws relating to private foundations is that of the *disqualified person*. Essentially, a disqualified person is a person (including an individual, corporation, partnership, trust, or estate) that has a particular, usually intimate, relationship with respect to a private foundation.[9]

TIP: When applying the intermediate sanctions rules (see Chapter 1), remember that the term *disqualified person* is defined somewhat differently (Q 1:14).

Thus, disqualified persons are commonly trustees, directors, officers, substantial contributors, members of their families, and controlling and controlled entities. The first three of these persons are collectively known as *foundation managers*. A controlling person is a *20 percent owner,* and controlled entities are corporations, partnerships, trusts, and estates.

Q 9:4   What is a *substantial contributor*?

One category of disqualified person[10] is a *substantial contributor* to a private foundation.[11] A substantial contributor generally is any person who contributes or bequeaths an aggregate amount of more than $5,000 to the private foundation involved, where the amount is more than 2 percent of the total contributions and bequests received by the foundation before the close of its year in which the contribution or bequest is received by the foundation from that person.[12] In making this computation, all contributions and bequests to the private foundation, made since its establishment, are taken into account.[13]

In the case of a trust, the term *substantial contributor* also means the creator of the trust.[14] The term *person* also includes tax-exempt organizations[15] (except as noted in a following paragraph) but does not include governmental units.[16] The term *person* also includes a decedent, even at the point in time preceding the transfer of any property from the estate to the private foundation.[17]

With one exception, once a person becomes a substantial contributor to a private foundation, it can never escape that status,[18] even though it might not be so classified if the determination were first made at a later date.[19] This exception enables a person's status as a substantial contributor to terminate in certain circumstances after 10 years with no connection with the private foundation.[20] For this lapse in status to occur, during the 10-year period, (1) the person (and any related persons) must not have made any contributions to the foundation, (2) the person (and any related persons) was not a foundation manager of the foundation, and (3) the aggregate contributions made by the person (and any related persons) must be determined by the IRS to be insignificant,[21] taking into account appreciation on contributions while held by the private foundation. The term *related person* means related disqualified persons, and in the case of a corporate donor includes the directors and officers of the corporation.[22]

For certain purposes,[23] the term *substantial contributor* does not include most organizations that are not private foundations or an organization wholly owned by a public charity. Moreover, for purposes of the self-dealing rules (Q 9:15), the term does not include any charitable organization—because to require inclusion of charities for this purpose would preclude private foundations from making large grants to or otherwise interacting with other private foundations.[24]

In determining whether a contributor is a substantial one, the total of the amounts received from the contributor and the total contributions and bequests received by the private foundation must be ascertained as of the last day of each tax year.[25] Each contribution and bequest is valued at its fair market value on the date received; an individual is treated as making all contributions and bequests made by his or her spouse.[26]

Q 9:5   What is a *foundation manager*?

Another category of disqualified person[27] is the *foundation manager*. A foundation manager is an officer, director, or trustee of a private foundation, or an individual having powers or responsibilities similar to one or more of these three positions.[28] An individual is considered an *officer* of a private foundation if he or she is specifically designated as such under the documents by which the foundation was formed or if he or she regularly exercises general authority to make administrative or policy decisions on behalf of the foundation.[29] Independent contractors acting in that capacity—such as lawyers, accountants, and investment managers and advisers—are not officers.[30]

An organization can be a foundation manager, such as a bank, a similar financial institution, or an investment advisor.[31]

Q 9:6   What is a *20 percent owner*?

An owner of more than 20 percent of the total *combined voting power* of a corporation, the *profits interest* of a partnership, or the *beneficial interest* of a trust or unincorporated enterprise, any of which is (during the ownership) a substantial contributor to a private foundation (Q 9:4), is a disqualified person with respect to that foundation.[32]

Combined voting power[33] includes voting power represented by holdings of voting stock, actual or constructive,[34] but does not include voting rights held only as a director or trustee.[35] Voting power includes outstanding voting power but does not include voting power obtainable but not obtained, such as voting power obtainable by converting securities or nonvoting stock into voting stock, or by exercising warrants or options to obtain voting stock. Voting power also includes the power that will vest in preferred stockholders only if and when the corporation has failed to pay preferred dividends for a specified period or has otherwise failed to meet specified requirements.[36]

The profits interest[37] of a partner is that equal to his, her, or its distributive share of income of the partnership as determined under special federal tax rules.[38] The term includes any interest that is outstanding but not any interest that is obtainable but has not been obtained.[39]

The beneficial interest in an unincorporated enterprise (other than a trust or estate) includes any right to receive a portion of distributions from profits of the enterprise or, in the absence of a profit-sharing agreement, any right to receive a portion of the assets (if any) upon liquidation of the enterprise, except as a creditor or employee.[40] A right to receive distribution of profits includes a right to receive any amounts from the profits other than as a creditor or employee, whether as a sum certain or as a portion of profits realized by the enterprise. Where there is no agreement fixing the rights of the participants in an enterprise, the fraction of the respective interest of each participant is determined by dividing the amount of all investments or contributions to the capital of the enterprise, made or obligated to be made by the participant, by the amount of all investments or contributions to capital made or obligated to be made by all of the participants.[41]

A person's beneficial interest in a trust is determined in proportion to the actuarial interest of the person in the trust.[42] The term *beneficial interest* includes any interest that is outstanding but not any interest that is obtainable but has not been obtained.[43]

Q 9:7   What is a *member of the family*?

Another category of disqualified person is a member of the family of an individual who is a substantial contributor (Q 9:4), a foundation manager (Q 9:5), or a 20 percent owner (Q 9:6).[44] The term *member of the family* is defined to include an individual's spouse, ancestors, children, grandchildren, great-grandchildren, and the spouses of children, grandchildren, and great-grandchildren.[45] Thus, these family members are themselves disqualified persons.

A legally adopted child of an individual is treated for these purposes as a child of the individual by blood.[46] A brother or sister of an individual is not, for these purposes, a member of the family.[47]

CAUTION: When applying the excess benefit transactions rules, remember that brothers and sisters are disqualified persons in that setting (Q 1:16).

However, for example, the spouse of a grandchild of an individual is a member of his or her family for these purposes.[48]

Q 9:8   When is a controlled corporation a disqualified person?

A corporation is a disqualified person if more than 35 percent of the total combined voting power in the corporation (including constructive holdings[49]) is owned by substantial contributors (Q 9:4), foundation managers (Q 9:5), 20 percent owners (Q 9:6), or members of the family of any of these persons (Q 9:7).[50]

Q 9:9   When is a controlled partnership a disqualified person?

A partnership is a disqualified person if more than 35 percent of the profits interest in the partnership (including constructive holdings[51]) is owned by substantial contributors (Q 9:4), foundation managers (Q 9:5), 20 percent owners (Q 9:6), or members of the family of any of these persons (Q 9:7).[52]

Q 9:10   When is a trust or estate a disqualified person?

A trust or estate is a disqualified person if more than 35 percent of the beneficial interest in the trust (including constructive holdings[53]) is owned by substantial contributors (Q 9:4), foundation managers (Q 9:5), 20 percent owners (Q 9:6), or members of the family of any of these persons (Q 9:7).[54]

Q 9:11   Can a private foundation be a disqualified person?

Yes, to a limited extent. A private foundation may be a disqualified person with respect to another private foundation—but only for purposes of the excess business holdings rules (Q 9:25).[55] The disqualified person private foundation must be effectively controlled,[56] directly or indirectly, by the same person or persons (other than a bank, trust company, or similar organization acting only as a foundation manager) who control the private foundation in question, or must be the recipient of contributions substantially all of which were made, directly or indirectly, by substantial contributors (Q 9:4), foundation managers (Q 9:5), 20 percent owners (Q 9:6), or members of their families (Q 9:7) who made, directly or indirectly, substantially all of the contributions to the private foundation in question.[57] One or more persons are considered to have made *substantially all* of the contributions to a private foundation for these purposes if the persons have contributed or bequeathed at least 85 percent of the total contributions and bequests that have been received by the private foundation during its entire existence, where each person has contributed or bequeathed at least 2 percent of the total.[58]

Q 9:12   Can a government official be a disqualified person?

Yes, but again only to a limited extent. A government official can be a disqualified person with respect to a private foundation—but only for purposes of the self-dealing rules (Q 9:15).[59]

The term *government official* means an elected public official in the U.S. Congress or executive branch, presidential appointees to the U.S. executive or judicial branches, certain higher compensated or ranking employees in one of these three branches, House of Representative or Senate employees earning at least $15,000 annually, elected or appointed public officials in the U.S. or District of Columbia governments (including governments of U.S. possessions or political subdivisions or areas of the United States) earning at least $20,000 annually, or the personal and executive assistant or secretary to any of the foregoing.[60]

In defining the term *public office* for purposes of the fifth category of governmental officials, this term must be distinguished from mere employment. Although holding a public office is a form of public employment, not every position in the employ of a state or other governmental subdivision constitutes a public office. Although a determination as to whether a public employee holds a public office depends on the facts and circumstances of the case, the essential element is whether a significant part of the activities of a public employee is the independent performance of policy-making functions. Several factors may be considered as indications that a position in the executive, legislative, or judicial branch of the government of a state, possession of the United States, or political subdivision or other area of any of the foregoing, or of the District of Columbia, constitutes a public office. Among these factors—in addition to the element of policy-making authority—are that the office is created by Congress, a state constitution, or a state legislature, or by a municipality or other governmental body pursuant to authority conferred by Congress, a state constitution, or a state legislature, and that the powers conferred on the office and the duties to be discharged by the official are defined either directly or indirectly by Congress, a state constitution, or a state legislature, or through legislative authority.[61]

NOTE: In one instance, a lawyer in private practice, who had been a director of a private foundation for more than 10 years and compensated in that capacity, was appointed by the president of the United States to be chair of a government entity. Reviewing this individual's status, the IRS concluded that the individual was not a government official, in that the individual was a special government employee because the employment would not be for more than 30 days over any 365-day period.[62]

PRIVATE FOUNDATION RULES

Q 9:13   Just what are the *private foundation rules*?

The federal tax law governing the operations of private foundations is a composite of rules pertaining to self-dealing, mandatory payout requirements, business holdings, investment practices, various types of expenditures, and more.

Q 9:14   What are the sanctions for violation of these rules?

The sanctions for violation of these rules are five sets of excise taxes, with each set entailing three tiers of taxation. The three tiers are known as the *initial tax*,[63] the *additional tax*,[64] and the *involuntary termination tax*.[65]

   In general, when there is a violation, the initial tax must be paid; the additional tax is levied only when the initial tax is not timely paid and the matter not timely corrected; the termination tax is levied when the other two taxes have been imposed and there continues to be willful, flagrant, or repeated acts or failures to act giving rise to one or more of the initial or additional taxes.

   The IRS generally has the authority to abate these initial taxes, where the taxable event was due to reasonable cause and not to willful neglect, and the event was timely corrected.[66] However, this abatement authority does not extend to the initial taxes imposed in the context of self-dealing.[67] Where a taxable event is timely corrected, any additional taxes that may have been assessed or paid are abated.[68]

   Because of the stringency of these rules, the sanctions are far more than merely taxes, being rather a system of absolute prohibitions.

Q 9:15   What are the rules concerning self-dealing?

In general, the federal tax law prohibits acts of self-dealing between a private foundation and a disqualified person.[69] An act of self-dealing may be direct or indirect. The latter generally is a self-dealing transaction between a disqualified person and an organization controlled by a private foundation.[70]

The sale or exchange of property between a private foundation and a disqualified person generally constitutes an act of self-dealing.[71] The transfer of real or personal property by a disqualified person to a private foundation is treated as a sale or exchange if the property is subject to a mortgage or similar lien that the foundation assumes, or if it is subject to a mortgage or similar lien that a disqualified person placed on the property within the 10-year period ending on the date of transfer.[72]

The following generally constitute acts of self-dealing: the leasing of property between a private foundation and a disqualified person,[73] the lending of money or other extension of credit between a private foundation and a disqualified person,[74] the furnishing of goods, services, or facilities between a private foundation and a disqualified person,[75] and the payment of compensation (or payment or reimbursement of expenses) by a private foundation to a disqualified person.[76]

The transfer to, or use by or for the benefit of, a disqualified person of the income or assets of a private foundation generally constitutes self-dealing.[77] Unlike the other sets of rules describing specific categories of acts of self-dealing, this one is a catch-all provision designed to sweep into the ambit of self-dealing a variety of transactions that might otherwise technically escape the discrete transactions defined to be those of self-dealing. Benefits to a disqualified person can occur when the foundation's assets are used by one or more parties that are not disqualified persons. There is no requirement that a disqualified person is intended to be benefited.

TIP 1:   This is the most dangerous aspect of the self-dealing rules, in that self-dealing can occur without the parties realizing it. Part of the problem is that the *benefit* involved can be intangible, such as increased goodwill,[78] enhanced reputation,[79] and the provision of marketing advantages[80]—all with respect to nondisqualified persons.

TIP 2:   This phraseology is also in the definition of *excess benefit transaction* (Q 1:7). As is the case with respect to much of the law defining self-dealing, developments in the private foundation arena can be used to interpret the intermediate sanctions rules.

An agreement by a private foundation to make a payment of money or other property to a government official generally constitutes self-dealing, unless the agreement is to employ the individual for a period after termination of his or her government service if the individual is terminating service within a 90-day period.[81]

Q 9:16   Are there any exceptions to the self-dealing rules?

There are many exceptions to the self-dealing rules. For example, in relation to the general prohibition on leasing transactions (Q 9:15), the leasing of property by a disqualified person to a private foundation without charge is not an act of self-dealing.[82] Likewise, in respect to the general prohibition on extensions of credit (Q 9:15), this rule does not apply to an extension of credit by a disqualified person to a private foundation if the transaction is without interest or other charge and the proceeds of the loan are used exclusively for charitable purposes.[83]

Concerning the general ban on furnishing of goods, services or facilities (Q 9:15), the furnishing of goods, services, or facilities by a disqualified person to a private foundation is not an act of self-dealing if they are furnished without charge and used exclusively for charitable purposes.[84] Moreover, the furnishing of goods, services, or facilities by a private foundation to a disqualified person is not self-dealing if the furnishing is made on a basis no more favorable than that on which the goods, services, or facilities are made available to the general public.[85]

As to the rules in respect to compensation (Q 9:15), except in the case of a governmental official (Q 9:12), the payment of compensation (or payment or reimbursement of expenses) by a private foundation to a disqualified person for the performance of personal services that are reasonable and necessary to carrying out the charitable purpose of the foundation is not self-dealing if the compensation (or payment or reimbursement) is not excessive.[86]

CAUTION: This exception is not necessarily as attractive as it might look. A court has held that the term *personal services* is confined to services that are "essentially professional and managerial in nature."[87] In that case, the services involved were found not to qualify for the exception, being general maintenance, janitorial, and custodial services.

As to the catch-all provision (Q 9:15), the fact that a disqualified person receives an incidental or tenuous benefit from a private foundation's use of its income or assets will not, by itself, make the use an act of self-dealing.[88] In the case of a government official, the self-dealing rules do not apply to the receipt of certain prizes and awards, scholarship and fellowship grants, annuities, gifts, and traveling expenses.[89]

By reason of another exception, a transaction between a private foundation and a corporation that is a disqualified person with respect to the foundation, is not an act of self-dealing if the transaction is engaged in pursuant to a liquidation, merger, redemption, recapitalization, or other corporate adjustment, organization, or reorganization.[90] For this exception to apply, all the securities of the same class as those held by the foundation prior to the transfer must be subject to the same terms and these terms must provide for receipt by the foundation of no less than fair market value.[91]

Q 9:17   When does an act of self-dealing *occur*?

An act of self-dealing *occurs* on the date on which all of the terms and conditions of the transaction and the liabilities of the parties have been fixed.[92]

Q 9:18   What is the *amount involved*?

The *amount involved* generally is the greater of the amount of money and the fair market value of the other property given or the amount of money and the fair market value of the other property received.[93]

Q 9:19   What does *correction* mean?

Correction of an act of self-dealing means undoing the transaction that constituted the act to the extent possible, but in no case may the resulting financial position of the private foundation be worse than would be the case if the disqualified person was dealing under the highest fiduciary standards.[94]

NOTE: For example, in the case of excessive compensation (Q 9:15, Q 9:16), correction of the act of self-dealing includes return to the foundation of the excess portion of the compensation paid. This is now the same standard applicable in the case of public charities (Q 1:20).

Q 9:20   What are the self-dealing tax penalties?

An initial tax is imposed on each act of self-dealing between a disqualified person and a private foundation; the tax is imposed on the self-dealer at a rate of 5 percent of the amount involved with respect to the act for each year in the taxable period or part of a period.[95] Where this initial tax is imposed, a tax of $2^1/_2$ percent of the amount involved is imposed on the participation of any foundation manager in the act of self-dealing, where the manager knowingly participated in the act.[96] However, this tax is not imposed where such participation is not willful and is due to reasonable cause.[97] This tax, which must be paid by the foundation manager, may not exceed $10,000.[98]

Where an initial tax is imposed and the self-dealing act is not timely corrected, an additional tax is imposed in an amount equal to 200 percent of the amount involved; this tax must be paid by the disqualified person (other than a foundation manager) who participated in the act of self-dealing.[99] An additional tax equal to 50 percent of the amount involved, up to $10,000,[100] is imposed on a foundation manager (where the additional tax is imposed on the self-dealer) who refuses to agree to all or part of the correction.[101]

In a case where more than one person is liable for any initial or additional tax with respect to any one act of self-dealing, all of the persons are jointly and severally liable for the tax or taxes.[102]

Willful repeated violations of these rules will result in involuntary termination of the private foundation's status and the imposition of additional taxes.[103] The termination tax thus serves as a third-tier tax.

Q 9:21   What are the mandatory distribution rules?

A private foundation is required to distribute, for each year, at least a minimum amount of money and/or property for charitable purposes.[104] The amount that must annually be distributed by a private foundation is the *distributable amount*.[105] That amount must be in the form of *qualifying distributions*, which essentially are grants, outlays for administration, and payments made to acquire charitable assets.[106] Generally, the distributable amount for a private foundation is an amount equal to 5 percent of the value of the noncharitable assets of the foundation;[107] this is the *minimum investment return*.[108] The distributable amount also includes amounts equal to repayments to a foundation of items previously treated as qualifying distributions (such as scholarship loans), amounts received on disposition of assets previously treated as qualifying distributions, and amounts previously set aside for a charitable project but not so used.[109]

Q 9:22   What are the *charitable assets* of a private foundation?

The *charitable assets* of a private foundation are those actually used by the foundation in carrying out its charitable objectives, or assets owned by the foundation where it has convinced the IRS that their immediate use for exempt purposes is not practical and that definite plans exist to commence a related use within a reasonable period of time.[110] Thus, the assets that are in the minimum investment return base are those held for the production of income or for investment (such as stocks, bonds, interest-bearing notes, endowment funds, and leased real estate).[111] Where property is used for both exempt and other purposes, it is considered to be used exclusively for tax-exempt purposes where the exempt use represents at least 95 percent of the total use; otherwise, a reasonable allocation between the two uses is required.[112]

Q 9:23   Are there any exceptions to the mandatory distribution rules?

No, not as such. There is, however, an exception to the *timing* of distributions by a private foundation for mandatory payout purposes. This is the *set-aside*, whereby funds are credited for a charitable purpose, rather than immediately granted; where the requirements are met, the set aside is regarded as a qualifying distribution.[113] One type of set aside is that referenced in the *suitability test*; this requires a specific project, a payment period not to exceed 60 months, and a ruling from the IRS.[114] The other type of set aside is the subject of the *cash distribution test*; this test entails set percentages of distributions over a multiyear period and does not require an IRS ruling.[115]

Q 9:24   What are the mandatory payout tax penalties?

An initial tax of 15 percent is imposed on the undistributed income of a private foundation that for any year has not been distributed on a timely basis in the form of qualifying distributions.[116] In a case in which an initial tax is imposed on the undistributed income of a private foundation for a year, an additional tax is imposed on any portion of the income remaining undistributed at the close of the taxable period.[117] This tax is equal to 100 percent of the amount remaining undistributed at the close of the period.[118]

Payment of these taxes is required in addition to, rather than in lieu of, making the required distributions.[119]

The termination taxes[120] serve as third-tier taxes.

Q 9:25   What are the excess business holdings rules?

Private foundations are limited as to the extent to which they can own interests in commercial business enterprises.[121] A private foundation and all disqualified persons with respect to it generally are permitted to hold no more than 20 percent of a corporation's voting stock or other interest in a business enterprise; these are *permitted holdings*.[122] If effective control of the business can be shown to be elsewhere, a 35 percent limit may be substituted for the 20 percent limit.[123] A private foundation must hold, directly or indirectly, more than 2 percent of the value of a business enterprise before these limitations become applicable.[124]

Q 9:26 Are there any exceptions to the excess business holdings rules?

There are three principal exceptions to these rules. The rules do not apply in the case of a business of which at least 95 percent of the gross income of which is derived from passive sources.[125] These sources generally include dividends, interest, annuities, royalties, and capital gain.[126]

The second exception is for holdings in a *functionally related business*.[127] This is a business that is substantially related to the achievement of the foundation's exempt purposes (other than merely providing funds for the foundation's programs); in which substantially all the work is performed for the private foundation without compensation; carried on by a private foundation primarily for the convenience of its employees; that consists of the selling of merchandise, substantially all of which was received by the foundation as contributions; or carried on within a larger aggregate of similar activities or within a larger complex of other endeavors that is related to the exempt purposes of the foundation.[128]

The third exception is for program-related investments (Q 9:30).[129]

Q 9:27 These excess business holdings rules seem strict; are there any relief provisions?

If a private foundation obtains holdings in a business enterprise, in a transaction that is not a purchase by the foundation or by disqualified persons with respect to it, and the additional holdings would result in the foundation's having an excess business holding, the foundation has five years to reduce the holdings to a permissible level without penalty.[130]

Moreover, the IRS has the authority to allow an additional five-year period for the disposition of excess business holdings in the case of an unusually large gift or bequest of diverse business holdings or holdings with complex corporate structures.[131] This latter rule entails several requirements, including a showing that diligent efforts were made to dispose of the holdings within the initial five-year period and that disposition within that five-year period was not possible (except at a price substantially below fair market value) by reason of the size and complexity or diversity of the holdings.

Q 9:28   What are the excess business holdings rules tax penalties?

An initial excise tax is imposed on the excess business holdings of a private foundation in a business enterprise for each tax year that ends during the taxable period.[132] The amount of this tax is 5 percent of the total value of all of the private foundation's excess business holdings in each of its business enterprises.[133]

If the excess business holdings are not disposed of during the period, an additional tax is imposed on the private foundation; the amount of this tax is 200 percent of the value of the excess business holdings.[134]

The termination taxes[135] serve as third-tier taxes.

Q 9:29   What are the jeopardizing investments rules?

There are rules governing the type of investments that a private foundation is allowed to make.[136] In general, a private foundation cannot invest any amount—income or principal—in a manner that would jeopardize the carrying out of any of its tax-exempt purposes.[137] An investment is considered to jeopardize the carrying out of the exempt purposes of a private foundation if it is determined that the foundation managers, in making the investment, failed to exercise ordinary business care and prudence, under the facts and circumstances prevailing at the time of the investment, in providing for the long-term and short-term financial needs of the foundation in carrying out its charitable activities.[138]

A determination as to whether the making of a particular investment jeopardizes the exempt purposes of a private foundation is made on an investment-by-investment basis, in each case taking into account the private foundation's portfolio as a whole.[139] Although the IRS will not rule as to an investment procedure governing investments to be made in the future, it will rule as to a currently proposed investment.[140]

No category of investments is treated as a per se violation of these rules. However, the types or methods of investment that are closely scrutinized to determine whether the foundation managers have met the requisite standard of care and prudence include trading in securities on margin, trading in commodity futures, investments in oil and gas syndications, the purchase of puts and calls (and straddles), the purchase of warrants, and selling short.[141]

Q 9:30   Are there any exceptions to these rules?

A *program-related investment* is not a jeopardizing investment. This is an investment the primary purpose of which is to accomplish one or more charitable purposes, and no significant purpose of which is the production of income or the appreciation of property.[142] No purpose of the investment may be the furthering of substantial legislative or political campaign activities.[143]

Q 9:31   What are the jeopardizing investments tax penalties?

If a private foundation invests an amount in a manner as to jeopardize the carrying out of any of its charitable purposes, an initial tax is imposed on the foundation on the making of the investment, at the rate of 5 percent of the amount so invested for each year or part of a year in the taxable period.[144]

In any case in which this initial tax is imposed, a tax is imposed on the participation of any foundation manager in the making of the investment, knowing that it is jeopardizing the carrying out of any of the foundation's exempt purposes, equal to 5 percent of the amount so invested for each year of the foundation (or part of the year) in the period.[145] With respect to any one investment, the maximum amount of this tax is $5,000.[146] This tax, which must be paid by any participating foundation manager, is not imposed where the participation was not willful and was due to reasonable cause.[147]

An additional tax is imposed in any case in which this initial tax is imposed and the investment is not removed from jeopardy within the period; this tax, which is to be paid by the private foundation, is at the rate of 25 percent of the amount of the investment.[148] In any case in which this additional tax is imposed and a foundation manager has refused to agree to all or part of the removal of the investment from jeopardy, a tax is imposed at the rate of 5 percent of the amount of the investment.[149] With respect to any one investment, the maximum amount of this tax is $10,000.[150]

Where more than one foundation manager is liable for an initial tax or an additional tax with respect to a jeopardizing investment, all of the managers are jointly and severally liable for the taxes.[151]

The termination taxes[152] serve as third-tier taxes.

Q 9:32   What are the taxable expenditures rules?

The federal tax law provides restrictions, in addition to those discussed earlier, on the activities and purposes for which private foundations may expend their funds.[153] These rules pertain to matters such as legislative activities, electioneering, grants to individuals, grants to noncharitable organizations, and grants for noncharitable purposes. Improper and, in effect, prohibited expenditures are termed *taxable expenditures*.

Q 9:33 What are the rules concerning lobbying?

One form of taxable expenditure is an amount paid or incurred by a private foundation to carry on propaganda or otherwise attempt to influence legislation.[154] Thus, the general rule by which charitable organizations can engage in a certain amount of legislative activity[155] is inapplicable to private foundations.

Attempts to influence legislation generally include certain communications with a member or employee of a legislative body or with an official or employee of an executive department of a government who may participate in formulating legislation, as well as efforts to affect the opinion of the general public or a segment of it.[156] An expenditure is an attempt to influence legislation if it is for a *direct lobbying communication* or a *grass roots lobbying communication*.[157]

Engaging in nonpartisan analysis, study, or research and making the results of this type of undertaking available to the general public (or a segment of it) or to governmental bodies or officials is not a prohibited form of legislative activity.[158] Likewise, amounts paid or incurred in connection with the provision of technical advice or assistance to a governmental body or committee (or subdivision of it) in response to a written request from the entity do not constitute taxable expenditures.[159] Another exception is that the taxable expenditures rules do not apply to any amount paid or incurred in connection with an appearance before or communication to a legislative body with respect to a possible decision of that body that might affect the existence of the private foundation, its powers and duties, its tax-exempt status, or the deductibility of contributions to the foundation.[160] Expenditures for examinations and discussions of broad social, economic, and similar issues are not taxable even if the problems are of the types with which government would be expected to deal ultimately.[161]

Q 9:34 What are the rules concerning electioneering?

The term *taxable expenditure* encompasses an amount paid or incurred by a private foundation to influence the outcome of a specific public election or to carry on, directly or indirectly, a voter registration drive.[162] The first of these prohibitions generally parallels the prohibition on political campaign activities by all charitable organizations.[163] However, a private foundation may engage in electioneering activities (including voter registration drives) without making a taxable expenditure, where a variety of criteria are satisfied, such as not confining the activity to one election period and carrying it on in at least five states.[164]

Q 9:35   What are the rules concerning grants to individuals?

The term *taxable expenditure* also encompasses an amount paid or incurred by a private foundation as a grant to an individual for travel, study, or other similar purposes.[165] However, this type of grant is not prohibited if it is awarded on an objective and nondiscriminatory basis pursuant to a procedure approved in advance by the IRS and the IRS is satisfied that the grant is one of three types. These are (1) a scholarship or fellowship grant that is excludable from the recipient's gross income and used for study at an educational institution; (2) a prize or award that is excludable from the recipient's gross income, where the recipient is selected from the general public; and (3) a grant for which the purpose is to achieve a specific objective, produce a report or similar product, or improve or enhance a literary, artistic, musical, scientific, teaching, or other similar capacity, skill, or talent of the grantee.[166]

The requirement as to objectivity and nondiscrimination generally necessitates that the group from which grantees are selected be chosen on the basis of criteria reasonably related to the purposes of the grant. The group must be sufficiently broad so that the making of grants to members of the group would be considered to fulfill a charitable purpose.[167] The individual or group of individuals who select grant recipients should not be in a position to derive a private benefit as the result of the selection process.[168]

These rules as to individual grants generally require (1) the receipt by a private foundation of an annual report from the beneficiary of a scholarship or fellowship;[169] (2) that a foundation investigate situations indicating that all or a part of a grant is not being used in furtherance of its purposes;[170] and (3) recovery or restoration of any diverted funds, and withholding of further payments to a grantee in an instance of improper diversion of grant funds.[171] A private foundation must maintain certain records pertaining to grants to individuals.[172]

Q 9:36   What are the rules concerning grants to noncharitable organizations?

A private foundation may make grants to an organization that is not a public charity;[173] however, when it does so it must exercise *expenditure responsibility* with respect to the grant.[174] A private foundation is considered to be exercising expenditure responsibility in connection with a grant as long as it exerts all reasonable efforts and establishes adequate procedures to see that the grant is spent solely for the purpose for which it was made, obtains full and complete reports from the grantee on how the funds are spent, and makes full and detailed reports with respect to the expenditures to the IRS.[175]

Q 9:37   What are the rules concerning grants for noncharitable purposes?

The term *taxable expenditure* encompasses an amount paid or incurred by a private foundation for a *noncharitable* purpose.[176] Ordinarily, only an expenditure for an activity that, if it were a substantial part of the organization's total activities, would cause loss of tax exemption is a taxable expenditure.[177]

Expenditures ordinarily not treated as taxable expenditures are (1) expenditures to acquire investments entered into for the purpose of obtaining income or funds to be used in furtherance of charitable purposes, (2) reasonable expenses with respect to investments, (3) payment of taxes, (4) any expenses that qualify as deductions in the computation of the unrelated business income tax,[178] (5) any payment that constitutes a qualifying distribution (Q 9:21) or an allowable deduction pursuant to the investment income tax rules (Q 9:39), (6) reasonable expenditures to evaluate, acquire, modify, and dispose of program-related investments (Q 9:30), or (7) business expenditures by the recipient of a program-related investment.

Conversely, expenditures for unreasonable administrative expenses, including compensation, consultants' fees, and other fees for services rendered, are ordinarily taxable expenditures, unless the private foundation can demonstrate that the expenses were paid or incurred in the good faith belief that they were reasonable and that the payment or incurrence of the expenses were in amounts consistent with ordinary care and prudence.[179]

Q 9:38   What are the taxable expenditures tax penalties?

An excise tax is imposed on each taxable expenditure of a private foundation, which is to be paid by the private foundation at the rate of 10 percent of the amount of each taxable expenditure.[180] An excise tax is imposed on the agreement of any foundation manager to the making of a taxable expenditure by a private foundation.[181] This latter initial tax is imposed only where the private foundation initial tax is imposed, the manager knows that the expenditure to which he or she agreed was a taxable one, and the agreement is not willful and is due to reasonable cause. This initial tax, which is at the rate of $2\frac{1}{2}$ percent of each taxable expenditure, must be paid by the foundation manager.[182]

An excise tax is imposed in any case in which an initial tax is imposed on a private foundation because of a taxable expenditure and the expenditure is not corrected within the taxable period; this additional tax is to be paid by the private foundation and is at the rate of 100 percent of the amount of each taxable expenditure.[183] An excise tax, in any case in which an initial tax has been levied, is imposed on a foundation manager if there has been a taxable expenditure and the foundation manager has refused to agree to part or all of the correction of the expenditure; this additional tax, which is at the rate of 50 percent of the amount of the taxable expenditure, is to be paid by the foundation manager.[184]

When more than one foundation manager is liable for an excise tax with respect to the making of a taxable expenditure, all the foundation managers are jointly and severally liable for the tax.[185] The maximum aggregate amount collectible as an initial tax from all foundation managers with respect to any one taxable expenditure is $5,000, and the maximum aggregate amount so collectible as an additional tax is $10,000.[186]

The second-tier excise taxes will be imposed at the end of the taxable period, which begins with the event giving rise to the expenditure tax and ends on the earlier of (1) the date a notice of deficiency with respect to the first-tier tax is mailed or (2) the date the first-tier tax is assessed if a deficiency notice is not mailed.[187]

The termination taxes[188] serve as third-tier taxes.

Q 9:39   Are there other private foundation rules?

An excise tax of 2 percent is generally imposed on the net investment income of private foundations for each tax year.[189] This tax must be estimated and paid quarterly, generally following the estimated tax rules for corporations.[190] Under certain circumstances, this tax rate is reduced to 1 percent in a year where the foundation's payout for charitable purposes (Q 9:21) is increased by an equivalent amount.[191]

As to certain of the private foundation rules, nonexempt charitable trusts[192] and split-interest trusts[193] are treated as private foundations.[194] A 4 percent tax is imposed on the gross investment income derived from sources within the United States by foreign organizations that constitute private foundations.[195]

Q 9:40   What are the consequences of private foundation status?

Because there are no advantages to a charitable organization in its classification as a private foundation, the organization almost always attempts (when it reasonably can) to become classified as a public
charity. The disadvantages to private foundation status are numerous,
and the importance of any of them largely depends on the circumstances of the particular charitable organization.

The disadvantages to private foundation status include (1) the
obligation of payment of a tax on net investment income (Q 9:39), (2)
probable inability of the organization to be funded by private foundations because of the requirement that grants of this nature be the subject of expenditure responsibility (Q 9:36), (3) a lesser degree of
deductibility of charitable contributions to the organization,[196] (4) the
fact that the charitable deduction for a gift of appreciated property to a
private foundation generally is confined to its basis rather than the full
fair market value of the property,[197] (5) requirement of compliance with
the earlier-described broad range of onerous rules and limitations as to
programs and investment policy, and (6) more extensive recordkeeping
and annual reporting requirements.[198]

It may be asserted that the ability of a small number of individuals to
preside over an aggregation of investment assets and "privately" determine how to distribute the income from the assets for charitable purposes
is an "advantage." However, the same opportunities can be available to a
charitable entity that is regarded by the federal tax law a public charity.

Q 9:41   Are the private foundation rules generally understood by now?

Unfortunately, no. One would think that, by now—since these rules
have been in existence for 30 years—the private foundation rules would
be mastered, both by the professional community and at least basically
by the public, including the media. But matters have not worked out
that way.

Two examples involving the media make the point. The *Kansas City
Star,* in an article published in June 1998, summarized most of the criti-
cisms levelled at private foundations these days. One of these complaints is that the annual mandatory payout amount (Q 9:21) is
inadequate. In the process, the journalist attempted to state that rule; it
came out this way: Private foundations must give away at least "5 percent of their total assets each year."[199] Were that true, a foundation
would disappear after its first 20 years or so. (To reiterate, the rule essentially is that, for a year, grants must be made out of income in an
amount equal to at least 5 percent of noncharitable assets.)

Another article fared far worse, however. The *Oregonian,* in an article published the same month, stated: "Self-sufficient and self-governing, the boards that govern foundations answer to no one."[200] The IRS and not a few courts, though, think otherwise. "And foundations don't pay a dime in taxes." Other than the tax on investment and unrelated income, that is (Q 9:39). "Their only requirement is to give away at least 5 percent of their assets each year to keep their nonprofit status." That is hardly the *only* requirement the law imposes on private foundations; their nonprofit status has nothing to do with this rule. As for the botching of the payout rule, see the preceding paragraph.

COMMENT: The law concerning private foundations is indeed complex. Nonetheless, although media scrutiny is to be applauded, journalists need to do a much better job in understanding the complicated and stringent legal environment in which foundations are forced to function.

CHAPTER 10

Ownership of Interests in Business Enterprises

Now more than ever, charitable organizations—and, to a lesser degree, other tax-exempt entities—have great flexibility in owning interests in for-profit businesses. These interests may be purchased, they may come to the exempt organization by gift, or they may arise out of the formation, involving the exempt organization, of a business enterprise. The law in this regard was considerably expanded as part of enactment of the Taxpayer Relief Act of 1997.

As is usually the case, expansion of the law brings additional complexities. Differing tax consequences are now associated with the holding of various types of interests in business enterprises. This is particularly the case with charitable organizations. Thus, these exempt organizations must, more so than before, be cautious when contemplating the ownership of an interest in a business enterprise.

Here are the questions most frequently asked (or should be asked) by clients about the tax considerations of ownership of an interest in a business enterprise—and the answers to them.

THE BASICS

Q 10:1   Is the tax law concerning the ownership of an interest in a business enterprise by a tax-exempt organization more complex in the case of charitable organizations?

Yes. Tax-exempt charitable organizations[1] can hold interests in business enterprises to a greater extent than is allowed for other categories of exempt organizations. This is the case for tax years beginning on or after January 1, 1998, so the considerations in this regard are recent and unfolding. This change concerns ownership in interests in small businesses, which is discussed later (Q 10:6). Accompanying this greater flexibility in the type of business interests that a charitable organization may own is greater complexity in the federal tax law.

CAUTION: This discussion of the ownership of interests in business enterprises by charitable organizations does not always apply to charities that are classified as *private foundations*.[2] This is because of special rules imposed on them regarding the extent to which they can own interests in business enterprises; these are the *excess business holdings* rules (Q 9:25–Q 9:28).

Q 10:2   What does the term *business enterprise* mean in this context?

For this purpose, the term *business enterprise* means a for-profit business conducted by a separate entity recognized as such in the law. There is one form of business entity that is not encompassed by this definition; this is the *sole proprietorship*. This type of business form is usually conducted by individuals without the benefit of a separate legal entity. However, a tax-exempt organization also can conduct an unrelated (or commercial) business as part of its operations;[3] when this is done, the exempt organization is operating a sole proprietorship.

Q 10:3   What are these separate entities that are used to house a for-profit business?

The separate entities that are used for the conduct of a for-profit business are corporations, limited liability companies, partnerships, and joint ventures. As to corporations, the federal tax law differentiates between C corporations and S corporations.

Q 10:4   What is the legal definition of a *corporation*?

Generally, the term *corporation* means a business entity that is organized under a state (or perhaps federal) statute, if the statute describes or refers to the entity as incorporated, as a corporation, or a body corporate.[4] This type of entity issues stock and the stockholders are the owners of the enterprise. Most corporations (other than certain small business corporations) are able to issue more than one class of stock (for example, common stock and preferred stock).

Some corporations issue stock that is publicly traded (that is, their stock is available for purchase and sale on an established securities market), whereas the stock of others is privately held (sometimes termed *closely held*).

Q 10:5   What is a *C corporation*?

The term *C corporation* is wholly a tax law concept (that is, it is not a type of corporation in a non-tax law setting). It means corporations (sometimes termed *regular corporations*) that are subject to the body of law found in Subtitle A (relating to income taxes), Chapter 1, Subchapter C, of the Internal Revenue Code.[5] It is this reference in this subchapter that has given rise to the term.

Fundamentally, a C corporation is, with respect to a tax year, a corporation that is not an S corporation (Q 10:6) for that year.[6]

Q 10:6   What is an *S corporation*?

The term *S corporation* is also wholly a tax law concept. It means corporations (sometimes termed *small business corporations*) that are subject to the body of law found in Subtitle A (relating to income taxes), Chapter 1, Subchapter S, of the Internal Revenue Code.[7] It is this reference in this subchapter that has given rise to this term. A corporation must elect to be an S corporation;[8] that election is a fundamental requirement for qualification as an S corporation.[9]

An S corporation may not have more than 75 shareholders, may not have a nonresident alien as a shareholder, and may not have more than one class of stock.[10] Traditionally, the shareholders of an S corporation were confined to individuals (as well as estates and certain trusts). However, for tax years beginning after December 31, 1997, a tax-exempt charitable organization (and a qualified pension, profit-sharing, or like plan) may be a shareholder in an S corporation.[11]

Q 10:7   What is the legal definition of a *limited liability company*?

A limited liability company is the newest of the business enterprise forms. This type of entity is a creature of state law. It is not a corporation. It is a business form that is taxed in the same fashion as a partnership (Q 3:5, Q 10:10).

NOTE: An unresolved issue is whether a limited liability company can qualify as a tax-exempt organization, including a charitable one.

Q 10:8   What is the legal definition of a *partnership*?

The term *partnership* means a syndicate, group, pool, joint venture, or other unincorporated organization, through or by means of which any business, financial operation, or venture is carried on.[12] A partnership must have at least two members,[13] who are its owners. Often, a partnership is evidenced by a formal partnership agreement.

There are two basic types of partnership: the general partnership and the limited partnership. A *general partnership* is much like a joint venture. A *limited partnership* is a partnership with both general and limited partners. These types of partnerships are more fully discussed elsewhere (Chapter 3).

Q 10:9   What is the legal definition of a *joint venture*?

The term *joint venture* is very broad and, as noted, is at least partially encompassed by the term *partnership* (Q 3:1, Q 10:8). Basically, a joint venture is regarded as a separate entity for tax purposes if the participants carry on a trade, business, financial operation, or venture and divide the profits of the undertaking.[14] In many instances a joint venture can be recognized for tax purposes, even though the parties do not realize they are, or do not wish to be, in a joint venture. This type of venture can arise out of the terms of a lease or other type of contract.

NOTE: In one instance, the working relationship between a charitable organization and a fund-raising company, evidenced by a contract, gave rise to a court finding of private inurement[15] because of the substantial control of and involvement in the charity by the company.[16] Although the court's opinion does not use the term, this relationship may be characterized as a "fund-raising joint venture."

Nonetheless, a joint undertaking merely to share expenses does not create a separate entity for tax purposes.[17] Likewise, mere co-ownership of property that is maintained, kept in repair, and leased does not constitute a separate entity for tax purposes.[18] This matter is more fully discussed elsewhere (Chapter 3).

Q 10:10   How are business enterprises taxed?

The tax treatment of a business enterprise is dependent on the type of enterprise. A C corporation is taxable as a separate legal entity.[19]

Generally, when a C corporation pays income to its shareholders, that income is taxable to them (Q 10:17). These tax consequences are known as *double taxation*.

An S corporation is a *pass-through entity*, which means that it is not taxable; instead, items of income, deductions, and credits are attributed to the shareholders.[20] Likewise, partnerships and joint ventures are not separately taxable; the entity's income, deductions, and credits are passed along to the partners.[21] A limited liability company is treated as a partnership for tax purposes.[22]

Q 10:11 How can a tax-exempt organization acquire an interest in a business enterprise?

There are essentially three ways a tax-exempt organization can acquire an interest in a business enterprise. One way is to purchase the interest. A simple example of this is the purchase by an exempt organization of shares of stock in a publicly traded corporation. Another example is the purchase of an interest in a limited partnership as a means of investment.

A second way an exempt organization can acquire an interest in a business enterprise is to create and then own, in whole or in part, the entity. This occurs, for example, when an exempt organization establishes a for-profit subsidiary (presumably a corporation) or becomes a partner in a partnership or joint venture.

The third way an exempt organization can acquire an interest in a business enterprise is to receive the interest as a gift. Acquisition of an interest in a business enterprise in this fashion is most likely to occur in the case of a charitable organization.

Q 10:12 What are the principal tax issues that an exempt organization should be concerned with when contemplating ownership of an interest in a business enterprise?

When contemplating ownership of an interest in a business enterprise, a tax-exempt organization should particularly consider three aspects of the matter: the impact of the ownership on the organization's tax-exempt status, the taxation of any income that will flow to it (or be attributed to it) from the business, and the taxation of any gain that may be recognized when it sells the ownership interest.

Q 10:13 Are there non-tax issues to be considered in this regard?

There are many considerations in this regard other than the tax issues. One obvious consideration is whether the interest in the business enterprise is a suitable investment for the exempt organization. This is particularly a concern in the case of an S corporation, which is a business in which success or failure is dependent primarily on the management skills of the corporation's directors and shareholders.

Continuing with the example of S corporation stock, a crucial issue is whether the stock looks like an attractive investment in relation to the potential burdens that owning the stock could impose. Questions to be asked include how soon the stock can be sold and converted into productive (or more productive) marketable investments, and if the stock is to be held for a period of time whether it can produce net cash flow (after payment of the unrelated business income tax (Q 10:18)) for use for charitable purposes. The tax consequences can be secondary to the basic economics of the transaction.

As a general rule, charities prefer to sell interests in closely held businesses that have been contributed to them, as these assets do not usually conform to charities' overall investment philosophy. Stock in an S corporation is not an exception to this basic policy; the charitable organization is almost certain to want to sell it (with imposition of the unrelated business income tax making the charity even more eager to sell the asset). This attitude may clash with that of the donor (Q 10:31).

Another general consideration in this regard is whether there is potential for legal liability arising out of the interest. There should also be a focus on the repercussions of being a sole owner, a majority owner, or a minority owner. From the standpoint of charitable organizations, a charity is not required to accept a gift, so it should carefully evaluate the consequences of ownership of every type of business interest offered to it. For example, S corporation stock may be subject to a transfer restriction that would prevent the charity from selling or granting the stock to another party without the other shareholders' approval. In this respect, in contrast, ownership of shares of stock in a publicly traded corporation presents the least of concerns.

Consequently, a charitable organization is well advised to not accept a gift of an interest in a business enterprise unless it is reasonably satisfied that there will not be any resulting material financial difficulties. In the case of S corporation stock, a charity should investigate the possibility of problems under state law concerning ownership of that type of stock. If the interest is to be sold several years after the contribution, the charity should be assured (including procurement of a timely and independent appraisal) that it is receiving a fair price for the stock.

CORPORATIONS IN GENERAL

Q 10:14 When could ownership of stock in a corporation potentially adversely affect an organization's tax-exempt status?

The principal way in which ownership of stock in a business corporation could adversely affect an organization's tax-exempt status is for the exempt organization to be so involved in the day-to-day management of the corporation, and to otherwise control it, that the law would regard the two entities as one. This is often referred to as a *sham arrangement*. In the sham situation, the activities of the business are attributed to, and treated for tax purposes as if they were carried out by, the exempt organization. Of course, the greater the extent of the business undertaking, the greater the likelihood of an adverse impact on the exempt organization's tax status.

Q 10:15 Should not this concern be greater when the corporation is not a publicly traded one?

That is certainly true. The chances of a tax-exempt organization's controlling a publicly traded corporation are remote. A holding of this nature is usually perceived to be a prudent investment. If the holding is in a small business (such as a closely held corporation (Q 10:4)), the likelihood of attribution of functions is clearly much greater.

Q 10:16 What about ownership of an interest in a limited liability company?

Ownership of an interest in a limited liability company, being treated the same as ownership in a partnership, is the ultimate in attribution. The look-through rule (Q 10:20) applies, so it is essential that the activities of the company be carefully scrutinized from the exempt organization's standpoint. Indeed, the limited liability company is emerging as the chief vehicle for an exempt organization, most notably a public charity, to participate in a joint venture (Q 3:6).

TAX TREATMENT OF INCOME

Q 10:17 What is the tax consequence to a tax-exempt organization of the receipt of income from a C corporation?

Generally, income paid to shareholders of a C corporation by the enterprise is a dividend (a distribution out of its earnings and profits).[23] For most shareholders this dividend income is taxable. However, dividends are not taxable to a tax-exempt organization,[24] even when they are paid from a subsidiary.[25]

NOTE: Dividends are not deductible by the payor corporation.

Q 10:18 What is the tax consequence to a tax-exempt organization of the receipt of income from an S corporation?

First, shareholders of an S corporation are taxable on their pro rata share of the corporation's income, irrespective of whether it was actually paid out to them (Q 10:10). So, for taxation, there is no requirement of actual *receipt* of the income.

Second, the income of an S corporation attributable to a tax-exempt charitable organization is, without exception, taxable as unrelated business income.[26]

NOTE: Other than pension plans and the like, charitable organizations are the only types of exempt organizations that can be shareholders in S corporations (Q 10:6).

Q 10:19 What is the tax consequence to a tax-exempt organization of the receipt of income from a limited liability company?

Because limited liability companies are treated as partnerships for tax purposes (Q 10:10), the answer to this question is the same as that pertaining to income from partnerships (Q 10:20).

Q 10:20 What is the tax consequence to a tax-exempt organization of the receipt of income from a general partnership?

Generally, items of income, deductions, credits, and the like, of partnerships are allocated to the partners; the partnership is not separately taxable (Q 10:10). Where the partner is a tax-exempt organization, the tax consequences are dependent on operation of what is known as a *look-through rule*.

This look-through rule requires an assessment of a business regularly carried on by a partnership, of which a tax-exempt organization is a member, to determine whether the business would be related or unrelated if conducted directly by the exempt organization. If the business is determined to be a related one, then the resulting income would not be taxable. In contrast, if the business would be an unrelated one, then the exempt organization would be required (subject to application of the various modifications, exceptions, and deductions[27]) to include its share (whether or not distributed) of the gross income of the partnership as unrelated trade or business.[28]

Q 10:21 What is the tax consequence to a tax-exempt organization of the receipt of income from a limited partnership?

The tax consequences of partnership income allocated or paid to an exempt organization as a limited partner are the same as those with respect to partnership income to an exempt organization as a general partner.[29] That is, the look-through rule (Q 10:20) applies irrespective of whether the tax-exempt organization is a general partner or a limited partner.

Q 10:22 What is the tax consequence to a tax-exempt organization of the receipt of income from a joint venture?

The income received by a tax-exempt organization from a joint venture (actually or by allocation) is regarded for tax purposes the same as income from a general partnership. That is, the look-through rule (Q 10:20) applies.

TAX TREATMENT OF GAIN

Q 10:23 What is the tax consequence to a tax-exempt organization of the receipt of gain from the sale of an interest in a C corporation?

When a tax-exempt organization sells its interest, in whole or in part, in a C corporation (that is, its stock), any resulting gain generally is not taxed.[30] The principal exception in this regard is where the unrelated debt-financed income rules[31] apply.[32]

Q 10:24 What is the tax consequence to a tax-exempt organization of the receipt of gain from the sale of an interest in an S corporation?

When a tax-exempt charitable organization sells its interest, in whole or in part, in an S corporation (that is, its stock), any resulting gain is, without exception, taxed as unrelated business income.[33] Other exempt organizations (other than pension plans and the like) (Q 10:6) are not eligible to hold stock in S corporations.

Q 10:25 What is the tax consequence to a tax-exempt organization of the receipt of gain from the sale of an interest in a limited liability company?

The gain from the sale of an interest (stock) in a limited liability company by a tax-exempt organization is, as a general rule, not taxable. This is because of the general rule excluding gain from taxation (Q 10:23).

Q 10:26 What is the tax consequence to a tax-exempt organization of the receipt of gain from the sale of an interest in a general partnership?

The gain from the sale of an interest in a general partnership by a tax-exempt organization is, as a general rule, not taxable. This is because of the general rule excluding gain from taxation (Q 10:23).

Q 10:27 What is the tax consequence to a tax-exempt organization of the receipt of gain from the sale of an interest in a limited partnership?

The gain from the sale of an interest in a limited partnership by a tax-exempt organization is, as a general rule, not taxable. This is because of the general rule excluding gain from taxation (Q 10:23).

Q 10:28 What is the tax consequence to a tax-exempt organization of the receipt of gain from the sale of an interest in a joint venture?

The gain from the sale of an interest in a joint venture by a tax-exempt organization is, as a general rule, not taxable. This is because of the general rule excluding gain from taxation (Q 10:23).

CHOICE OF BUSINESS ENTITY INTEREST

Q 10:29 Where a tax-exempt organization is contemplating purchase of an interest in a business enterprise, which enterprise form should it favor?

When a tax-exempt organization is investing its money, it should seek the highest rate of return with the lowest degree of risk—the same standard followed by nearly all prudent investors. However, a tax-exempt organization has a great advantage that most investors do not have: generally, its investment income (principally, dividends, interest, and capital gain) is not taxable.

Thus, an exempt organization can invest in the stock of a C corporation and not worry about the double taxation feature: the resulting income is not taxable (Q 10:17) unless the for-profit company is a subsidiary of the exempt organization (Q 10:12). This is the outcome notwithstanding the fact that the corporation conducts a business that is an unrelated one with respect to the exempt organization (which usually is the case).

In contrast, an exempt charitable organization probably would not want to invest in an S corporation. There are several reasons for this. First, the charity is likely to be a minority shareholder in the corporation, and thus at the mercy of those who control the small business. Second, income from the enterprise is taxable as unrelated business income—even when the charity does not actually receive the income (Q 10:18). Third, capital gain on the sale of the stock is also taxable to the charity (Q 10:24). Thus, although S corporations do not carry with them the double taxation feature, they cause income and gain to be taxable to the charity when that would not be the case were the stock that of a C corporation.

An exempt organization may invest as a limited partner in a limited partnership. When it is this type of partner, its liability is limited to the scope of its investment. The taxation of income is dependent on the look-through rule (Q 10:20).

Q 10:30 What about acquisition by a charitable organization of an interest in a business enterprise by gift?

At first blush, a charitable organization may want to accept a gift of an interest in a business enterprise without much thought, on the premise that it would be better off than it would be absent the gift. In some instances—such as a contribution of publicly traded stock—this would be true.

However, some interests are less desirable than others, even if obtained as the result of a contribution. For example, income and gain derived from S corporation stock is taxable to the charitable organization that is the shareholder (Q 10:18, Q 10:24). It may be thought that this is of scant concern, in that the charity still receives the after-tax income and gain. Although this is true, the fact that income from an S corporation is taxable to a charitable organization, even though the income is not actually distributed (Q 10:18), can cause the charity to have to pay the tax out of other resources, which can cause financial stress. There is also the problem of being a minority shareholder (Q 10:31).

Gifts of interests in general partnerships can also be problematic. The income from this type of business enterprise can be taxable (Q 10:20). Moreover, general partners are subject to calls for additional capital and can be liable as a result of the affairs of the partnership.

Q 10:31 Do potential donors have concerns in this regard?

They can. For example, the change in the law regarding ownership of S corporation stock by charitable organizations (Q 10:6) provides an opportunity for many business owners to make charitable gifts of this type of stock. At the same time, the potential donor should think about whether he or she would be comfortable with a charity having the legal rights of a (presumably minority) shareholder.

In the case of a gift of S corporation stock, the charitable deduction will usually be less than the appraised value of the stock. The law provides that the income tax deduction for a charitable gift of S corporation stock should be reduced under rules that are analogous to those governing charitable gifts of partnership interests.[34] It may be possible to avoid a reduced deduction by having the donor terminate the S corporation status shortly before making the gift of the stock, although the *step transaction doctrine*[35] may foil this approach.

In addition, with respect to S corporation stock, a donor may expect the charity to hold the stock for a significant period of time. Moreover, there is usually a very restricted market for selling this type of stock; it is frequently confined to the issuer corporation itself, existing shareholders, or purchasers who have been preapproved by the existing shareholders. Inasmuch as the charity is almost certain to be a minority shareholder, it must rely on the controlling shareholders for fair treatment. For example, the prospective donee charity should satisfy itself that the control group will not engage in practices that may prove damaging to the charity.

Q 10:32 What about acquisition of an interest in a business enterprise as the result of creation by the exempt organization of the business entity?

The creation of a business entity by a tax-exempt organization is a growing practice, with health care providers engaged in most of the activity.[36] Here are the common models: (1) creation of a for-profit subsidiary (corporation),[37] (2) involvement as a general partner in a limited partnership, (3) creation of a for-profit subsidiary and causing it to be a general partner in a limited partnership,[38] and (4) investment as an owner of a limited liability company.

Usually, the reasons for this type of a business enterprise have little to do with investing as such. Frequently, the exempt organization is endeavoring to earn a profit from a business undertaking and/or seeking to attract additional funding in support of its exempt functions.[39] The resulting structure is selected, at least in part, for tax reasons.

In choosing the business enterprise form, the exempt organization should take into account all of the tax considerations noted earlier. For active involvement in business enterprises, the most favorable vehicles are limited liability companies and limited partnerships. These usually advance exempt ends, so the look-through rule (Q 10:20) works to prevent taxation of income. S corporations are not suitable vehicles in this regard because of the inevitability of taxation and the other disadvantages noted earlier.

Q 10:33 Can the interests of a taxable partner and those of an exempt partner be in conflict?

Absolutely. When tax considerations are taken into account, it can be safely said that the organizations involved that are taxable will be interested in minimized taxation. A principal way to do this is to avoid double taxation arrangements. This means that the taxable persons will be shying away from use of a C corporation.

Those that are to be taxed will want to use a pass-through entity, such as a limited liability company or partnership. This way, the income they are to receive will be taxed only once. But the tax-exempt organization may favor the C corporation, so that it can receive income, in the form of dividends, without taxation. For the exempt participant, a pass-through entity can be troublesome because of the potentiality of taxation of income as unrelated income—even where it is not actually received. The use of an S corporation is, from a charitable organization's standpoint, the worst of approaches, because of the automatic taxation of income, whereas a taxable person may favor it as a means of avoiding double taxation.

CHAPTER 11

Annual Return Preparation— In General

The federal tax law requires that nearly all tax-exempt organizations file an annual information return with the IRS. This document, which is generally accessible by the public, has become quite extensive in recent years. It is far more than a tax return, in that much of the information required to be submitted goes beyond financial information and involves a considerable amount of descriptive material (sentences and paragraphs). Too many organizations devote an insufficient amount of thought and care in the preparation of the return, and too often overlook or ignore the importance of this document. Congress and the IRS are of the view that this return is infrequently adequately prepared or filed late or not at all. Consequently, recent legislation has brought disclosure and dissemination requirements, and an increase in penalties.

Here are the questions most frequently asked by clients about the basic annual information return filing rules—and the answers to them.

GENERAL REQUIREMENTS

Q 11:1 Do tax-exempt organizations have to file an annual return with the IRS?

In almost all instances, yes. The federal tax law requires the filing of an annual information return by just about every type of tax-exempt organization.[1] This includes charitable organizations,[2] associations and other business leagues (see Chapter 5), social welfare organizations (Chapter 6), social clubs (Chapter 7), fraternal organizations,[3] labor unions,[4] and veterans' organizations.[5] In addition, certain nonexempt charitable trusts are required to file.[6]

NOTE: This type of trust may also have to file the tax return generally required of trusts (Form 1041). However, if the trust does not have any taxable income, Form 1041 is not required, although the annual information return still is. Even if the trust has gross receipts below $25,000 (Q 11:3), it must nonetheless file the annual return for the purpose of complying with a special requirement (Q 11:3).

There are, however, some organizations that are excused from the filing obligation (Q 11:3). Moreover, there are certain tax-exempt organizations that, although not obligated to file an annual information return of this nature, must file another information return or a tax return (Q 11:7).

The fundamental purpose of the annual information return is to provide the IRS with the required information. However, the return may also be used to transmit elections that are required to be transmitted to the IRS, such as the election to capitalize costs.[7]

Q 11:2   Is there any significance to use of the term *annual information return*?

Yes. The document involved is not an *annual report* (such as may be required under state law), and it is not a *tax return*. As to the latter, these documents are not publicly accessible. The document that must be filed is an *information return*, which means, among other things, it is a return that contains much more than financial information and it must be made available to the public (Q 13:1–Q 13:7).

Q 11:3   What organizations are not required to file an annual return?

Some tax-exempt organizations do not have to file because of their exemption classification. These are:

1. Instrumentalities of the United States[8]
2. State institutions the gross income of which is excluded from income taxation[9]
3. Other governmental units and tax-exempt organizations that are affiliated with them[10]

4. Churches, interchurch organizations of local units of a church, conventions or associations of churches, and integrated auxiliaries of a church[11]

5. Church-affiliated organizations that are exclusively engaged in managing funds or maintaining retirement programs[12]

6. A school below college level affiliated with a church or operated by a religious order[13]

7. A mission society sponsored by or affiliated with one or more churches or church denominations, if more than one half of the society's activities are conducted in, or directed at persons in, foreign countries[14]

8. An exclusively religious activity of a religious order[15]

NOTE: Some organizations that are not required to file annual information returns because of a tax law exception may find they need to prepare them in satisfaction of state reporting requirements (Q 11:41).

Other tax-exempt organizations are excused from filing an annual return because of the size of their gross receipts. There are two categories in this regard: organizations normally receiving $25,000 or less in gross receipts annually[16] and foreign organizations the annual gross receipts of which from sources within the United States are normally $25,000 or less.[17]

TIP: An organization with gross receipts that are normally not more than $25,000 should consider filing with the IRS anyway. This is done by completing the top portion of the return (name, address, and the like) and checking the box on line K. The purpose of this is to be certain that the IRS has the organization's correct address and realizes that the organization is not filing because it is not required to, rather than because it is unaware of or is ignoring the requirement. The IRS also requests that, when an organization of this type receives a Form 990 package in the mail, the top portion of the return be filed using the mailing label.

NOTE: The statute provides a filing exception only where an organization's gross receipts normally do not exceed $5,000.[18] However, the IRS, on its own initiative, increased the threshold to $25,000.

An organization that has been filing annual information returns and then becomes no longer required to file them, because of qualification under an exemption, should notify the IRS of the change in filing status. Failure to do this is likely to result in inquiries from the IRS as to why returns are not being filed; a large expenditure of time and effort may then be required in resolving the matter.

Q 11:4   What constitutes gross receipts?

A distinction must be made between the term *gross receipts* and the term *gross revenue*.

NOTE: The reader may wish to have a copy of Form 990 handy while reviewing the rest of this chapter and Chapters 12 and 13. The discussions are based on the Form 990 for 1997.

On Form 990 (Q 11:7), for example, *gross revenue* means all revenue referenced in Part I, lines 1 to 12 (Q 11:16). This includes contributions, grants, exempt function revenue, investment income, and unrelated business income.

NOTE: For the most part, *gross* revenue must be taken into account in determining total revenue (that is, expenses are irrelevant). However, there are four exceptions, where only net (gross less expenses) income is taken into account for this purpose: rental income (or loss) (Form 990, Part I, lines 6a to c), gain from sale of assets (or loss) (lines 8a to d), income from special events (or loss) (lines 9a to c), and gain from sales of inventory less certain items (or loss) (lines 10a to c).

TIP: Consistency is very important when reporting these numbers. In this instance, these four net revenue items must be reported again in the context of the analysis of income-producing activities (Q: 12:5) (Form 990, Part VII, lines 97 to 102).

In contrast, gross receipts are the total amount the organization received from all sources during its annual accounting period, without subtraction of any costs or expenses.

NOTE: Thus, the four exceptions noted earlier are irrelevant in computing gross receipts. Consequently, on Form 990, gross receipts are the sum of lines 1d, 2 to 5, 6a, 7, 8a (both columns), 9a, 10a, and 11. Gross receipts can also be calculated by adding back the amounts subtracted in ascertaining gross revenue.

Q 11:5   What does the term *normally* mean?

The term *normally* in this context generally means an average of the most recent three tax years of the organization (including the year relating to the return). Thus, to be entitled to this reporting exception, it is not necessary that the organization be below the $25,000 threshold each year. Specifically, an organization is considered to meet the $25,000 gross receipts test if one of the following tests apply:

1. The organization has been in existence for one year and has received, or donors have pledged to give, $37,500 or less during its first year.
2. The organization has been in existence between one and three years and averaged $30,000 or less in gross receipts during each of its first two years.
3. The organization has been in existence three or more years and averaged $25,000 or less in gross receipts for the immediately preceding three years (including the year for which the return would be filed).[19]

Q 11:6   What happens once this $25,000 gross receipts test is exceeded?

Once it is determined that the organization's gross receipts for the measuring period (Q 11:5) are such that it has exceeded the $25,000 threshold, it has 90 days within which to file the appropriate annual return (unless another exception is available (Q 11:3)).[20]

Q 11:7   What IRS form is this annual information return?

For most organizations, it is Form 990.

NOTE: Thus, the rest of the questions and answers in this chapter and Chapter 12 will focus exclusively on that return.

Small organizations—those with gross receipts of less than $100,000 and total assets of less than $250,000—are allowed to file a simpler (two-page) version of the return, which is Form 990-EZ.

TIP: An organization that is eligible to file Form 990-EZ may nonetheless file Form 990 if it wishes (perhaps to provide more specific information) or if necessary (such as to meet state law reporting requirements).

Private foundations (Chapter 9) file Form 990-PF, and black lung benefit trusts[21] file Form 990-BL.

There are other tax-exempt organizations that are not required to file this annual information return but are nonetheless required to file either another information return or a tax return. These are political organizations (Chapter 8) (Form 1120-POL), homeowners' associations[22] (Form 1120-H), apostolic organizations[23] (Form 1065), and stock bonus, pension, or profit-sharing trusts[24] (Form 5500).

NOTE: Form 1120 is the tax return generally filed by corporations. Thus, technically, Forms 1120-POL and 1120-H are tax returns, not information returns. Form 1065 is the information return filed by partnerships; apostolic organizations are treated as partnerships for tax purposes. (Partnerships, being *pass-through entities* (Q 3:5), do not pay federal income tax.)

Charitable organizations that are not private foundations are required to also file Schedule A to accompany Form 990 (or Form 990-EZ).[25]

Q 11:8   Is there any reason to file the simpler version of the annual information return when the organization is exempt from the filing requirement because of the amount of its gross receipts?

As noted, an organization with gross receipts that do not normally exceed $25,000 annually is excused from filing an annual information return (Q 11:3). Certain organizations with gross receipts of less than $100,000 can file a simpler version of the annual return—the Form 990-EZ (Q 11:7). The question thus is whether an organization with less than $25,000 in annual gross receipts should nonetheless file Form 990-EZ.

One reason for the filing of Form 990-EZ in this situation—or at least preparing it—is so that the organization can have the benefit of understanding what its items of income, expense, assets, and liabilities are.

From a legal standpoint, however, there is a very good reason for filing Form 990-EZ even though it is not required as a matter of law. This pertains to the running of the statute of limitations on the assessment and collection of taxes. The general rule is that income taxes must be assessed within the three-year period following the filing of the return.[26] If a return is not filed, the statute of limitations does not start to run and the tax may be assessed at any time.[27]

As noted, the annual information return is not a tax return (Q 11:2). The original position of the IRS was that the filing of an information return did not trigger the running of the statute of limitations for purposes of assessment of the unrelated business income tax—which is to be calculated and reported on a tax return, Form 990-T.[28] However, the Tax Court held that the statute of limitations does begin to run in this circumstance where the information in the annual information return clearly revealed the possibilities of unrelated business income.[29] Thereafter, the IRS relented, announcing that it would adhere to the Tax Court's approach where adequate facts as to the presence of unrelated business income are disclosed in the annual information return and it was filed in good faith.[30]

Of course, a small organization may not have any unrelated business income, or it may have a small amount that it shielded from tax by the $1,000 specific deduction.[31] In many instances, however, comfort can be gained by filing an annual information return despite the fact it is not required. At least the filing puts the IRS on notice that the organization exists.

Although its utility is remote, there is another reason for filing an annual information return. The statute of limitations begins to run when an organization, believing in good faith that it is a tax-exempt entity, files an annual information return and is subsequently held to be a taxable organization. This can be the outcome even where the organization has not yet been recognized as an exempt entity (Q 4:2–Q 4:4).[32] Thus, there may be a measure of protection to be obtained in this connection.

Q 11:9   When is this annual information return due?

The annual information return is required to be filed with the IRS by the 15th day of the fifth month following the close of its accounting period.[33] Thus, for exempt organizations using the calendar year as the accounting period, the return is due by May 15. An organization with a fiscal year ending June 30 is expected to file by November 15. An organization with a fiscal year ending October 31 must file by March 15.

If the regular due date falls on a Saturday, Sunday, or legal holiday, the due date is the next business day.

NOTE: If the organization is liquidated, dissolved, or terminated, the return should be filed by the 15th day of the fifth month after the liquidation, dissolution, or termination.

Q 11:10 Are extensions of this filing due date available?

Yes. It is common for exempt organizations to obtain an extension of the annual information return due date. The proper way to request this extension is the filing of Form 2758.

Generally, the IRS will not grant an extension of time to file the annual information return for more than 90 days, unless sufficient need for an extended period is clearly shown. The IRS will not, in any event, grant an extension of more than six months to any domestic organization.

Q 11:11 Where is the annual information return filed?

All annual information returns filed by tax-exempt organizations are required to be filed with the Internal Revenue Service Center in Ogden, Utah 84201-0027.[34]

NOTE: Historically, annual information returns were filed with the appropriate IRS service center. Now that the IRS has centralized this function, that system has been abandoned.

Q 11:12 How does an organization amend its return?

To change its return for a year, the organization must file a new return, including any required attachments. It should use the version of the annual information return applicable to the year involved. The amended return must provide all of the information called for by the return and its instructions, not just the new or corrected information. The organization should check the "Amended Return" box in the heading of the return (Q 11:17) or, if the version of the return being used lacks the box, "Amended Return" should be written at the top of the return.

The organization may file an amended return at any time to change or add to the information reported on a previously filed return for the same year. It must make the amended return available for public inspection for three years from the date of filing or three years from the date the original return was due, whichever is later (Q 13:1).

The organization must also send a copy of the amended return to any state with which it filed a copy of the return originally to meet that state's filing requirement (Q 11:41).

Q 11:13 Does the IRS provide copies of previously filed annual information returns?

Yes. A tax-exempt organization may request a copy of an annual information return it has previously filed by filing Form 4506-A with the IRS.

Q 11:14 What if the return is a final return?

In the case of a complete liquidation of a corporation or termination of a trust, the "Final Return" box in the heading of the annual information return should be checked (Q 11:17). An explanatory statement should be attached to the return.

This statement should indicate whether the assets have been distributed and the date of the distribution. A certified copy of any resolution, or plan of liquidation or termination, should be attached, along with all amendments or supplements not already filed. In addition, a schedule should be attached listing the names and addresses of all persons who received the assets distributed in liquidation or termination, the kinds of assets distributed to each one, and each asset's fair market value.

OVERVIEW OF RETURN CONTENTS

Q 11:15 How are the contents of the annual information return determined?

Some of the contents of the return are mandated by statute.[35] These elements are very general. Most of the information required to be submitted on the return has been developed by the IRS on its own.

Q 11:16 What are the contents of the annual information return?

That question cannot be responded to in a single answer. The best way to survey the contents of the return is to break it down by its portions.

The document consists of six pages, comprising nine parts. The accompanying Schedule A also constitutes six pages, comprising seven parts. Let us proceed part by part, beginning with the basic information required on page 1, before Part I. The IRS regards this as the *heading* of the return.

REMINDER: The reader should refer to a copy of Form 990 in tandem with the rest of the questions and answers. The discussion is based on the return and Schedule A for 1997.

Q 11:17 What items of information are required in the heading of the return, preceding Part I?

There are ten items of information that are to be supplied:

1. Identification of the organization's accounting period.
2. The nature of the return: initial, final, or amended. Any change of address is to be noted.

TIP: The IRS prefers that an address change be communicated to it by the filing of Form 8822.

---

3. The organization's name and address.
4. The organization's employer identification number.

NOTE: Presumably, the organization has been assigned this number by the time it begins filing annual information returns. If the number has not yet been obtained, the organization acquires it by the filing of Form SS-4.

---

5. State registration number. The state or local jurisdiction number should be entered for each jurisdiction in which the organization files the Form 990 in lieu of a state or local form.
6. The organization is required to indicate whether it has an application for recognition of tax exemption pending.
7. The organization is to identify its tax status as an exempt organization (by completing the Internal Revenue Code citation) or a nonexempt charitable trust (see Q 11:1).

8. Information to be provided by organizations for which the tax exemption is based on a group exemption (Q 4:36 to 4:44), including the group exemption number.

9. The accounting method used by the organization (see Q 11:26).

10. Indication that the organization is below the $25,000 threshold (see Q 11:3).

REVENUE, EXPENSES, BALANCES, ASSETS

Q 11:18 Since the classification of government grant revenues is somewhat different for tax and accounting purposes, what issues must be considered in determining whether an item of revenue of this nature is reportable as a grant or program service revenue?

The dilemma here is whether to report the revenue item as a grant on Part I, line 1, or as program service revenue on Part I, line 2 (Q 11:19). The latter categorization is used when the underlying document is a contract for services. Sometimes, this distinction is difficult to make.

NOTE: This is not merely a reporting issue. The distinction between a grant and an item of exempt function revenue must be made in computing public support in the case of many publicly supported organizations.[36]

One aspect of this matter is clear: The fact that the document is designated as a grant agreement or a contract for services is basically irrelevant. It is the substance of the arrangement that is controlling.[37]

A *grant* is a payment that is akin to a gift, where the recipient of the funds is essentially free to use them as it deems appropriate. Normally, a grant is made to encourage the grantee to carry on certain programs in furthermore of its exempt purposes. There may be a grant agreement imposed by the grantor to ensure that the grantee's programs are conducted in a manner that is compatible with the grantor's programs and policies, and is beneficial to the public. The grantee may also perform a service or produce a work product that incidentally benefits the grantor.[38]

An item of revenue is properly characterized as *exempt function revenue* (assuming the underlying activity is not an unrelated business) if a specific service, facility, or product is provided by the payee to serve the direct and immediate needs of the payor. In general, payments made primarily to enable the payor to realize or receive some economic or physical benefit as a result of the service, facility, or product obtained, are treated as items of exempt function revenue with respect to the payee.

TIP: The fact that a for-profit organization would, primarily for its own economic or physical betterment, contract with a nonprofit organization for the rendition of a comparable service, facility, or product from the organization is evidence that any payments received by the tax-exempt payee for the services, facilities, or products are primarily for the economic or physical benefit of the payor, and thus are forms of exempt function revenue and not grants.[39]

Q 11:19 What information as to revenue is required on the annual information return?

The return, in Part I, requires the reporting of all items of revenue that the organization received during the year. This requires the reporting of items of *gross* revenue; however, as indicated (see Q 11:4), four items of revenue are netted, in whole or in part, in this portion of the return).

1. Line 1. On this line, the organization reports revenue that it received during the year in the form of contributions, grants, and the like.

NOTE: The return references *contributions* and *gifts*. For return reporting purposes, these words mean the same.

This can involve distinguishing between these items and exempt function revenue. For example, an organization may have to determine whether a payment was in the form of a *grant* or made pursuant to a *contract* (Q 11:18).

This financial information must be further broken down into direct and indirect public support. *Direct public support* (line 1a) means contributions to the organization from all sources: individuals, corporations, trusts, and the like; it also includes grants from private foundations. *Indirect public support* (line 1b) means a grant from a publicly supported charity; the gifts made to this grantor are deemed to be embodied in the grant, so that they are considered made indirectly to the grantee (the organization preparing the return). Government grants are also separately identified (line 1c).

This financial information is totaled (line 1d). A schedule of contributors and donors must be attached. However, the information on this schedule need not be made accessible to the public (see Q 13:1). In addition, there must be a breakdown of these items between those made in the form of cash and those that are in noncash form. These two numbers combined should be equal to the total figure (on line 1d).

NOTE: Not all noncash items are eligible to be listed as this form of revenue. Basically, the reference to *noncash* items is to tangible personal and real property, and intangible property such as securities. Items that are *not* to be reported in this portion of the return are (1) donated services or (2) the use of materials, equipment, or facilities at no charge or at substantially less than fair rental value. These items are reported elsewhere on the return (Q 11:34).

---

2. Lines 2 and 3. On these lines, the organization reports its *exempt function revenue*, which essentially is revenue derived from related business activities. That is, this is revenue derived from the performance of a service (such as admission to a facility or an activity pursuant to a government grant) or the sale of one or more goods (such as publications).

The return terms this type of income *program service revenue* (line 2). These types of revenue are detailed elsewhere on the return (see Q 12:5), and the total is inserted in this portion of the return. Another type of exempt function revenue is membership dues and assessments, which is separately reported (line 3). Membership income must also be reported elsewhere on the return (see Q 12:5).

3. Line 4. Interest on savings and temporary cash investments is reported here.

4. Line 5. Dividends and interest from securities are reported here.

5. Line 6. Gross rental income less expenses is reported here.

6. Line 7. Other investment income is reported here.

7. Line 8. Gross amounts from the sale of assets (other than inventory), including capital assets such as securities (that give rise to capital gain or loss), less their cost basis and sales expenses, are reported here. A schedule of these sales transactions must be attached.

NOTE: For organizations that engage in large numbers of securities and other sales transactions, this schedule can be sizable, amounting to several inches of paper, which can cause reproduction of the return to be expensive and time-consuming (Q 13:2).

---

8. Line 9. Gross income from special events, less expenses other than those for fund-raising, is reported here. A *special event* is defined in the annual return instructions as an activity the sole or primary purpose of which is to raise funds (that are not contributions) to finance the organization's activities (such as dinners, dances, carnivals, and gambling activities). A schedule of these activities must be attached.

9. Line 10. Gross sales of inventory, less returns, allowances, and costs of goods sold (yielding gross profit (or loss)), is reported here. A schedule of these sales must be attached.

10. Line 11. Other revenue is reported here. This category of revenue, which includes unrelated business income, is detailed elsewhere on the return (Q 12:5).

11. Line 12. The organization's total revenue (taking into account the four instances where a form of netting is permitted) is reported here.

TIP: The information provided as to the sources of the organization's revenue should correlate, in terms of both the accuracy of the numbers and the classification of the revenue items, with the reporting of public support (Q 12:16) and the analysis of income-producing activities (Q 12:5).

Q 11:20 What information as to expenses is required on the annual information return?

The various categories of the organization's expenses are reported on the annual information return, in Part I. Most of this information is presented in greater detail elsewhere in the return, so this portion is a summary of the four categories of expenses. The expenses of most tax-exempt organizations are allocated across three categories: related business activities (expenditures for program), management, and fund-raising.

1. Line 13. The total of the expenses associated with the organization's program activities is reported here.
2. Line 14. The total of the expenses associated with management of the organization is reported here.
3. Line 15. The total of the expenses associated with fund-raising for the organization is reported here.
4. Line 16. Any payments to affiliated organizations are reported here. A schedule of these payments must be attached.

NOTE: An organization's expenses for program services, management and general, and fund-raising are calculated using a method by which costs are allocated across the three functions (Q 12:3).

---

5. Line 17. Expenses are totaled and reported here.

NOTE: There are two controversial matters as to an organization's expenses that are reflected elsewhere on the return. One is the issue of joint costs (Q 12:4). The other is the matter of compensation of key employees, independent contractors, and others, and the correlation of this with the intermediate sanctions rules (Chapter 1).

Q 11:21 How does a public charity report a program-related investment?

First, it is necessary to define this term. A *program-related investment* is an investment that is made primarily to accomplish an exempt purpose of the investing organization rather than to produce income. This type of investment is expressly recognized in the private foundation setting (Q 9:30).

There are three aspects of reporting program-related investments. One concerns the activity itself. A program-related investment should be reported as a program service accomplishment (Q 12:2).

The second aspect pertains to the reporting of income from the program-related investment (such as interest paid in connection with loans to victims of a disaster or rent paid in connection with a charitable lease). This income should be reported as program service revenue (Part I, line 2) (Q 11:19, Q 12:5).

Third, the asset involved in the program-related investment (equity or debt) should be reported on the balance sheet (Part IV) (Q 11:23). It should be characterized as an "other asset" (line 58).

Q 11:22 What information as to net income or loss is required on the annual information return?

The reporting organization must calculate its net revenue (what the return terms *excess* revenue) or net loss (deficit) for the year. This is reported on line 18 of Part I of the return. This number is the organization's total revenue (Q 11:19) less total expenses (Q 11:20).

Q 11:23 What information as to net assets is required on the annual information return?

The reporting organization must calculate its *net assets or fund balances* at the beginning of the year and report this item on line 19 of Part I of the return. It must likewise calculate its net assets and fund balances at the end of the year and report this item on line 21 of the return. Any other changes in this item must be reported (on line 20), along with an explanation.

The determination as to net assets or fund balances at the beginning of the year is derived from the balance sheet that constitutes Part IV of the return. This portion of the return requires the organization to ascertain, as of the beginning of the year and the end of the year, the following:

1. Assets
   a. Cash (non-interest bearing) (line 45).
   b. Savings and temporary cash investments (line 46).
   c. Accounts receivable, less allowance for doubtful accounts (line 47).

d. Pledges receivable, less allowance for doubtful accounts (line 48).

e. Grants receivable (line 49).

f. Receivables due from trustees, directors, officers, and key employees (line 50). A schedule of end-of-the-year amounts must be attached.

NOTE: For tax-exempt organizations (other than, in some instances, private foundations), loans, advances, and the like to individuals of this nature are not prohibited (although they may be subject to special scrutiny, which is the purpose of this line). This aspect of the return verifies the point.

---

g. Other notes and loans receivable, less an allowance for doubtful accounts (line 51). A schedule for end-of-the-year amounts must be attached.

h. Inventories for sale or use (line 52).

i. Prepaid expenses and deferred charges (line 53).

j. Investments involving securities (line 54). A schedule for end-of-the-year amounts must be attached.

k. Investments involving land, buildings, and equipment, less accumulated depreciation (line 55). A schedule for end-of-the-year depreciation amounts must be attached.

l. Other investments (line 56). A schedule for end-of-the-year amounts must be attached.

m. Land, buildings, and equipment, less accumulated depreciation (line 57). A schedule for end-of-the-year depreciation amounts must be attached.

n. Other assets, accompanied by a description of them (line 58).

o. Total assets (line 59).

2. Liabilities

a. Accounts payable and accrued expenses (line 60).

b. Grants payable (line 61).

c. Deferred revenue (line 62).

d. Loans from trustees, directors, officers, and key employees (line 63). A schedule for end-of-the-year amounts must be attached.

  e. Tax-exempt bond liabilities (line 64a). A schedule for end-of-the-year amounts must be attached.

  f. Mortgages and other notes payable (line 64b). A schedule for end-of-the-year amounts must be attached.

  g. Other liabilities, accompanied by a description of them (line 65).

  h. Total liabilities (line 66).

3. Net assets or fund balances for organizations that follow *Financial Statements of Not-for-Profit Organizations*, issued by the Financial Accounting Standards Board (SFAS 117).

  a. Unrestricted (line 67).

  b. Temporarily restricted (line 68).

  c. Permanently restricted (line 69).

  d. Total net assets or fund balances (line 73). This amount for the beginning of the year (column (A)) is entered on line 19 of Part I of the return. This amount for the end of the year (column (B)) is entered on line 21 of Part I of the return.

  e. Total liabilities and net assets/fund balances (line 74).

TIP: The amount on line 74 should equal the total on lines 66 (total liabilities) and 73 (total net assets or fund balances), and should be the same as the amount on line 59 (total assets). The amount entered on line 21 of the return should also be the sum of the amounts on lines 18-20.

---

4. Net assets or fund balances for organizations that do not follow SFAS 117.

  a. Capital stock, trust principal, or current funds (line 70).

  b. Paid-in or capital surplus, or land, building, and equipment fund (line 71).

  c. Retained earnings, endowment, accumulated income, or other funds (line 72).

  d. Total net assets or fund balances (line 73). Again, this amount for the beginning of the year (column (A)) is entered on line 19 of Part I of the return. This amount for the end of the year (column (B)) is entered on line 21 of Part I of the return.

  e. Total liabilities and net assets/fund balances (line 74).

TIP: Again, the amount on line 74 should equal the total on lines 66 (total liabilities) and 73 (total net assets or fund balances), and should be the same as the amount on line 59 (total assets). Again, the amount entered on line 21 of the return should also be the sum of the amounts on lines 18-20.

Q 11:24 Should organizations be concerned about a large amount of net assets or fund balance?

They should be somewhat concerned. There is no law that places a restriction on the amount of money or property that an exempt organization can accumulate. At the same time, a large and growing accumulation of assets can be a signal that inadequate or infrequent exempt functions are taking place.

NOTE: The IRS occasionally applies what is known as the *commensurate test*. The agency compares an organization's program activities with the extent of its financial resources to see if it is doing enough in the way of exempt functions. (So far, this test has been applied only to public charities.[40]) A large fund balance accumulation is an element that the IRS would take into consideration in applying this test.

A factor to take into account in this context is the reason for the accumulation. The organization may denominate some or all of these assets as an endowment fund, a building fund, or some other reserve. This can go a long way in dispelling concerns about what may otherwise appear to be an unreasonable accumulation.

Some organizations avoid this dilemma by transferring some or all of their fund balance to another, controlled, entity. This organization is often generically referred to as a *foundation*; it may technically be a *supporting organization*.[41] This entity can hold the funds as an endowment fund or for a similar function. Whatever the use that is made of this type of separate entity, it causes what might otherwise appear to be an excessive accumulation of funds or property to be removed from the "bottom line" of the reporting tax-exempt organization.

Q 11:25 Under what circumstances should an amended return be filed when an organization finds that a prior year annual information return contains an error?

Technically, an amended return should be filed whenever there is an error in the original return. The annual information return applicable to the year involved should be used.

NOTE: Blank forms for prior years may be obtained from the IRS by calling 1-800-TAX-FORM (1-800-829-3676).

The "Amended Return" box in the heading of the return should be checked (Q 11:12).

However, if the error is insignificant or incidental, the common practice is not to bother with the filing of an amended return. In contrast, if the error is a significant one, a failure to correct it may result in penalties (Q 12:17–Q 12:20) and/or a cessation of the running of the statute of limitations (Q 11:8).

Q 11:26 It appears that the annual information return is based on the cash basis method of accounting.

That is true. Despite the trends in the field of accounting, neither Congress nor the IRS has endeavored to cause preparation of the annual return to be on an accrual basis, which is what is called for in the body of accounting rules known as *generally accepted accounting principles*.

Q 11:27 Aren't financial statements of exempt organizations prepared on another basis of accounting?

Yes. These audited financial statements are prepared in accordance with generally accepted accounting principles, which means—among other things—that they are prepared on the accrual basis of accounting.

Q 11:28 Doesn't this use of two accounting systems require exempt organizations to maintain two sets of financial records?

Basically, yes. What the IRS has done to date in this regard is to create a segment of the annual information return, by which items on the audited financial statement are reconciled with items on the annual return. One portion of the annual return is devoted to the reconciliation of revenue items (Part IV-A) and another is used to reconcile expense items (Part IV-B).

GENERAL OPERATIONS

Q 11:29 What happens when an organization is engaging in an activity that was not previously disclosed to the IRS?

If a tax-exempt organization has a determination letter or ruling from the IRS recognizing its tax exemption, the organization as part of that process presumably apprised the IRS of all of its program or other activities at that time (Q 4:11).

NOTE: It is possible, of course, that an organization did not disclose all of its activities to the IRS as part of the application process. If that is the case, it could have an adverse impact on the organization's exempt status. A ruling of this nature is only as valid as the material facts on which it is based; if material facts were omitted, the IRS may have occasion to revoke the ruling, either prospectively or retroactively.

An organization may have previously reported one or more activities to the IRS on a prior annual information return or during an audit. Indeed, the law requires that an exempt organization provide the IRS with contemporaneous notice of any *material* change in the facts concerning it (Q 4:9). This is required, of course, to accord the IRS the opportunity to review these facts, so as to determine whether the organization is no longer primarily engaged in exempt functions. It is intended to be part of the IRS's ongoing enforcement of the *operational test.*

Thus, there can be several occasions when the IRS was informed of an organization's activities. If, however, there is an activity engaged in by the organization, which it did not previously report to the IRS, the entity is required to check a "Yes" box and disclose it as part of the return (Form 990, Part VI, line 76). A detailed description of each activity of this nature must be attached to the return. Otherwise, the question is answered "No."

Q 11:30 What happens when an organization changed its operating documents but did not previously report this to the IRS?

Any changes made in the organizing or governing documents not reported to the IRS are to be disclosed as part of the return (Part VI, line 77). The organization is required to check a "Yes" box and a conformed copy of the amendments must be attached to the return. Otherwise, the question is answered "No."

The same problem can arise here as in respect to activities. A change in one of these documents can be a *material* change; an illustration is a substantial modification of the organization's statement of purposes. If this entailed a material change, the organization is obligated to communicate the change to the IRS contemporaneously. Again, this is required to accord the IRS the opportunity to review these facts, so as to determine whether the organization is no longer primarily engaged in exempt functions. It is intended to be part of the IRS's ongoing enforcement of the *organizational test.*[42]

Q 11:31 How does the filing of the annual information return relate to the receipt of unrelated business income?

As noted, this return is an annual information return, not a tax return (Q 11:2). Thus, the details as to unrelated business income are not reported on this return, but on the unrelated business income tax return, which is Form 990-T.

Nonetheless, the annual information return requires the tax exempt organization to answer "Yes" or "No" to the question as to whether it had unrelated business gross income of $1,000 or more during the year covered by the return (Part VI, line 78a). If the answer is truthfully "No," that is the end of the matter. If the answer is "Yes," the organization must answer "Yes" or "No" to the question as to whether it filed a Form 990-T for the year (line 78b). The correct answer is "Yes," because that is the basic criterion for filing the unrelated business income tax return. If the organization is forced to respond to this question with a "No," it is best advised to quickly remedy the deficiency and/or seek professional assistance.

Q 11:32 What if the organization dissolved or substantially contracted during the year?

Dissolution or substantial contraction of an organization is a material change warranting reporting of it even if there were not a separate question on the point (see Q 11:29).

The organization is required to answer the question—"Yes" or "No"—as to whether, during the year, there was a liquidation, dissolution, termination, or substantial contraction of it (Part VI, line 79). An explanatory statement must be attached when the answer is "Yes."

Q 11:33 What about relationships with other organizations?

A question on the annual information return inquires as to whether the organization is related (other than by association with a statewide or nationwide organization) through common membership, governing bodies, trustees, officers, or other means, to another organization (Part VI, line 80a). If the answer is "Yes," a box indicating that answer must be checked, and the name of the organization must be provided, along with an indication as to whether the other organization is tax-exempt (line 80b). Otherwise, the question is answered "No."

There are, however, other questions on this subject. These include ownership of taxable subsidiaries[43] (Q 12:13), involvement in partnerships (Chapter 3) (Q 12:14), grants and loans by public charities to other organizations (Q 12:10), and transactions and relationships between public charities and other tax-exempt organizations (Q 12:15).

Q 11:34 What if the organization received a contribution of services or a gift of the use of property?

The organization must answer "Yes" or "No" to the question as to whether it received donated services or the use of materials, equipment, or facilities at no charge or at substantially less than fair rental value (Part VI, line 82a). If it did, it may indicate the value of these items on the return (line 82b).

TIP: As discussed (Q 11:19), the value of gifts of this nature cannot be included as revenue. Yet the IRS has allowed an organization to disclose this value if it can be of importance to the organization or its constituency.

Q 11:35 What about the public inspection requirements?

These are discussed elsewhere (Chapter 13). However, it may be noted here that there is a question on the return, which must be answered "Yes" or "No," inquiring as to whether the organization complied with the public inspection requirements, in respect to both applications for recognition of exemption and annual information returns (Part VI, line 83a). Inasmuch as the law requires compliance with these requirements, the organization is well advised to answer this question in the affirmative if it possibly (and truthfully) can. The answer is "Yes" even if there were no requests for the documents. If the answer must be "No," the assistance of a lawyer is advised.

Q 11:36 What about fund-raising practices?

Expenses of fund-raising, in the form of professional fund-raising fees, are accorded a line on the statement of expenses (Q 11:20). Other fund-raising costs must be reported as well. In the case of public charities, social welfare organizations, and nonexempt charitable trusts, fund-raising expenses must be derived using the functional method of accounting (Q 12:3). There is reporting in the case of joint costs incurred in connection with an educational campaign and a fund-raising solicitation (Q 12:4).

One of the elements of federal fund-raising regulation involves certain disclosure requirements with respect to quid pro quo contributions (Q 13:19). One of the questions on the return, which requires a "Yes" or "No" answer, is whether these disclosure requirements were complied with (Part VI, line 83b). Inasmuch as the law requires compliance with these requirements, the organization is well advised to answer this question in the affirmative if it possibly (and truthfully) can. The answer is "Yes" even if there were no quid pro quo contributions during the year. If the answer must be "No," professional assistance is advised.

Moreover, there are certain rules about the solicitation of gifts that are not tax deductible (Q 13:17). Basically, the law requires that the solicitation material contain an express statement that these contributions are not deductible. The return requires a "Yes" or "No" answer to a question as to whether any contributions of this nature were solicited (line 84a). If the answer is "No," that is the end of the matter (assuming that answer is truthful). If the answer is "Yes," the organization must answer "Yes" or "No" to the question of whether the statement as to nondeductibility was included (line 85b). Of course, the desired answer to that question is "Yes." Again, if this answer must be "No," professional assistance is advised.

If a public charity, social welfare organization, or nonexempt charitable trust performs fund-raising services for a tax-exempt organization, certain information must be reported (Q 12:15).

Q 11:37 Are there any special requirements for social clubs?

Yes. A tax-exempt social club (Chapter 7) must report two unique items of financial information. One is the amount of initiation fees and capital contributions received during the year (Part VI, line 86a). The other is the amount of gross receipts for public use of club facilities (line 86b).

NOTE: Both of these items must also be reported as part of the club's revenue for the year (Q 11:19) (Part I, lines 3 or 11).

CAUTION: As discussed (Q 7:13), there are limits on the amount of revenue an exempt social club can receive from the public for the use of its facilities.

Q 11:38 How does a tax-exempt organization change its accounting period (tax year)?

A tax-exempt organization can change its accounting period whenever it wishes, without permission from the IRS or any other government agency. However, when this is done, it must file an annual information return for the short period resulting from the change.

TIP: Write "Change of Accounting Period" at the top of this short-period return.

If an organization changes its accounting period within the 10-calendar-year period that includes the beginning of one of these short periods, and it had an annual information return filing requirement at any time during that 10-year period, it must prepare and attach an IRS form (Form 1128) to the short-period return.[44]

NOTE: When affiliated organizations authorize their central organization to file a group return for them (Q 4:40), the accounting period of each affiliated organization and of the central organization must be the same.

Q 11:39 How does a tax-exempt organization change its accounting method?

A tax-exempt organization that wishes to change its accounting method generally must prepare and file an IRS form (Form 3115).

NOTE 1: Whatever accounting method is used, it must be one that clearly reflects income.

NOTE 2: The annual information return is based on the cash basis method of accounting (Q 11:26).

However, this form is not required for tax-exempt organizations that change their methods of accounting to comply with *Accounting for Contributions Received and Contributions Made*, issued by the Financial

Accounting Standards Board (SFAS 116).[45] A change in accounting method may result in the need to make certain adjustments in the computation of income and expenses for tax purposes.[46] An adjustment of this nature should be reported as a net asset adjustment made during the year the change is made.

NOTE: This adjustment should be identified as the effect of changing to the method provided in SFAS 116.

Q 11:40 Are there any special requirements for benevolent and mutual organizations?

Yes. These organizations[47] are required to report the amount of gross income received from their members or shareholders (Part VI, line 87a). They must also report gross income from other sources; the IRS admonishes that they should not net amounts due or paid to other sources against amounts due or received from them (line 87b).

Q 11:41 Don't some states require that copies of the annual return be filed with them?

That is true. Nearly all of the states have a charitable solicitation act which, among other requirements, mandates registration and annual reporting.[48] As part of these processes, some states require the filing of a copy of this annual information return. Other states permit the filing of this return instead of all or part of separate financial information if the organization wishes to do that. The organization is required to list the states in which a copy of the annual return is filed (Part VI, line 90).

Because the IRS has developed the annual information return in conjunction with state fund-raising regulation officials, it devotes a considerable amount of space in the return instructions advising about state and local filing requirements—even though the subject has no bearing whatsoever on the federal filing obligations. For example, the IRS advises organizations to consult the appropriate officials of state and local jurisdictions in which the organization does business to determine their filing requirements there. It is the view of the IRS that *doing business* in a jurisdiction may include any of the following:

1. Soliciting contributions or grants by mail or otherwise from individuals, businesses, or other charitable organizations
2. Conducting programs
3. Having employees within the jurisdiction
4. Maintaining a checking account in the jurisdiction
5. Owning or renting property in the jurisdiction

NOTE: The IRS is acting beyond the scope of its authority in proclaiming on this subject. Moreover, it is by no means clear that solicitation of gifts by mail alone constitutes doing business in a jurisdiction.

Q 11:42 Does the annual information return require any additional information concerning general operations?

Yes. The organization must identify who has the care of its books and records, this person's telephone number, and the location of these books and records (Part VI, line 91). In addition, a nonexempt charitable trust that is filing this return (Q 11:1) must check a box to this effect and report the amount of any tax-exempt interest that it received or accrued during the course of the year (line 92).

ADMINISTRATIVE MATTERS

Q 11:43 How is the annual information return form obtained?

Most tax-exempt organizations that are required to file an annual information return receive the return each year in the mail, with the return containing a mailing label (Q 11:3). Officially, they are available at IRS offices, but, in practice, they are hard to find there. They can be obtained by telephone—call 1-800-TAX-FORM (1-800-829-3676). Many organizations rely on their accountant or lawyer for the return.

The return may be available by computer. Those who subscribe to an on-line service should ask the provider if IRS information is available and, if so, how to access it. Tax forms, instructions, publications, and other IRS information are available through Internal Revenue Information Services (IRIS) on FedWorld, a government bulletin board. The IRIS menus offer information on available file formats and software needed to read and print files.

TIP: The return must be printed to use it. We are not yet at the point where it can be filled out on-screen.

IRIS is directly accessible by modem at 703-321-8020. On the Internet, connect to iris.irs.ustreas.gov or, for file transfer protocol services, connect to ftp.irs.ustreas.gov. A user of the World Wide Web can connect to http://www.irs.ustreas.gov. FedWorld's help desk offers technical assistance on accessing IRIS during regular business hours at 703-487-4608.

NOTE: Tax advice or assistance is not available at this location.

Tax forms, instructions, and publications are also available on CD-ROM, including prior-year forms starting with the 1991 form. For ordering information and software requirements, contact the Government Printing Office's Superintendent of Documents (202-512-1800) or Federal Bulletin Board (202-512-1387).

Q 11:44 How much time should we plan on spending to maintain the records necessary to prepare this return?

It is nearly impossible to generalize as to how much time it takes to maintain the necessary records. The IRS estimates that the average time needed to keep the requisite records for preparation of the Form 990, each year, is 94 hours and 28 minutes. The recordkeeping for Schedule A separately is estimated to entail 49 hours and 59 minutes. Organizations that file Form 990-EZ should plan on investing 28 hours and 28 minutes of their time for this purpose.

Q 11:45 Is that the only significant amount of time we should plan for?

I'm afraid not. The IRS estimates that it takes 19 hours and 52 minutes to learn about the law or the return, 25 hours and 5 minutes to prepare the return, and 48 minutes for photocopying, assembling, and sending the return to the IRS. The comparable data for the Schedule A is 9 hours and 14 minutes, 10 hours and 28 minutes, and 0 minutes. The data with respect to Form 990-EZ is 9 hours and 12 minutes, 11 hours and 1 minute, and 16 minutes.

Q 11:46 Does the IRS accept a form as a substitute for the annual information return?

Generally, no. There are two exceptions, which allow for partial substitutions:

1. A tax-exempt labor organization that files Form LM-2 (Labor Organization Annual Report), or the shorter Form LM-3, with the Department of Labor (DOL) can attach a copy of the completed DOL form to the annual information return to provide some of the information required by the annual return. This substitution is not permitted if the organization files a DOL report that consolidates its financial statements with those of one or more separate subsidiary organizations.

2. An employee benefit plan may be able to substitute Form 5500, or Form 5500-C/R, for part of the annual information return. This substitution can be made if the organization filing the annual return and the plan filing the required form meet all of the following requirements:

   a. The filer of the information return is one of three types of tax-exempt employee benefit plans.

   b. This tax-exempt organization and the form filer are identical for financial reporting purposes and have identical receipts, disbursements, assets, liabilities, and equity accounts.

   c. The employee benefit plan does not include more than one tax-exempt organization and that exempt organization is not a part of more than one employee benefit plan.

   d. The organization's accounting year and the employee plan year are the same.

TIP: If this exception is important to the organization, it may want to change its accounting year to make it coincide with the plan year.

Q 11:47 What are the allowable substitution areas?

Whether the organization involved is a labor organization or an employee benefit plan, the allowable substitution areas are (on Form 990):

1. Part I, lines 13 to 15 (Q 11:20). Nonetheless, lines 16 to 21 should be completed.

2. Part II (Q 12:3).

3. Part IV (Q 11:23). Nonetheless, lines 59, 66, and 74, columns (A) and (B) should be completed.

If an organization substitutes Form LM-2 or LM-3 for any portions of the annual information return, it must attach a reconciliation sheet to show the relationship between the amounts on the DOL forms and the amounts on the annual return. This is particularly true of the relationship of disbursements shown on the DOL forms and the total expenses on the annual information return. The organization must make this reconciliation because the cash disbursements section of the DOL forms includes nonexpense items. If the organization substitutes Form LM-2, it should be certain to complete its separate schedule of expenses.

CHAPTER 12

Annual Return Preparation—
Special Considerations

The foregoing chapter is a review of the general requirements concerning preparation of the annual information return. However, there is far more to the substance of this return, because it reflects a number of significant tax-exempt organization topics and issues that are of current concern to the IRS and others.

Here are the questions most frequently asked (or should be asked) by clients about these topics and issues—and the answers to them.

Q 12:1 It was previously advised that to be tax-exempt, an organization must primarily engage in the appropriate exempt functions. Is this rule of law reflected in the annual information return?

Very much so. One of the most important questions constituting the annual return is this: "What is the organization's primary exempt purpose?" (Form 990, Part III). An organization should be thoughtful and careful when responding to this question. This is the heart of the *operational test* as that test is applied to the organization.[1] The answer to this question provides the general framework for most of the other questions and sets the tone for the other portions of the return. The sophisticated reader of an annual information return is likely to turn to the answer to this question first.

There is not much space on the return itself for an adequate an-swer, so a full response will likely have to be made on an attachment. While a general answer may suffice (such as "higher education," "trade association," or "social club"), the organization should go beyond very vague terminology (such as "charitable" or "social welfare"). Given that this is a public document (Chapter 13), the response to this question is an opportunity to tout the organization, to cast it in the most favorable light (staying within the bounds of veracity). It is an opportunity that is frequently overlooked.

TIP: This last observation is applicable to many other portions of the annual information return, which are referenced in this or the previous chapter.

NOTE: The annual information return now contains much factual in-formation other than financial data. It is no longer a document to be prepared solely by an accountant. The answers to this and most of the other questions should be conscientiously considered by the organiza-tion's management and reviewed by at least some of the volunteer leadership, the organization's lawyer, and perhaps others, such as a fund-raising and/or public relations professional.

Q 12:2   What about the organization's programs? How should they be discussed?

The programs of a tax-exempt organization are the heart of the entity. The organization exists to conduct its programs. All other functions are (or should be) conducted in support of its primary activities, which are its programs. Here is one place where the annual information return should read like an annual report. The return amply provides opportu-nity for the organization to summarize its programs—what the return terms the organization's *program service accomplishments.*

The organization must describe its exempt purpose achievements (Part III). There is adequate room on the return to describe the four most important ones (lines a to d), although the organization should not hesitate to use one or more attachments. If more than four program service accomplishments are to be discussed, a schedule describing them should be attached (line e).

There are no bounds to creativeness here (other than accuracy). The organization should exuberantly and fully portray its programs.

Specificity is in order. The return supplies some hints in this regard: the organization can state the number of clients served or publications issued. As the IRS puts it, the organization should also "discuss achievements that are not measurable."

NOTE: In the instructions accompanying the annual information return, the IRS observes that "some members of the public rely on . . . [the annual return] as the primary or sole source of information about a particular organization. How the public perceives an organization in such cases may be determined by the information presented on its return. Therefore, please make sure the return is complete and accurate and fully describes the organization's programs and accomplishments."

This portion of the return involves some financial information, because one way to describe program services is by citing grants and allocations to others. This financial information is mandatory for charitable and social welfare organizations, and nonexempt charitable trusts; it is optional for all other tax-exempt organizations.

Following this descriptive and financial information, the organization's program service expenses should be totaled (line f). Of course, this number should be the same as that inserted on the face of the return for program service expenses (Q 11:20).

TIP 1: Some have the attitude that the IRS should be given as little information as legally possible. Although in some settings this approach can be the correct one, this is not the place. Indeed, skimpy entries can be the basis for suspicions. Explicate!

TIP 2: An organization may develop excellent descriptions of its programs and then simply reuse them over the years. This is fine as long as the summaries remain accurate and reflect contemporary priorities. However, there is the danger that the material facts will change so that the descriptions are no longer appropriate; they may even be false or misleading. Thus, these statements should be reviewed and considered anew each year.

Q 12:3   Surely there is more to the reporting of expenses than simply reporting program, management, and fund-raising costs.

There certainly is. As noted, these three categories of expenses must be reported on the face of the return (Q 11:20). However, there are some complexities to work through in arriving at those three numbers.

The tax law recognizes that an expenditure may not simply be for one function. For example, payments for telephone services may all be program expenditures; or they may be part program and part management; or all management; or part program, part management, and part fund-raising; or all for fund-raising; Thus, an outlay can range over more than one function, and this has given rise to the concept of *functional expense reporting*.

However, not all tax-exempt organizations are required to report their expenses functionally. Public charities and social welfare organizations are required to do so, as are nonexempt charitable trusts. This type of reporting is optional for all other exempt entities. Every reporting exempt organization must report total expenses by category (Part II, column (A)). The return is structured to also accommodate functional reporting of expenses (columns (B) to (D)).

NOTE: There is an oddity in the return in this regard. As noted, for many categories of tax-exempt organizations, functional reporting of expenses is said to be "optional." Yet, as noted, on the face of the return, the organization is required to separately report expenses for program services, management, and fund-raising.

There are 21 categories of expenses that must be reported. They are as follows:

CAUTION: When preparing this portion of the return, the expenses already taken into account in netting four items on the face of the return (Q 11:19) should not be repeated. Moreover, payments to affiliates are separately reported (Q 11:20) and thus should not be reflected here.

---

1. Grants and allocations (line 22). A schedule of these items is required. Total cash items and noncash items must be reported. These items are always allocated to program services.

2. Specific assistance to individuals (line 23). A schedule is required. These items are always allocated to program services.

3. Benefits paid to or for members (line 24). A schedule is required. These items are always allocated to program services.

4. Compensation of trustees, directors, and officers (line 25).

NOTE: Additional information in this regard is required elsewhere in the return (Q 12:6).

---

5. Other salaries and wages (line 26).

6. Pension plan contributions (line 27).

7. Other employee benefits (line 28).

8. Payroll taxes (line 29).

9. Professional fund-raising fees (line 30). This item may not be allocated to either program services or management.

10. Accounting fees (line 31).

11. Legal fees (line 32).

12. Supplies (line 33).

13. Telephone (line 34).

14. Postage and shipping (line 35).

15. Occupancy (line 36).

16. Equipment rental and maintenance (line 37).

17. Printing and publications (line 38).

18. Travel (line 39).

19. Conferences, conventions, and meetings (line 40).

20. Interest (line 41).

21. Depreciation, depletion, and the like (line 42). A schedule is required.

There is space on the return to list other expenses (line 43). An attachment may be used if necessary.

The organization's expenses are totaled (line 44). This number is carried over and inserted in the total expense line on the face of the return. If expenses are reported functionally, they are likewise carried forward and inserted in the appropriate expense line on the face of the return. (Q 11:20)

Q 12:4   There has been some controversy about allocating what some regard as fund-raising costs to programs. Is this reflected on the return?

Yes. The IRS refers to this situation as involving *joint costs*. Specifically, this arises where there is a combined educational campaign and a fund-raising solicitation. The organization must answer, on a "Yes" or "No" basis, whether any such joint costs are being reported as part of program services expenses (Part II). If the answer is "Yes," the organization must report the aggregate amount of these joint costs, the amount allocated to program, the amount allocated to management, and the amount allocated to fund-raising.

NOTE: The controversy, of course, arises when there is a perception that an organization is treating as program costs an amount of expenses that ought to be regarded as being for fund-raising. This may be done to augment the size of the entity's program or reduce the amount of fund-raising outlays. Critics of this type of allocation prefer a *primary purpose rule*, which would cause all of the expenses to be regarded as fund-raising expenses. The principal champions of this primary purpose rule are, not surprisingly, state regulatory agencies and watchdog groups.

Q 12:5   Does the annual return require any additional information about an organization's expenses?

Yes, much more. One of the most critical portions of the return is the analysis of income-producing activities (Part VII). This segment of the return must be prepared with considerable care and understanding of the underlying points of law.

The first step is for the organization to list each of its sources of program service revenue. This information has already been gathered and reported elsewhere on the return (Q 11:20). Here is the list:

1. Program service revenue (line 93). The return provides space for the listing of six sources; an attachment may be necessary. Fees and contracts from government agencies are expressly identified (line 93g), as are membership dues and assessments (line 94).

2. Interest on savings and temporary cash investments (line 95).

3. Dividends and interest from securities (line 96).

4. Net rental income (or loss) from real estate (line 97). There must be a differentiation between revenue derived from debt-financed property and property that is not debt-financed.

5. Net rental income (or loss) from personal property (line 98).

6. Other investment income (line 99).

7. Gain (or loss) from sales of assets other than inventory (line 100).

8. Net income (or loss) from special events (line 101).

9. Gross profit (or loss) from sales of inventory (line 102).

10. Other revenue (line 103). The return provides space for the listing of five items; an attachment may be used if necessary.

Once these sources of revenue are identified, they must be classified in accordance with the unrelated business income rules.[2] Specifically, the organization must decide whether an item of income is derived from a related business or an unrelated business, or whether the income, although not from a related business, is nonetheless not taxable because it is excluded from taxation by statute.

If the organization is reporting income as being from an exempt function, that item of income, matched up with the appropriate source (as in the preceding list), is inserted in the appropriate line in column (E). Thus, all items that are considered related income are entered in column (E). Then the organization must provide a written explanation as to how each of these activities is a related one, that is, how it contributed importantly to the accomplishment of the organization's exempt purposes. Of course, these explanations should be carefully thought through; this is one place where the assistance of a tax professional may well be advisable. An attachment may be required.

NOTE: It is not sufficient that the income from an activity is used for exempt purposes. The activity must inherently be an exempt function.

If the organization is reporting income from an unrelated business, this amount or these amounts must be reported in column (B). Each unrelated business activity must be assigned a business code, which is inserted in the appropriate line in column (A). These codes are found in the Form 990-T instructions.

If the organization is reporting income that is not from a related source but is sheltered from taxation by statute, this amount or these amounts must be reported in column (D). The organization must determine which section of the Internal Revenue Code provides the exclusion, correlate that exclusion with an exclusion code, and insert that code in the appropriate line in column (C). These codes are found in the Form 990 instructions.

Then the subtotals for these three groupings of income are reported (line 104), followed by their total (line 105).

NOTE: As noted, most of these revenue items have been previously ascertained and reported. Thus, the total on line 105, plus the amount of any contributions and grants (Q 11:19), should equal the amount of total revenue reported on the face of the return (Q 11:19).

Q 12:6   What about expenses for compensation?

This is another subject of great concern to the IRS. Thus, it should not be a surprise to learn that the annual information return devotes considerable space to the reporting of compensation.

As noted, as part of the listing of its expenses, the organization is required to make a line entry for the compensation of trustees, directors, and officers, as well as for other salaries and wages. In addition to those forms of compensation, the organization must report its payments for pension plan contributions and other employee benefits (Q 12:3).

In addition, the organization must provide a list of its trustees, directors, officers, and key employees (Part V). This list is required even if any individual(s) is not compensated.

Specifically, the name and address of each of these individuals must be listed, along with his or her title, the average hours per week devoted to the position, the amount of compensation, the amount contributed to employee benefit plans, the amount of deferred compensation, and information as to expense account and other allowances.

For many tax-exempt organizations, the doctrine of *private inurement* is applicable.[3] One way to have private inurement is for the exempt organization to pay an amount of compensation that is excessive. This portion of the return is used by the IRS as part of the process of ascertaining whether there may be an unreasonable compensation package.

Sometimes a compensation package of an individual is reasonable when evaluated alone, but the total compensation of the individual may be excessive when combined with compensation from a related organization. That is why the IRS asks the question, which must be answered "Yes" or "No," as to whether any trustee, director, officer, or key employee received aggregate compensation of more than $100,000 from the organization and all related organizations, where more than $10,000 was provided by one or more related organizations (line 75). If the answer is "Yes," an explanatory schedule must be attached.

Q 12:7   How does this matter of compensation relate to the intermediate sanctions rules?

There is a direct connection between this matter of compensation and the intermediate sanctions rules.

To recapitulate (see Chapter 1): If a public charity or a social welfare organization participates in an excess benefit transaction with a disqualified person, tax penalties are imposed on that person and on the organization managers who knew that the transaction gave rise to an excess benefit. Providing excessive compensation is one way to have an excess benefit transaction. Compensation arrangements involving trustees, directors, officers, and/or key employees are suspect under these rules because these individuals are almost always disqualified persons.

A public charity or a social welfare organization must answer "Yes" or "No" to a question as to whether it engaged in an excess benefit transaction during the year (Part VI, line 89b). If the answer is "Yes," it must attach a statement explaining each transaction. Moreover, the organization must report the amount of tax paid, during the year, by its organization managers or disqualified persons with respect to it (line 89c) and the amount of any of these taxes that the organization reimbursed (line 89d).

The reporting rules in this regard are more extensive for public charities. This is because these organizations are required to file Schedule A of Form 990.

This supplemental form requires much more detail as to the payment of compensation. Thus, a public charity must provide information as to the compensation of its five highest paid employees—if they were paid more than $50,000—other than trustees, directors, and officers (Schedule A, Part I). Specifically, the organization must supply the names and addresses of these employees, their titles, the average hours per week devoted to their positions, the amount of their compensation, the amount of contributions to employee benefit plans, deferred compensation, and expense accounts, and other allowances. If there are no employees of this nature, the organization should insert "None" on the first line.

NOTE: The way the schedule is constructed, the organization need only provide this information for 10 employees. It then inserts the total number of other employees paid over $50,000. If there are more than 10, there is no guidance as to which 10 to select for detailed reporting.

A public charity must also provide information as to the highest-paid independent contractors for professional services. It is required to list the name and address of each independent contractor paid more than $50,000, the type of service provided, and the compensation paid. If there are no independent contractors of this nature, the organization should insert "None" on the first line.

NOTE: Again, the organization need only provide this information for 10 independent contractors. It then inserts the total number of other independent contractors paid over $50,000. As with employees, if there are more than 10, there is no guidance as to which 10 to select for detailed reporting.

A public charity is also asked whether, during the year, it, directly or indirectly, paid compensation (or paid or reimbursed expenses if more than $1,000) to any of its trustees, directors, officers, creators, key employees, or members of their families, or to any taxable organization with which any of these persons is affiliated as a trustee, director, officer, majority owner, or principal beneficiary (Schedule A, Part III, line 2d). This is a "Yes" or "No" question. If the answer is "Yes," a detailed explanation is required.

Q 12:8 But the intermediate sanctions rules relate to much more than excessive compensation, don't they?

Absolutely. The concept of the excess benefit transaction embraces much more than compensation arrangements. It covers the provision of excess benefits by means of sales, loans, renting, and other transactions.

There is a set of questions on the annual return that predate the intermediate sanctions rules but that are being used to ferret out possible excess benefit transactions with public charities. These questions pertain to transactions during the year, whether direct or indirect, between the public charity and any of its trustees, directors, officers, creators, key employees, or members of their families, or with any taxable organization with which any of these persons is affiliated as a trustee, director, officer, majority owner, or principal beneficiary (Schedule A, Part III).

These transactions are the following:

1. Sales or exchanges of property (line 2a)
2. Leasing of property (line 2a)
3. Lending of money or other extension of credit (line 2b)
4. Furnishing of goods, services, or facilities (line 2c)
5. Compensation arrangements (line 2d) (Q 12:6)
6. Transfer of any part of the organization's income or assets (line 2e)

Each of these questions must be answered "Yes" or "No." In each instance where the answer is "Yes," a detailed explanation is required.

Q 12:9 Are there reporting requirements for public charities that make grants to individuals?

Yes. A public charity is asked whether it makes grants for scholarships, fellowships, student loans, and the like (Form 990, Schedule A, Part III, line 3). This is a "Yes" or "No" question. If the answer is "Yes," the organization must attach a statement explaining how it determines that individuals receiving grants or loans from it, in furtherance of its charitable programs, qualify to receive the payments (line 4).

In addition, all organizations are required to report expenses that constitute grants (Q 12:3). Further, a grant, loan, or similar program is a program service, and a statement about the program(s) is likely to be required, including the amount of the grants (Q 12:3). A grant payable should be identified on the organization's balance sheet (Q 11:23).

Q 12:10 There must be reporting requirements for grants to organizations, as well.

Yes, although there is not a specific "Yes" or "No" question on the point for all tax-exempt organizations. Nonetheless, if a public charity makes grants or loans to organizations, it must attach a statement explaining how it determines that the recipients of its support, in furtherance of its charitable programs, qualify to receive the payments (Form 990, Schedule A, Part III, line 4).

A public charity may also make grants or loans to other exempt organizations that are not charitable ones. If that is the case, there are other reporting requirements (Q 12:3).

Moreover, all tax-exempt organizations are required to report expenses that constitute specific assistance to individuals (Q 12:9). A scholarship, loan, or similar program is also a program service, and a statement about the program(s) is likely to be required, including the amount of the grants (Q 12:3). As noted, a grant payable should be identified on the organization's balance sheet (Q 11:23).

Q 12:11 Does the annual information return ask any questions about lobbying activities?

Yes. The IRS is very curious about lobbying activities by tax-exempt organizations, and this is mirrored in the amount of space the annual information return devotes to the subject. There are essentially two sets of questions about this subject. One set pertains to public charities. The other involves membership associations, principally social welfare organizations, labor organizations, and business leagues (Chapters 5 and 6). There are no questions about lobbying by other types of tax-exempt organizations.

NOTE: The portion of the annual return that focuses on an organization's expenses (Q 11:20) does not contain any express reference to lobbying expenditures.

A public charity is asked whether it, during the year, attempted to influence national, state, or local legislation, including any attempt to influence public opinion on a legislative matter or referendum (Form 990, Schedule A, Part III, line 1). This is a "Yes" or "No" question. If the answer is "Yes," the organization is required to report the expenses paid or incurred in this connection.

By reason of the *substantial part test*,[4] a charitable organization is prohibited from engaging in substantial amounts of lobbying activity. An organization that is subject to this test must also complete another portion of the return which requests more specific information about the lobbying activities. If a public charity has made an election and thus is bound by the rules of the *expenditure test*,[5] it must complete another portion of the return.

Charitable organizations that are bound by the substantial part test must answer "Yes" or "No" to eight questions pertaining to lobbying activities during the year (Schedule A, Part VI-B). These activities embrace direct lobbying, grass roots lobbying, and referenda. The questions pertain to lobbying through the use of the following:

1. Volunteers (line a).
2. Paid staff or management (line b).
3. Media advertisements (line c).
4. Mailings to members, legislators, or the public (line d). The amount of these expenses must be provided.
5. Publications, or published or broadcast statements (line e). The amount of these expenses must be provided.
6. Grants to other organizations for lobbying purposes (line f). The amount of these expenses must be provided.
7. Direct contact with legislators, their staffs, government officials, or a legislative body (line g). The amount of these expenses must be provided.
8. Rallies, demonstrations, seminars, conventions, speeches, lectures, or other means (line h). The amount of these expenses must be provided.

Total lobbying expenses are reported (line i). For each type of lobbying engaged in, the organization is required to attach a statement giving a detailed description of the activities.

A charitable organization that is subject to the expenditure test must indicate whether it belongs to an affiliated group (Schedule A, Part VI-A, box a) and, if so, whether the *limited control* provisions are applicable.

The focus and purpose of this portion of the return is the provision of an opportunity to make the various calculations that the expenditure test requires. Thus, the charity must report the following, for the year involved, both for the organization itself and for any affiliated group:

1. Total lobbying expenditures to influence public opinion (grass roots lobbying) (line 36).
2. Total lobbying expenditures to influence a legislative body (direct lobbying) (line 37).
3. Total lobbying expenditures (line 38, which is a total of the amounts on lines 36 and 37).
4. Other exempt purpose expenditures (line 39).

5. Total exempt purpose expenditures (line 40, which is a total of lines 38 and 39)

6. Direct lobbying nontaxable amount (line 41). The return includes a table for determining that amount.

7. Grass roots lobbying nontaxable amount (line 42). This amount is a maximum of 25 percent of the amount on line 41.

8. Grass roots lobbying taxable amount, if any (line 43, which is line 36 less line 42).

9. Direct lobbying taxable amount, if any (line 44, which is line 38 less line 41).

NOTE: If there is an amount in the eighth or ninth of these items, the organization must file Form 4720, which is used to pay the expenditure test tax on lobbying outlays.

Most organizations that are subject to the expenditure test must also report lobbying amounts for the current year and the three immediately previous years, because these calculations are made on the basis of four-year averaging. Thus, there must be reporting of the numbers for the four years, plus the total, for the following:

1. Direct lobbying nontaxable amount (line 45)

2. Direct lobbying ceiling amount (line 46)

3. Total direct lobbying expenditures (line 47)

4. Grass roots lobbying nontaxable amount (line 48)

5. Grass roots lobbying ceiling amount (line 49)

6. Grass roots lobbying expenditures (line 50)

In addition, a public charity must report the amount of any tax paid during the year because of lobbying expenditures (Part VI, line 89a). This involves both the tax imposed by reason of the substantial part test and the one imposed as part of the expenditure test.

As noted, a separate body of law concerns lobbying by membership associations, principally social welfare organizations, labor groups, and business leagues.

From the standpoint of tax-exempt status, these organizations are free to attempt to influence legislation without restraint. Indeed, lobbying can be their primary or even sole purpose. However, amounts expended for lobbying are not deductible. This rule "flows through" these membership entities and has an impact on the dues members pay; a ratio of lobbying expenses to total expenses is created, and that ratio is applied to the dues, rendering the portion of the dues attributed to lobbying nondeductible. For example, if a business association expended 25 percent of its revenue during the year for lobbying, then only 75 percent of the dues paid to it are deductible as a business expense.

This ratio must be timely communicated to the members. If this is not done, there is a penalty on the organization in the form of a *proxy tax*. However, the organization can voluntarily pay the proxy tax, thereby allowing the members to fully deduct the dues payments.

Under certain circumstances, an organization can be given, by the IRS, a waiver for the proxy tax owed for the prior year. Under certain circumstances, if an incorrect notice was sent to the membership in good faith, the organization can elect to add the taxable amount of its lobbying expenditures to its reasonable estimate of dues allocable to nondeductible lobbying expenditures for the following year.

However, these rules do not apply where substantially all of the dues paid to the organization by its members were not deductible in any event. Moreover, certain in-house lobbying expenditures are disregarded for this purpose if they do not exceed $2,000.

All of this is reflected on the annual information return. (This portion of the return need be completed only by social welfare organizations, labor organizations, and business leagues.) Thus, an organization must answer "Yes" or "No" to the question as to whether substantially all of the dues were nondeductible by its members (Part VI, line 85a).

NOTE: This is not an easy standard to meet. The phrase *substantially all* in this context means at least 90 percent.

The organization must also answer "Yes" or "No" to the question of whether it made only in-house lobbying expenditures of $2,000 or less (line 85b). If the answer to either question is "Yes," the organization should not complete the rest of the question unless it received a waiver for proxy tax owed for the prior year.

Assuming the organization must continue with this area of inquiry, it is required to report the amount of dues, assessments, and/or similar amounts paid by its members during the year (line 85c), as well as the amount of its lobbying expenditures (line 85d). It must report the nondeductible amount of the dues as shown on the notices (line 85e) and the taxable amount of lobbying (line 85f). The organization must answer

"Yes" or "No" to the question as to whether it elected to pay the proxy tax (line 85g). The organization must also answer "Yes" or "No" to the question of whether, if dues notices were sent, the organization agrees to add the taxable amount of lobbying expenditures to its reasonable estimate of dues allocable to nondeductible lobbying expenditures for the following year (line 85h).

Q 12:12 Does the annual information return ask any questions about political activities?

Yes. The law makes a distinction between *political activities* and *political campaign activities*. Political campaign activities are participations or interventions on behalf of or in opposition to candidates for public office.[6] Political activities include political campaign activities and also embrace efforts such as support of or opposition to nominations for public office (Q 8:4)

Every tax-exempt organization that files the annual information return is required, if it, directly or indirectly, made any political expenditures during the year, to enter the amount on the return (Part VI, line 81a). The organization must also state, by a "Yes" or "No" answer, whether it filed the political organization tax return (Form 1120-POL) for the year (line 81b). This is because these political expenditures may be taxable and that is the form by which the tax is reported.

Membership associations that are caught up in the rules concerning the nondeductibility of dues because of lobbying expenditures (Q 12:11) have those rules applicable to them in the event of political expenditures.

Public charities are prohibited from engaging in political campaign activities. One tax sanction that can be applied if they do this is a tax. A public charity must report the amount of any tax paid during the year because of political campaign expenditures (Part VI, line 89a).

Q 12:13 What about the ownership by a tax-exempt organization of a taxable subsidiary?

An organization must answer "Yes" or "No" to the question as to whether, at any time during the year, the organization owned a 50 percent or greater interest in a taxable corporation (Part VI, line 88).[7] If the answer is "Yes," another portion of the return must be completed.

This other portion of the return (Part IX) requires reporting of the name, address, and employer identification number of the corporation. The exempt organization is also required to state the percentage of its ownership interest in the corporation, as well as the nature of the corporation's business activities, total income, and end-of-year assets.

Remember, there is a question generally inquiring into the organization's relationship with another organization (Q 11:33). That question would be answered "Yes" in the instance of ownership of a taxable subsidiary, and the other information sought by that question would have to be provided.

Q 12:14 What about the involvement of a tax-exempt organization in a partnership?

An organization must answer "Yes" or "No" to the question as to whether, at any time during the year, the organization owned a 50 percent or greater interest in a partnership (Part VI, line 88) (Chapter 3). If the answer is "Yes," another portion of the return must be completed.

This other portion of the return (Part IX) requires reporting of the name, address, and employer identification number of the partnership. The exempt organization is also required to state the percentage of its ownership interest in the partnership, as well as the nature of the partnership's business activities, total income, and end-of-year assets.

Again, remember, there is a question generally inquiring into the organization's relationship with another organization (Q 11:33). That question would be answered "Yes" in the instance of involvement of the organization in a partnership, and the other information sought by that question would have to be provided.

Q 12:15 What about the organization's relationship to other tax-exempt organizations?

This has been touched on elsewhere, involving situations where the organizations are related (Q 11:33) or, in the case of public charities, are the recipients of grants or loans (Q 12:16).

However, public charities are additionally required to provide information regarding transfers to, and transactions and relationships with, other tax-exempt organizations that are not charities (Form 990, Schedule A, Part VII).

NOTE: For this purpose, political organizations (Chapter 8) are included as tax-exempt organizations.

The public charity is required to answer "Yes" or "No" to the question as to whether it, directly or indirectly, engaged in any of the following transactions with noncharitable exempt organizations:

1. Transfers of cash (line 51a(i))
2. Transfers of other assets (line 51a(ii))
3. Sales of assets (line 51b(i))
4. Purchases of assets (line 51b(ii))
5. Rental of facilities or equipment (line 51b(iii))
6. Reimbursements (line 51b(iv))
7. Loans or loan guarantees (line 51b(v))
8. Performance of services or membership or fund-raising solicitations (line 51b(vi))
9. Sharing of facilities, equipment, mailing lists, other assets, or paid employees (line 51c)

If the answer to any of these nine questions is "Yes," the organization must complete a schedule. This schedule must provide in columns, for each of the transactions being reported, the amount involved, the name of the noncharitable exempt organization, and a description of the transfers, transactions, and sharing arrangements. The *amount involved* (column (b)) can be the fair market value of the goods, other assets, or services provided by the organization. If the organization received less than fair market value in any transaction or sharing arrangement, it should reflect in the description (column (d)) the value of the goods, other assets, or services received.

TIP: For purposes of the intermediate sanctions rules (Chapter 1), a noncharitable tax-exempt organization can be a disqualified person with respect to a public charity. Thus, the information provided in this portion of the return should be evaluated from that perspective.

The organization must also answer "Yes" or "No" to a question as to whether it is, directly or indirectly, affiliated with or otherwise related to one or more noncharitable tax-exempt organizations (line 52a). If the answer is "Yes," a schedule must be completed (line 52b). This schedule must provide the name of the noncharitable entity, its tax-exempt status, and a description of the relationship.

Q 12:16 What information must be reported concerning the organization's public charity status?

A charitable organization that is a public charity is required to report information about its public charity status.[8]

There are eleven ways for a charitable organization to constitute a public charity. These ways are enumerated in the return (Form 990, Schedule A, Part IV); the organization is required to indicate which one of the categories it is in. The categories are:

1. A church, convention of churches, or association of churches (line 5).
2. A school (line 6).

NOTE: Schools are required to complete another portion of Schedule A (Part V, the Private School Questionnaire).

---

3. A hospital or a cooperative service organization (line 7).
4. A federal, state, or local government or governmental unit (line 8).
5. A medical research organization operated in conjunction with a hospital (line 9). The hospital's name, city, and state must be provided.
6. An organization operated for the benefit of a college or university that is owned or operated by a governmental unit (line 10). There is a public support requirement for these organizations; a support schedule must be completed (Part IV-A).
7. An organization that is a publicly supported charity because it is the donative type (line 11a). A support schedule must be completed (Part IV-A).
8. A community trust (or community foundation) (line 11b). A support schedule must be completed (Part IV-A).
9. An organization that is a publicly supported charity because it is the service provider type (line 12). A support schedule must be completed (Part IV-A).
10. A supporting organization (line 13). The supported organization(s) must be identified by name and public charity status (the latter by selecting the appropriate line number).
11. An organization that is organized and operated to test for public safety (line 14).

SANCTIONS

Q 12:17 What can give rise to penalties on organizations concerning annual information returns?

Penalties can be imposed for failure to file the return, for a late filing, an incorrect filing, or an incomplete filing.

Q 12:18 What are these penalties?

The basic penalty is $20 per day, not to exceed the smaller of $10,000 or 5 percent of the gross receipts of the organization for the year. A penalty will not be imposed in an instance of reasonable cause for the violation.

However, an organization with annual gross receipts in excess of $1 million is subject to a penalty of $100 for each day the failure continues. The maximum penalty per return is $50,000.

These penalties begin on the due date for filing the annual return.

TIP: One way to avoid penalties is to complete all applicable line items. Each question on the return should be answered "Yes," "No," or "N/A" (not applicable). An entry should be made on all total lines (including a zero when appropriate). "None" or "N/A" should be entered if an entire part does not apply.

Q 12:19 Are there any other consequences for nonfiling and the like?

Yes. The IRS takes the position that it can remove an organization from its Publication 78 if an annual information return is not filed.

NOTE: Publication 78 is titled *Cumulative List of Organizations Described in Section 170(c) of the Internal Revenue Code.* It thus is a registry of organizations to which deductible charitable gifts can be made. It is often relied on by donors and grantors, so removal from this publication can be of dire consequences to an organization.

TIP: Contributions to an organization in this position continue to be deductible until the IRS publishes a notice to the contrary in the *Internal Revenue Bulletin.*

Obviously, the potential of this sanction is of no consequence to organizations that are not qualified charitable donees.

Q 12:20 Are there penalties on individuals as well as organizations for nonfiling and the like?

Yes. There is a separate penalty that may be imposed on *responsible persons*. This penalty is $10 per day, not to exceed $5,000. This penalty will not be levied in an instance of reasonable cause.

TIP: If an organization does not file a complete return or does not furnish correct information, it is the practice of the IRS to send the organization a letter that includes a fixed time to fulfill these requirements. After that period expires, the person failing to comply will be charged the penalty.

If more than one person is responsible, they are jointly and individually liable for the penalty.

There are other penalties, in the form of fines and imprisonment, for willfully not filing returns when they are required, and for filing fraudulent returns and statements with the IRS.

CHAPTER 13

Disclosure and Distribution Rules

The federal tax law embodies a variety of disclosure and distribution rules that are imposed on tax-exempt organizations. The most significant of these are the requirements with respect to annual information returns and applications for recognition of tax exemption. Other disclosure rules pertain to private letter rulings, the availability of certain information or services, and certain solicitations of charitable gifts.

Here are the questions most frequently asked by clients about disclosure and distribution requirements—and the answers to them.

ANNUAL INFORMATION RETURNS

Q 13:1   It was mentioned earlier that the annual information returns are public documents. What does that mean?

There are two aspects of this matter. One is that these documents are available from the IRS. The other is that an exempt organization is required to make copies of them accessible to whoever asks to see them. Let us focus on the second of these aspects first.

Tax-exempt organizations must make their annual information returns available for public inspection.[1] The requirement pertains to the three most recent annual information returns.

NOTE: There are separate publicity requirements for private foundations.[2]

This requirement does not cause disclosure of the names or addresses
of donors.[3]

An exempt organization is required to make a copy of each return available for inspection, during regular business hours, at its
principal office, by any individual. If an exempt organization regularly
maintains one or more regional or district offices having at least three
employees, this distribution requirement applies with respect to
each office.[4]

It is not necessary, under these rules, that copies be provided for
retention by those who request them; the documents need only be provided for review.

However, this body of law is about to be significantly augmented,
when new distribution rules take effect.

Q 13:2   What are the coming distribution rules?

Congress, in 1996, enacted distribution rules in this context. These
rules will be amplified by tax regulations. However, the new statutory
rules will not take effect until 60 days following their issuance in final
form. The regulations in proposed form were issued in the fall of 1997.[5]

CAUTION: Thus, this body of law (including that discussed in Q 13:3
to Q 13:7) is not yet effective. The rules described earlier (Q 13:1) remain the applicable law. However, it is anticipated that the regulations
in this regard will be finalized in late 1998.

TIP: However, it has been the "expectation" of Congress, since mid-
1996, that exempt organizations will "voluntarily" comply with these
rules until the effective date.

Generally, under these emerging rules, anyone who requests a copy of
one or more of the three most recent annual returns, in person or in
writing, will have to be provided these copies. The individual requesting them will be able to retain these copies.[6]

If a request for copies is made in person, the organization will have
to provide them immediately.[7] Response to a request in writing will

have to be made within 30 days. The only charge that can be imposed for these copies is a reasonable fee for photocopying and mailing costs.

This annual return distribution requirement will extend to all schedules and attachments filed with the IRS. For charitable organizations, this includes Schedule A. An organization will not be required, however, to disclose the parts of the return that identify names and addresses of contributors to the organization. Moreover, a tax-exempt organization will not be required to disclose its unrelated business income tax return (Form 990-T).

There will be rules concerning the documents that must be made available by an organization that is recognized as tax-exempt under a group exemption (Q 4:36–4:45).

A tax-exempt organization will have to make the specified documents available for public inspection at its principal, regional, and district offices. The documents generally will have to be available for inspection on the day of the request during the organization's normal business hours. An office of an organization will be considered a regional or district office only if it has three or more paid full-time employees (or paid employees, whether part-time or full-time, whose aggregate number of paid hours per week is at least 120).

Certain sites where the organization's employees perform solely exempt function activities will be excluded from consideration as a regional or district office. The rules will prescribe how an organization that does not maintain a permanent office or whose office has very limited hours during certain times of the year can comply with the public inspection requirements.

A tax-exempt organization will have to accept requests for copies made in person at the same place and time that the information must be available for public inspection. An organization will generally be required to provide the copies on the day of the request. In unusual circumstances, an organization will be permitted to provide the requested copies on the next business day.

Where a request is made in writing, an exempt organization will have to furnish the copies within 30 days from the date the request is received. If an organization requires advance payment of a reasonable fee for copying and mailing, it may provide the copies within 30 days from the date it receives payment (rather than from the date of the request).

There will be rules that provide guidance as to what constitutes a *request*, when a request is considered *received*, and when copies are considered *provided*. Instead of requesting a copy of an entire annual return, individuals may request a specific portion of the document. A principal, regional, or district office of an organization will be able to use an agent to process requests for copies.

The reasonable fee a tax-exempt organization will be permitted to charge for copies may be no more than the fees charged by the IRS for copies of exempt organization returns and related documents. This is currently $1.00 for the first page and $.15 for each subsequent page. In addition, actual postage costs can be charged. An organization will be permitted to collect payment in advance of providing the requested copies.

If an organization receives a written request for copies with payment not enclosed, and the organization requires payment in advance, the organization will have to request payment within seven days from the date it receives the request. Payment will be deemed to occur on the day an organization receives the money, check (provided the check subsequently clears), or money order. An organization will be required to accept payment made in the form of money or money order and, when the request is made in writing, to accept payment by personal check. An organization will be permitted, though not required, to accept other forms of payment. To protect requesters from unexpected fees where an exempt organization does not require prepayment and where a requester does not enclose prepayment with a request, an organization will have to receive consent from a requester before providing copies for which the fee charged for copying and postage is in excess of $20.

Q 13:3   What will an individual be able to do if denied a copy of the return?

The tax regulations will provide guidance for an individual denied inspection, or a copy, of an annual return. Basically, the individual will be able to provide the IRS with a statement that describes the reason that the individual believes the denial was in violation of legal requirements.[8]

Q 13:4   Are there any exceptions to the inspection requirement?

Not really. No excuses are allowed. As noted, certain donor information need not be provided (Q 13:1). Otherwise, as long as the request is made during regular business hours, copies of the returns must be made available for inspection.

Q 13:5   Will there be any exceptions to the distribution requirement?

Yes, under two circumstances an exempt organization will be relieved of the obligation to provide copies of the returns. An exception will be available where the organization has made the documents *widely avail-*

able. The other exception will obtain where the IRS determines, following application by the organization, that the organization is subject to a *harassment campaign* and that a waiver of the disclosure obligation is in the public interest.[9]

Q 13:6   What will the term *widely available* mean?

Under the proposed regulations, a tax-exempt organization will not be required to comply with requests for copies of its annual returns if the organization has made them widely available.[10] An organization will be able to make its annual information return *widely available* by posting the document on its World Wide Web page on the Internet or by having the applicable document posted on another organization's Web page as part of a data base of similar materials.

However, for this exception to be available, the following criteria will have to be followed:

1. The entity maintaining the Web page must have procedures for ensuring the reliability and accuracy of the application or return that is posted.
2. This entity must take reasonable precautions to prevent alteration, destruction, or accidental loss of the posted document.
3. The application or return must be posted in the same format used by the IRS to post forms and publications on the IRS's Web page.
4. The Web page that is used must clearly inform readers that the document is available and provide instructions for downloading it.
5. When downloaded and printed in hard copy, the document must be in substantially the same form as the original application or return and contain the same information as provided in the original document filed with the IRS (other than information that can be lawfully withheld).
6. A person can access and download the document without payment of a fee to the organization maintaining the Web page.

The IRS will be authorized to prescribe, by revenue procedure or other guidance, other methods that an organization can use to make its annual return widely available.

An organization that makes its return widely available will have to inform individuals who request copies how and where to obtain the requested document.

Q 13:7 What will the term *harassment campaign* mean?

Under the proposed regulations, generally, a *harassment campaign* will exist where an organization receives a group of requests, and the relevant facts and circumstances show that the purpose of the group of requests is to disrupt the operations of the exempt organization rather than to collect information.[11]

These facts and circumstances will include a sudden increase in the number of requests, an extraordinary number of requests made through form letters or similarly worded correspondence, evidence of a purpose to significantly deter the organization's employees or volunteers from pursuing the organization's exempt purpose, requests that contain language hostile to the organization, direct evidence of bad faith by organizers of the purported harassment campaign, evidence that the organization has already provided the requested documents to a member of the purported harassing group, and a demonstration by the exempt organization that it routinely provides copies of its documents upon request.

The regulations will contain examples that evaluate whether particular situations constitute a harassment campaign and whether an organization has a reasonable basis for believing that a request is part of this type of campaign.

TIP: Organizations will not be able to suspend compliance with a request for copies from a representative of the news media even though the organization believes or knows that the request is part of a harassment campaign.

An organization will be able to disregard requests in excess of two per 30-day period or four per year from the same individual or from the same address. There will be procedures for requesting a determination that an organization is subject to a harassment campaign and the treatment of requests for copies while a request for a determination is pending.

NOTE: These two exceptions are to be exceptions only from the rules concerning *distribution* of returns. They will not be exceptions from the *inspection* requirements (Q 13:1).[12]

Q 13:8   How are these returns available from the IRS?

Copies of exempt organizations' annual information returns are available for public inspection and photocopying from the IRS, although trade secrets, and names and addresses of contributors, cannot be disclosed.[13]

A request for inspection must be in writing, include the name and address (city and state) of the organization that filed the return, and include the type (number) of the return and the year(s) involved. The request may be sent to the IRS district director (Attention: Disclosure Officer) of the district in which the requester desires to inspect the return. If inspection at the IRS National Office is desired, the request should be sent to the Commissioner of Internal Revenue, Attention: Freedom of Information Reading Room, 1111 Constitution Avenue, N.W., Washington, DC 20224.

A copy of one or more annual information returns is available through the IRS. Form 4506-A is used for this purpose. There is a fee for photocopying.

EXEMPTION APPLICATIONS

Q 13:9   What is the disclosure requirement with respect to applications for recognition of exemption?

The inspection requirement described earlier (Q 13.1) is likewise applicable with respect to applications for recognition of exemption. Again, certain information will be withheld from public inspection, such as trade secrets and patents.

Q 13:10 Will the coming distribution requirements apply to exemption applications?

Yes. All of the rules as to distribution of documents, and the exceptions to them, (Q 13:2–Q 13:7) will be applicable with respect to applications for recognition of exemption.

Q 13:11 Are copies of exemption applications available from the IRS?

Yes. The application for recognition of tax exemption and any supporting documents filed by most tax-exempt organizations must be made accessible to the public by the IRS where a favorable determination letter is issued to an organization.[14]

NOTE: This disclosure rule applies only to documents filed by the exempt organization. It does not extend to documents submitted by third parties (such as members of Congress) in support of or opposition to the application.[15]

An organization, for which application for recognition of exemption is open to public inspection, may request in writing that information relating to a trade secret, patent, process, style of work, or apparatus be withheld. The information will be withheld from public inspection if the IRS determines that its disclosure would adversely affect the organization.[16]

An application and related materials may be inspected at the appropriate field office of the IRS. Inspection may also occur at the National Office of the IRS; a request for inspection may be directed to the Assistant to the Commissioner (Public Affairs), 1111 Constitution Avenue, N.W., Washington, DC 20224.[17]

Once an organization's exemption application, and related and supporting documents, become open to public inspection, the determination letter issued by the IRS becomes publicly available as well. Also open to inspection are any technical advice memoranda issued with respect to any favorable ruling.

NOTE: A favorable ruling recognizing an organization's tax-exempt status may be issued by the IRS's National Office. These rulings and the underlying applications for recognition of tax exemption are available for inspection in the IRS's Freedom of Information Reading Room in Washington, D.C.[18]

DISCLOSURE AND DISTRIBUTION SANCTIONS

Q 13:12 What is the penalty on organizations for failure to comply with the public inspection requirements?

The penalty is $10 per day for each day that inspection is not permitted, up to a maximum of $5,000 for each return.[19] In the case of exemption applications, the penalty is $10 per day as long as the failure to comply continues.[20] This penalty is inapplicable in instances of reasonable cause.[21]

Q 13:13 What is the penalty on individuals for failure to comply with the public inspection requirements?

An individual who willfully fails to comply with the inspection requirements is subject to a penalty of $5,000.[22]

PROVISION OF GOODS AND SERVICES

Q 13:14 What are the disclosure rules regarding the availability of goods or services?

There are disclosure rules that become applicable if a tax-exempt organization offers to sell or solicits money for specific information or a routine service for an individual that could be readily obtained by the individual without charge or for a nominal charge from an agency of the federal government.

A penalty can be imposed when the tax-exempt organization, in making the offer or solicitation, fails to make an express statement—in a conspicuous and easily recognizable format—that the information or service can be so obtained. Imposition of this penalty requires an intentional disregard of these requirements.[23]

Q 13:15 What are the parameters of this type of *solicitation*?

This requirement of disclosure applies only if the information to be provided involves the *specific individual* solicited. Thus, for example, the requirement applies with respect to obtaining the Social Security earnings record or the Social Security identification number of an individual solicited, but is inapplicable with respect to the furnishing of copies of newsletters issued by federal agencies or providing copies of or descriptive material on pending legislation. Moreover, this requirement is not applicable to the provision of professional services (such as tax return preparation, grant application preparation, or medical services), as opposed to routine information retrieval services, to an individual even if they may be available from the federal government without charge.[24]

Q 13:16 What is the penalty for violation of this rule?

The penalty for violation of this disclosure rule is applicable for each day on which the failure occurred. This penalty is the greater of $1,000 or 50 percent of the aggregate cost of the offers and solicitations that occurred on any day on which the failure occurred and with respect to which there was this type of failure.[25]

FUND-RAISING DISCLOSURE

Q 13:17 What are the fund-raising disclosure rules for noncharitable organizations?

There are rules designed to prevent noncharitable organizations from engaging in gift-solicitation activities under circumstances in which donors will assume, or be led to assume, that the contributions are tax-deductible when, in fact, they are not.

NOTE: These rules are targeted principally at tax-exempt social welfare organizations (Chapter 6).

However, these rules do not apply to an organization that has annual gross receipts that are normally no more than $100,000.[26]

Under these rules, each *fund-raising solicitation* by or on behalf of an exempt noncharitable organization must contain an express statement, in a "conspicuous and easily recognizable format," that gifts to it are not deductible as charitable contributions for federal income tax purposes. A fund-raising solicitation is any solicitation of gifts made in written or printed form, or by television, radio, or telephone. There is an exclusion for letters or calls not part of a coordinated fund-raising campaign soliciting more than 10 persons during a calendar year.

CAUTION: Despite the reference in the statute to *contributions and gifts*, the IRS interprets this rule to mandate disclosure when any noncharitable organization seeks funds, such as dues from members. Thus, for example, it applies with respect to dues solicitations by membership associations (Chapter 5) and social clubs (Chapter 7) and contribution solicitations by political organizations (Chapter 8).

Q 13:18 What are the penalties for violation of these rules?

The penalty for failure to satisfy this disclosure requirement for noncharitable organizations is $1,000 per day (maximum of $10,000 per year), albeit with a reasonable cause exception.[27] However, in an instance of "intentional disregard" of these rules, the penalty for the day on which the offense occurred is the greater of $1,000 or 50 percent of the aggregate cost of the solicitations that took place on that day; the $10,000 limitation is inapplicable.

Q 13:19 What are the fund-raising disclosure rules for charitable organizations?

One disclosure rule is that if a charitable organization receives a quid pro quo contribution in excess of $75, the organization must, in connection with the solicitation or receipt of the solicitation, provide a written statement that

1. Informs the donor that the amount of the contribution that is deductible for federal income tax purposes is limited to the excess of the amount of any money and the value of any property other than money contributed by the donor over the value of any goods or services provided by the organization, and
2. Provides the donor with a good-faith estimate of the value of the goods or services.[28]

A *quid pro quo contribution* is a payment "made partly as a contribution and partly in consideration for goods or services provided to the payor by the donee organization."

NOTE: This term does not include a payment made to an organization, operated exclusively for religious purposes, in return for which the donor receives solely an intangible religious benefit that generally is not sold in a commercial transaction outside the donative context.

There are also charitable gift *substantiation* rules, whereby the charitable donee must provide certain information pertaining to the gift in writing to donors, where the contribution is $250 or more in a year.[29]

Q 13:20 What are the penalties for violation of these rules?

The penalty for violation of the rules concerning *quid pro quo contributions* is $10 per contribution, capped at $5,000 per particular fund-raising event or mailing, absent reasonable cause.[30] The penalty for transgressing the charitable gift substantiation rules is denial of the charitable contribution deduction to the donor—even though the deduction may otherwise be allowable in full.

Endnotes

CHAPTER 1

1   Throughout, the Internal Revenue Service is referred to as the IRS. See *The Legal Answer Book for Nonprofit Organizations,* (LAB 1) (New York: John Wiley & Sons, 1996), Chapter 1, note 7.

2   Proposed Regulation section (Prop. Reg. §) 53.4958-1(g)(1).

3   Prop. Reg. § 53.4958-1(g)(2).

4   Internal Revenue Code of 1986, as amended, section 4958. Throughout, "IRC § " is used to designate sections of the Code. The intermediate sanctions rules are detailed in Hopkins and Tesdahl, *Intermediate Sanctions: Curbing Nonprofit Abuse* (New York: John Wiley & Sons, 1997).

5   H. Rep. 104-506, 104th Cong., 2d Sess. (1996).

6   REG-246256-96.

7   IRC § 4958(e). Prop. Reg. § 53.4958-2.

8   Prop. Reg. § 53.4958-2(c).

9   Prop. Reg. § 53.4958-2(a)(2).

10 Prop. Reg. § 53.4958-2(b), (c).

11 IRC § 4958(c).

12 Prop. Reg. § 53.4958-4.

13 Prop. Reg. § 53.4958-4(b)(2).

14 Prop. Reg. § 53.4958-4(c).

15 Prop. Reg. § 53.4958-4(a)(2).

16 IRC § 4958(c)(2).

17 Prop. Reg. § 53.4958-5(a).

18 Prop. Reg. § 53.4958-4(a)(3)(i).

19 Prop. Reg. § 53.4958-4(a)(3)(ii).

20 Prop. Reg. § 53.4958-4(a)(3)(iii).

21 IRC § 162.

22 Prop. Reg. § 53.4958-4(b)(3)(i).

23 *Id.*

24 *Anclote Psychiatric Center, Inc. v. Commissioner,* 76 T.C.M. 175 (1998).

25 Prop. Reg. § 53.4958-4(b)(3)(ii).

26   Prop. Reg. § 53.4958-6(d)(1)(i).
27   Prop. Reg. § 53.4958-6(a).
28   Prop. Reg. § 53.4958-6(d)(2)(i).
29   Prop. Reg. § 53.4958-6(d)(2)(ii), (iii).
30   Prop. Reg. § 53.4958-6(d)(3).
31   Prop. Reg. § 53.4958-6(d)(1)(iii).
32   Prop. Reg. § 53.4958-3(a).
33   IRC § 4958(f)(1); Prop. Reg. § 53.4958-3(a), (b).
34   Prop. Reg. § 53.4958-3(c)(2).
35   Prop. Reg. § 53.4958-3(c)(3).
36   Prop. Reg. § 53.4958-3(c)(1).
37   IRS General Counsel Memorandum (Gen. Couns. Mem.) 39862.
38   Prop. Reg. § 53.4958-3(d)(1).
39   Prop. Reg. § 53.4958-3(d)(2).
40   Prop. Reg. § 53.4958-3(e)(1).
41   Prop. Reg. § 53.4958-3(e)(2).
42   Prop. Reg. § 53.4958-3(e)(3).
43   IRC § 4958(f)(2).
44   Prop. Reg. § 53.4958-1(d)(2)(i).
45   Prop. Reg. § 53.4958-1(d)(2)(i)(B).
46   Prop. Reg. § 53.4958-1(d)(2)(ii).
47   IRC § 4958(f)(4); Prop. Reg. § 53.4958-3(b)(1).
48   IRC § 4958(f)(3); Prop. Reg. § 53.4958-3(b)(2).
49   Prop. Reg. § 53.4958-3(b)(2)(iii).
50   IRC § 4958(a); Prop. Reg. § 53.4958-1(a)–(e).
51   IRC § 4958(f)(6).
52   Prop. Reg. § 53.4958-1(c)(1)(ii).
53   Prop. Reg. § 53.4958-1(d)(3).
54   Prop. Reg. § 53.4958-1(d)(4)(i).
55   Prop. Reg. § 53.4958-1(d)(4)(ii).
56   Prop. Reg. § 53.4958-1(d)(5).
57   Prop. Reg. § 53.4958(d)(6).
58   Prop. Reg. § 53.4958-1(d)(7).
59   *Id.*
60   IRC § 4958(d)(1); Prop. Reg. § 53.4958-1(d)(9).
61   Prop. Reg. § 53.4958-1(c)(2)(ii).
62   IRC §§ 4961, 4962; Prop. Reg. § 53.4958-1(c)(2)(iv).
63   Prop. Reg. § 53.4958-4(a)(4).
64   *Id.*
65   Prop. Reg. § 53.4958-1(f).
66   Prop. Reg. § 53.4958-7(a).

CHAPTER 2

1   These are organizations described in IRC § 501(c)(14).
2   "Should Credit Unions Be Taxed," CRS Analysis No. I B 89066 (Sept. 18, 1990).
3   That is, organizations described in IRC § 501(c)(8).
4   "Report to the Congress on Fraternal Beneficiary Societies," Department of the Treasury (Jan. 15, 1993).
5   See LAB 1, Chapter 10.
6   *American Medical Association v. United States,* 887 F.2d 760, 772 (7th Cir. 1989).
7   *Louisiana Credit Union League v. United States,* 693 F.2d 525, 540 (5th Cir. 1982).
8   That is, entities described in IRC § 501(c)(20).
9   E.g., *Hi-Plains Hospital v. United States,* 670 F.2d 528 (5th Cir. 1982); *Carle Foundation v. United States,* 611 F.2d 1192 (7th Cir. 1979), *cert. den.,* 449 U.S. 824 (1980).

10 IRS Revenue Ruling (Rev. Rul.) 85-110, 1985-2 C.B. 166.

11 E.g., IRS Private Letter Ruling (Priv. Ltr. Rul.) 9739043.

12 E.g., IRS Technical Advice Memorandum (Tech. Adv. Mem.) 9803001.

13 Rev. Rul. 79-361, 1979-2 C.B. 237.

14 IRS Priv. Ltr. Rul. 8626080.

15 E.g., IRS Tech. Adv. Mem. 9702004. The IRS proposed travel tour regulations in the unrelated business income context on April 20, 1998 (Prop. Reg. § 1.513-7).

16 IRC § 513(c), (i).

17 E.g., IRS Tech. Adv. Mem. 9550003.

18 E.g., payments with respect to securities loans (IRC § 512(b)(1)); treatment of associate member dues (IRC § 512(d)); conduct of trade shows, state fairs, and the like (IRC § 513(d)); sponsorship payments (IRC § 513(i)).

19 IRC § 513(a)(2).

20 See LAB 1, Q 10:13.

21 E.g., IRS Tech. Adv. Mem. 9712001.

22 IRC § 513(a)(3).

23 IRC § 513(a)(1).

24 IRC § 513(i).

25 IRC § 513(h).

26 IRC § 513(d).

27 IRC § 513(f).

28 IRC § 513(h).

29 IRC § 512(b)(2).

30 This doctrine is the subject of Hopkins, *The Law of Tax-Exempt Organizations,* 7th ed. (New York: John Wiley & Sons, 1998), Chapter 25.

31 *Trinidad v. Sagrada Orden de Predicatores de la Provincia del Santisimo Rosario de Filipinas,* 263 U.S. 578, 581, 582 (1924).

32 *Better Business Bureau of Washington, D.C. v. United States,* 326 U.S. 279, 283-284 (1945).

33 *Scripture Press Foundation v. United States,* 285 F.2d 800, 803, 805 (Ct. Cl. 1961).

34 *American Institute for Economic Research v. United States,* 302 F.2d 934, 937 (Ct. Cl. 1962).

35 *The Golden Rule Church Association v. Commissioner,* 41 T.C. 719, 731 (1964).

36 *Elisian Guild, Inc. v. United States,* 292 F. Supp. 219, 221 (D. Mass. 1968).

37 *Greater United Navajo Development Enterprises, Inc. v. Commissioner,* 74 T.C. 69, 79 (1980).

38 *Incorporated Trustees of Gospel Worker Society v. United States,* 510 F. Supp. 374, 381 (D.D.C.), *aff'd,* 672 F.2d 894 (D.C. Cir. 1981), *cert. den.,* 456 U.S. 944 (1981).

39 *Presbyterian and Reformed Publishing Co. v. Commissioner,* 743 F.2d 148, 152 (3d Cir. 1984).

40 *United Missionary Aviation, Inc. v. Commissioner,* 60 T.C.M. 1152 (1990), *rev. and rem'd,* 985 F.2d 564 (8th Cir. 1989), *cert. den.,* 506 U.S. 816 (1992).

41 *Public Industries, Inc. v. Commissioner,* 61 T.C.M. 1626 (1991).

42 *New Faith, Inc. v. Commissioner,* 64 T.C.M. 1050 (1992).

43 *Living Faith, Inc. v. Commissioner,* 60 T.C.M. 710, 713 (1990).

44 *Living Faith, Inc. v. Commissioner,* 950 F.2d 365, 373–375 (7th Cir. 1991).

45 McGraw, Rock, and Dillon, "Money Games: Inside the NCAA" (subtitled "Revenues dominate college sports world"), *Kansas City Star,* Oct. 5, 1997.

46 Nordheimer and Frantz, "Testing Giant Exceeds Roots, Drawing Business Rivals' Ire," *The New York Times,* Sept. 30, 1997.

47 IRC § 501(m).

48 IRC § 501(n).

49 Income Tax Regulations (Reg.) §§ 1.513-1(c)(1), 1.513-1(c)(2)(ii).

50 The carrying on of a program simply to raise money in support of exempt purposes does not make that program an exempt function.

51 See the discussions in LAB 1, Chapter 3, and in Chapter 1 of this book.

52   E.g., *National League of Postmasters v. Commissioner,* 69 T.C.M. 2569 (1995), *aff'd,* 86 F.3d 59 (4th Cir. 1996).

CHAPTER 3

1   IRC § 7701(a)(2); Reg. § 301.7701-2(a).
2   Reg. § 301.7701-2(c)(1).
3   *Whiteford v. United States,* 61-1 U.S.T.C. ¶ 9301, at 79,762 (D. Kan. 1960).
4   Rev. Rul. 54-369, 1954-2 C.B. 364; Rev. Rul. 54-170, 1954-1 C.B. 213.
5   Reg. § 301.7701-3(a).
6   IRC §§ 701, 702.
7   *Whiteford v. United States, supra* note 3.
8   *Stevens Brothers Foundation, Inc. v. Commissioner,* 324 F.2d 633 (8th Cir. 1963).
9   *Commissioner v. Tower,* 327 U.S. 280, 286-287 (1946).
10   *Id.* at 287.
11   *Harlan E. Moore Charitable Trust v. United States,* 812 F. Supp. 130, 132 (C.D. Ill. 1993), *aff'd,* 9 F.3d 623 (7th Cir. 1993).
12   *Trust U/W Emily Oblinger v. Commissioner,* 100 T.C. 114 (1993).
13   *Id.* at 118.
14   *Id.*
15   *Id.* at 118–119.
16   *Id.* at 119.
17   See LAB 1, Chapter 6.
18   E.g., Priv. Ltr. Rul. 9608039.
19   See LAB 1, Q 1:19.
20   Rev. Rul. 98-15, 1998-12 I.R.B. 6.
21   E.g., Priv. Ltr. Rul. 8338127.
22   Priv. Ltr. Rul. 8938001.
23   See LAB 1, Chapter 3.
24   See Hyatt and Hopkins, *The Law of Tax-Exempt Healthcare Organizations* (New York: John Wiley & Sons, 1995), Chapter 22.
25   See Sanders, *Partnerships and Joint Ventures Involving Tax-Exempt Organizations* (New York: John Wiley & Sons, 1994).
26   Priv. Ltr. Rul. 7820058.
27   Priv. Ltr. Rul. 7952002.
28   *Plumstead Theatre Society, Inc. v. Commissioner,* 74 T.C. 1324 (1980), *aff'd,* 675 F.2d 244 (9th Cir. 1982).
29   Gen. Couns. Mem. 39005.
30   Gen. Couns. Mem. 39862.
31   *Id.* Also Rev. Rul 98-15, *supra* note 20.
32   E.g., *Butler v. Commissioner,* 36 T.C. 1097 (1961).
33   Rev. Rul 98-15, *supra* note 20.
34   Priv. Ltr. Rul. 8541108.
35   Gen. Couns. Mem. 39444.
36   Priv. Ltr. Rul. 9438030.
37   IRS Audit Guidelines for Hospitals, Manual Transmittal 7(10)69-38 for *Exempt Organizations Examinations Guidelines Handbook* (Mar. 27, 1992).
38   Rev. Rul 98-15, *supra* note 20.
39   Gen. Couns. Mem. 39732.
40   The efficacy of this rule was never clear: under general partnership law, a person is either a general partner or not.
41   Gen. Couns. Mems. 39005, 39444, 39546, 39732.
42   Rev. Rul 98-15, *supra* note 20.
43   IRC § 512(c)(1).
44   IRC § 168(h)(6)(A)(i).

45   See Hopkins, "Tax Consequences of a Charity's Participation as a General Partner in a Limited Partnership Venture: A Commentary on the McGovern Analysis," 30 *Tax Notes* 361 (1986), written in response to McGovern, "The Tax Consequences of a Charity's Participation as a General Partner in a Limited Partnership Venture," 29 *Tax Notes* 1261 (1985).

46   IRC § 512(c)(1).

47   E.g., *Service Bolt & Nut Co. Profit Sharing Trust v. Commissioner,* 724 F.2d 519 (6th Cir. 1983).

48   IRC § 469(k)(2).

49   Former IRC § 512(c)(2).

50   See LAB 1, Chapter 6.

51   Priv. Ltr. Rul. 8817039.

52   Priv. Ltr. Rul. 8521055.

53   Priv. Ltr. Rul. 8833038.

54   E.g., Priv. Ltr. Rul. 9249026.

55   E.g., Priv. Ltr. Rul. 9637050.

56   *United States v. Myra Foundation,* 382 F.2d 107 (8th Cir. 1967).

57   See LAB 1, Q 10:24.

58   *Id.,* Q 10:25.

59   E.g., *Sierra Club, Inc. v. Commissioner,* 103 T.C. 307 (1994).

60   Gen. Couns. Mem. 39862.

61   Rev. Rul 98-15, *supra* note 20.

62   A favorable ruling concerning use of a management contract is Priv. Ltr. Rul. 9715031.

63   This issue is currently in litigation (*Redlands Surgical Services v. Commissioner* (Tax Ct. 11025-97X)). Cf. Priv. Ltr. Rul. 9709014.

64   IRC § 6031(b).

65   Temp. Reg. § 1.6031(b)-1T.

66   IRC § 6031(d).

67   IRC § 6031. E.g., Priv. Ltr. Rul. 8925092.

CHAPTER 4

1   See Hopkins, *The Law of Tax-Exempt Organizations,* 7th ed. (New York: John Wiley & Sons, 1998), Appendix C.

2   IRC § 501(e).

3   *HCSC-Laundry v. United States,* 450 U.S. 1 (1981).

4   IRC § 501(m).

5   IRC § 501(c)(20) (exemption expired as to years after July 1, 1992).

6   *Maryland Savings-Share Insurance Corporation v. United States,* 400 U.S. 4 (1970).

7   IRC § 501(c)(14)(B), (C).

8   IRC § 501(c)(18).

9   IRC § 501(c)(27)(A).

10   IRC § 501(c)(23).

11   Reg. §§ 601.201(a)(1), 601.201(d)(1).

12   That is, organizations described in IRC § 501(c)(3).

13   IRC § 508(a).

14   That is, entities described in IRC § 501(c)(9), (17), and (20).

15   IRC § 505(c)(1).

16   IRS Revenue Procedure (Rev. Proc.) 90-27, 1990-1 C.B. 514.

17   Reg. § 601.201(a)(3).

18   Reg. § 601.201(a)(2).

19   Reg. § 1.501(a)-1(a)(2).

20   This rule is inherent in the previously cited regulation and is stated in determination letters and rulings issued by the IRS.

21   Reg. § 601.201(n)(1)(ii).
22   Reg. § 601.201(n)(1)(ii); Rev. Proc. 90-27, *supra* note 16 § 5.02.
23   Reg. § 601.201(n)(1)(ii).
24   *Pius XII Academy, Inc. v. Commissioner,* 43 T.C.M. 634, 636 (1982).
25   *Id.*
26   *Public Industries, Inc. v. Commissioner,* 61 T.C.M. 1626, 1629 (1991).
27   *National Association of American Churches v. Commissioner,* 82 T.C. 18, 32 (1984).
28   Rev. Proc. 90-27, *supra* note 16 § 5.02.
29   E.g., *The Church of the Visible Intelligence That Governs the Universe v. United States,* 83-2 U.S.T.C. ¶ 9726 (Ct. Cl. 1983).
30   *American Science Foundation v. Commissioner,* 52 T.C.M. 1049, 1051 (1986).
31   E.g., *New Concordia Bible Church v. Commissioner,* 49 T.C.M. 176 (1984).
32   Rev. Proc. 90-27, *supra* note 16 § 5.02.
33   *Id.* §§ 5.05, 5.06.
34   Rev. Proc. 98-8, 1998-1 I.R.B. 225.
35   Reg. § 601.201(n)(2)(ii); Rev. Proc. 90-27, *supra* note 16 § 6.02.
36   Reg. § 601.201(n)(2)(iv); Rev. Proc. 98-5, 1998-1 I.R.B. 155.
37   Rev. Proc. 90-27, *supra* note 16 § 6.03.
38   *Id.* § 7.01.
39   See LAB 1, Q 4:15–Q 4:23.
40   Reg. § 1.501(h)-3(d)(1).
41   Reg. § 601.201(n)(3)(i); Rev. Proc. 90-27, *supra* note 16 § 13.01.
42   Rev. Proc. 90-27, *supra* note 16 § 13.01.
43   Reg. § 601.201(n)(3)(ii); Rev. Proc. 90-27, *supra* note 16 § 13.02.
44   See LAB 1, Chapters 4 and 5.
45   *Id.* Chapter 6.
46   IRC §§ 508(a)(2), 508(d)(2)(B); Reg. § 1.508-2.
47   Reg. § 1.508-1(a)(2)(i).
48   Rev. Proc. 92-85, 1992-2 C.B. 490 § 4.01.
49   *Id.* § 5.01.
50   Reg. § 1.9100-1.
51   Rev. Proc. 92-85, *supra* note 48, modified by Rev. Proc. 93-28, 1993-2 C.B. 344.
52   Rev. Rul. 80-108, 1980-1 C.B. 119.
53   IRC § 508(c)(1), (2); Reg. § 1.508-1(a)(3)(i)(A).
54   IRC § 508(c)(1).
55   Reg. § 1.508-1(a)(3)(ii).
56   *Id.*
57   IRC § 508(c)(1)(A).
58   See LAB 1, Chapter 6.
59   As to the latter, see IRC § 7428.
60   Rev. Proc. 80-27, 1980-1 C.B. 677.
61   See LAB 1, Q 1:5, Q 3:4.
62   *National Association of American Churches v. Commissioner, supra* note 27.
63   Rev. Proc. 96-40, 1996-2 C.B. 301.
64   Reg. § 1.6033-2(d).
65   Priv. Ltr. Rul. 8337094.
66   Tech. Adv. Mem. 9711004.

CHAPTER 5

1   LAB 1, Q 2:39–Q 2:42.
2   IRC § 501(a).
3   See Chapter 6.
4   See Chapter 7.
5   IRC § 501(c)(6). The private inurement doctrine is the subject of LAB 1, Chapter 3.

6 Reg. § 1.501(c)(6)-1.

7 See LAB 1, Q 10:6.

8 Rev. Rul. 70-641, 1970-2 C.B. 119.

9 Rev. Rul. 67-264, 1967-2 C.B. 196.

10 E.g., *American Kennel Club, Inc. v. Hoey,* 148 F.2d 920 (2d Cir. 1945).

11 Rev. Rul. 77-112, 1977-1 C.B. 149.

12 Reg. § 1.501(c)(6)-1.

13 Rev. Rul. 73-567, 1973-2 C.B. 178.

14 Rev. Rul. 74-147, 1974-1 C.B. 136.

15 Rev. Rul. 74-553, 1974-2 C.B. 168.

16 Rev. Rul. 75-287, 1975-2 C.B. 211.

17 Rev. Rul. 76-400, 1976-2 C.B. 153.

18 Rev. Rul. 82-138, 1982-2 C.B. 106.

19 Rev. Rul. 59-391, 1959-2 C.B. 151.

20 *American Automobile Association v. Commissioner,* 19 T.C. 1146 (1953).

21 E.g., Rev. Rul. 69-632, 1969-2 C.B. 120.

22 *National Muffler Dealers Association v. United States,* 440 U.S. 472 (1979).

23 *Guide International Corporation v. United States,* 948 F.2d 360 (7th Cir. 1991); *National Prime Users Group, Inc. v. United States,* 667 F. Supp. 250 (D. Md. 1987); Rev. Rul. 83-164, 1983-2 C.B. 95. Cf. Rev. Rul. 74-147, *supra,* note 14.

24 Rev. Rul. 58-294, 1958-1 C.B. 244.

25 Rev. Rul. 67-77, 1967-1 C.B. 138.

26 E.g., *Crooks v. Kansas City Hay Dealers Association,* 37 F.2d 83 (8th Cir. 1929); *Associated Industries of Cleveland v. Commissioner,* 7 T.C. 1449 (1946); *Washington State Apples, Inc. v. Commissioner,* 46 B.T.A. 64 (1942).

27 Rev. Rul. 76-410, 1976-2 C.B. 155.

28 Rev. Rul. 72-211, 1972-1 C.B. 150.

29 Rev. Rul. 71-504, 1971-2 C.B. 231.

30 Rev. Rul. 71-505, 1971-2 C.B. 232.

31 Gen. Couns. Mem. 39721.

32 See LAB 1, Q 4:27–Q 4:31.

33 *Id.,* Q 5:20.

34 *Northwestern Jobbers' Credit Bureau v. Commissioner,* 37 F.2d 880 (8th Cir. 1930).

35 Rev. Rul. 67-251, 1967-2 C.B. 196.

36 *National Chiropractic Association, Inc. v. Birmingham,* 96 F. Supp. 874 (N.D. Iowa 1951).

37 *Wholesale Grocers Exchange, Inc. v. Commissioner,* 3 T.C.M. 699 (1944).

38 *Crooks v. Kansas City Hay Dealers Association, supra* note 26.

39 Rev. Rul. 81-60, 1981-1 C.B. 335.

40 Rev. Rul. 77-206, 1977-1 C.B. 149.

41 Rev. Rul. 81-175, 1981-1 C.B. 337.

42 *Associated Master Barbers and Beauticians of America, Inc. v. Commissioner,* 69 T.C. 53 (1977).

43 Rev. Rul. 81-174, 1981-1 C.B. 335.

44 Rev. Rul. 81-175, *supra* note 41.

45 *Engineers Club of San Francisco v. United States,* 791 F.2d 686 (9th Cir. 1986).

46 *MIB, Inc. v. Commissioner,* 734 F.2d 71 (1st Cir. 1984).

47 Rev. Rul. 64-315, 1964-2 C.B. 147.

48 Rev. Rul. 65-14, 1965-1 C.B. 236.

49 *Automotive Electric Association v. Commissioner,* 168 F.2d 366 (6th Cir. 1948).

50 Rev. Rul. 55-444, 1955-2 C.B. 258.

51 *Washington State Apples, Inc. v. Commissioner, supra* note 26.

52 Rev. Rul. 72-211, *supra* note 28.

53 *Professional Insurance Agents of Michigan v. Commissioner,* 726 F.2d 1097, 1104 (6th Cir. 1984).

54 *Id.*
55 Priv. Ltr. Rul. 8524006.
56 Rev. Rul. 72-211, *supra* note 28.
57 Rev. Rul. 56-84, 1956-1 C.B. 201.
58 Rev. Rul. 57-453, 1957-2 C.B. 310.
59 *Apartment Operations Association v. Commissioner,* 136 F.2d 435 (9th Cir. 1943); *Uniform Printing & Supply Co. v. Commissioner,* 33 F.2d 445 (7th Cir. 1939); *Indiana Retail Hardware Association, Inc. v. United States,* 366 F.2d 998 (Ct. Cl. 1966); Rev. Rul. 66-338, 1966-2 C.B. 226.
60 Rev. Rul. 68-264, 1968-1 C.B. 264.
61 *.Florists Telegraph Delivery Association, Inc. v. Commissioner,* 47 B.T.A. 1044 (1942).
62 Rev. Rul. 67-176, 1967-1 C.B. 140.
63 *United States v. Oklahoma City Retailers Association,* 331 F.2d 328 (10th Cir. 1964); Rev. Rul. 68-265, 1968-1 C.B. 265.
64 Rev. Rul. 71-175, 1971-1 C.B. 153.
65 Rev. Rul. 70-591, 1970-2 C.B. 118.
66 Rev. Rul. 76-409, 1976-2 C.B. 154.
67 Rev. Rul. 65-164, 1965-1 C.B. 238.
68 Rev. Rul. 66-260, 1966-2 C.B. 225.
69 Rev. Rul. 69-634, 1969-2 C.B. 124.
70 Rev. Rul. 55-715, 1955-2 C.B. 263.
71 Rev. Rul. 69-387, 1969-2 C.B. 124.
72 Tech. Adv. Mem. 9550001.
73 *Washington State Apples, Inc. v. Commissioner, supra* note 26.
74 *American Plywood Association v. United States,* 267 F. Supp. 830 (W.D. Wash. 1967).
75 Rev. Rul. 70-80, 1980-1 C.B. 130.
76 IRC § 501(c)(5).
77 E.g., Rev. Rul. 67-252, 1967-2 C.B. 195.
78 Rev. Rul. 70-31, 1970-1 C.B. 130.
79 *Engineers Club of San Francisco v. United States, supra* note 45.
80 IRC § 4958(e). A business league can be a *disqualified person* with respect to a public charity if it is in a position to exercise substantial influence over the affairs of the charitable organization (IRC § 4958(f)(1)(A)). The same is true with respect to the private inurement doctrine (see *supra* note 5), where a business league may be an *insider* with respect to a charitable organization if it is in a position to exercise substantial control over the charitable organization (*United Cancer Council, Inc. v. Commissioner,* 109 T.C. 326 (1997)).
81 IRC § 6033(a)(1).
82 IRS Announcement (Ann.) 82-88, 1982-25 I.R.B. 23.
83 Priv. Ltr. Rul. 9141050.
84 IRC § 277.
85 IRC § 513(c).
86 IRC § 501(c)(6).
87 Rev. Rul. 78-51, 1978-1 C.B. 165.
88 Rev. Rul. 66-338, 1966-2 C.B. 226.
89 Rev. Rul. 66-151, 1966-1 C.B. 152.
90 Rev. Rul. 74-81, 1974-1 C.B. 135.
91 Tech. Adv. Mem. 8524006.
92 Rev. Rul. 82-139, 1982-2 C.B. 108.
93 Priv. Ltr. Rul. 7902006.
94 *Texas Apartment Association v. United States,* 869 F.2d 884 (5th Cir. 1989).
95 Rev. Rul. 66-151, *supra* note 89.
96 *Professional Insurance Agents of Michigan v. Commissioner, supra* note 53.
97 *American Academy of Family Physicians v. United States,* 91 F.3d 1155 (8th Cir. 1996).

98 The IRS ruled to the contrary in Priv. Ltr. Rul. 9029047.

99 *Independent Insurance Agents of Northern Nevada, Inc. v. United States,* 79-2 U.S.T.C. ¶ 9601 (D. Nev. 1979).

100 *National League of Postmasters v. Commissioner,* 86 F.3d 59 (4th Cir. 1996).

101 Rev. Proc. 95-21, 1995-1 C.B. 686.

102 IRC § 512(d).

103 Rev. Proc. 97-12, 1997-1 C.B. 631.

104 Federal Election Commission Advisory Opinion 1984-12.

105 *American Bar Association v. United States,* 84-1 U.S.T.C. ¶ 9179 (N.D. Ill. 1984); Rev. Rul. 58-293, 1958-1 C.B. 146.

106 IRC § 501(c)(3).

107 IRC § 509(a)(2). See LAB 1, Q 6:8.

108 IRC § 509(a)(1). See LAB 1, Q 6:7.

109 IRC § 509(a)(3). See LAB 1, Q 6:15, Q 6:22.

110 IRC § 527. See Chapter 9.

111 LAB 1, Q 5:16–Q 5:23.

112 LAB 1, Chapter 11.

113 E.g., Tech. Adv. Mem. 9338003; Priv. Ltr. Rul. 9506046.

114 IRC § 318

115 IRC § 501(c)(2).

CHAPTER 6

1 LAB 1, Q 2:39–Q 2:42.

2 IRC § 501(a).

3 IRC § 170.

4 Reg. § 1.501(c)(4)-1(a)(2)(ii).

5 Reg. § 1.501(c)(4)-1(a)(2)(ii).

6 *Id.*

7 Reg. § 1.501(c)(4)-1(a)(2)(i).

8 *New York State Association of Real Estate Boards Group Insurance Fund v. Commissioner,* 54 T.C. 1325 (1970).

9 *People's Educational Camp Society, Inc. v. Commissioner,* 331 F.2d 923 (2d Cir. 1964), *aff'g* 39 T.C. 756 (1963), *cert. den.,* 379 U.S. 839 (1964).

10 *Id.* at 932.

11 Rev. Rul. 65-299, 1965-2 C.B. 165.

12 Rev. Rul. 78-50, 1978-1 C.B. 155.

13 Rev. Rul. 66-148, 1966-1 C.B. 143.

14 See *infra* note 25.

15 Rev. Rul. 72-102, 1972-1 C.B. 149, modified by Rev. Rul. 76-147, 1976-1 C.B. 151.

16 Rev. Rul. 74-99, 1974-1 C.B. 131.

17 *Id.*

18 *Id.*

19 Rev. Rul. 75-286, 1975-2 C.B. 210.

20 Rev. Rul. 75-386, 1975-2 C.B. 211.

21 Rev. Rul. 80-63, 1980-1 C.B. 116.

22 E.g., *Flat Top Lake Association, Inc. v. United States,* 86-2 U.S.T.C. ¶ 9756 (S.D. W. Va. 1986); *Lake Petersburg Association v. Commissioner,* 33 T.C.M. 259 (1974).

23 *Rancho Sante Fe Association v. United States,* 84-2 U.S.T.C. ¶ 9536 (S.D. Cal. 1984).

24 Rev. Rul. 74-17, 1974-1 C.B. 130.

25 IRC § 528.

26 *Eden Hall Farm v. United States,* 389 F. Supp. 858 (W.D. Penn. 1975).

27 *Id.* at 866.

28 Rev. Rul. 80-205, 1980-2 C.B. 184.

29 Rev. Rul. 66-273, 1966-2 C.B. 222.

30 Rev. Rul. 67-294, 1967-2 C.B. 193.

31 Rev. Rul. 61-153, 1961-2 C.B. 114.

32 Rev. Rul. 78-69, 1978-1 C.B. 156.

33 Rev. Rul. 78-131, 1978-1 C.B. 156.

34 Rev. Rul. 67-109, 1967-1 C.B. 136.

35 Rev. Rul. 65-195, 1965-2 C.B. 164.

36 Rev. Rul. 68-118, 1968-1 C.B. 261.

37 See Chapter 2.

38 *Los Angeles County Remount Association v. Commissioner,* 27 T.C.M. 1035 (1968).

39 The *public policy doctrine* is a rule of law that has been engrafted by the courts onto the statutory criteria for tax exemption by reason of IRC § 501(c)(3). This doctrine requires that the organization "demonstrably serve and be in harmony with the public interest" and have a purpose that is not "so at odds with the common community conscience as to undermine any public benefit that might otherwise be conferred" (*Bob Jones University v. United States,* 461 U.S. 574, 591-592 (1983) (holding that racial discrimination in private education is contrary to public policy and that the IRS has the authority to determine what is *public policy*)).

40 Rev. Rul. 75-384, 1975-2 C.B. 204.

41 Rev. Rul. 70-535, 1970-2 C.B. 117.

42 Rev. Rul. 77-273, 1977-2 C.B. 195.

43 *Club Gaona, Inc. v. United States,* 167 F. Supp. 741 (S.D. Cal. 1958).

44 Rev. Rul. 78-429, 1978-2 C.B. 178.

45 See LAB 1, Chapter 3.

46 IRC § 501(c)(4)(B), added by § 1311(b) of the Taxpayer Bill of Rights 2 (P.L. 104-168, 104th Cong., 2d Sess. (1996)).

47 Taxpayer Bill of Rights 2, *supra* note 46, § 1311(d)(3)(B).

48 Rev. Rul. 69-385, 1969-2 C.B. 123.

49 *Consumer-Farmer Milk Cooperative v. Commissioner,* 186 F.2d 68 (2d Cir. 1950), *aff'g* 13 T.C. 150 (1949), *cert. den.,* 341 U.S. 931 (1951).

50 *Mutual Aid Association of the Church of the Brethren v. United States,* 663 F. Supp. 275 (M.D. Ala. 1987), *aff'd,* 850 F.2d 1510 (11th Cir. 1988).

51 Rev. Rul. 81-58, 1981-1 C.B. 331.

52 *Smyth v. California State Automobile Association,* 175 F.2d 752 (9th Cir. 1949).

53 Rev. Rul. 61-158, 1961-2 C.B. 115.

54 Rev. Rul. 66-360, 1966-2 C.B. 228.

55 Rev. Rul. 73-349, 1973-2 C.B. 179.

56 Rev. Rul. 78-132, 1978-1 C.B. 157.

57 Rev. Rul. 64-313, 1964-2 C.B. 146.

58 Rev. Rul. 57-297, 1957-2 C.B. 307.

59 Rev. Rul. 80-206, 1980-2 C.B. 185.

60 Rev. Rul. 73-306, 1973-2 C.B. 179.

61 Rev. Rul. 79-316, 1979-2 C.B. 228.

62 *Contracting Plumbers Cooperative Restoration   Corporation v. United States,* 488 F.2d 684 (2d Cir. 1973), *cert. den.,* 419 U.S. 827 (1974).

63 IRC § 501(m).

64 That is, organizations described in IRC § 501(c)(3).

65 See LAB 1, Chapter 10.

66 IRC Subchapter L.

67 H. Rep. 99-841, 99th Cong., 2d Sess. II-345 (1986).

68 See Chapter 2.

69 Gen. Couns. Mem. 39829.

70 *Paratransit Insurance Corporation v. Commissioner,* 102 T.C. 745, 754 (1994).

71 Gen. Couns. Mem. 39828.

72 IRC § 501(m)(4).

73 IRC § 501(m)(3).
74 Rev. Rul. 71-529, 1971-2 C.B. 234.
75 IRC § 514(c)(5).
76 IRC §§ 501(m)(3)(E), 501(m)(5).
77 *Paratransit Insurance Corporation v. Commissioner, supra* note 70, at 754.
78 *Nonprofits' Insurance Alliance of California v. United States,* 94-2 U.S.T.C. ¶ 50,593 (Ct. Fed. Cl. 1994).
79 *Florida Hospital Trust Fund v. Commissioner,* 103 T.C. 140, 158 (1994), *aff'd,* 71 F.3d 808 (11th Cir. 1996).
80 This legislation was enacted as part of the Small Business Job Protection Act (P.L. 104-188, 104th Cong., 2d Sess. (1996)).
81 IRC § 501(n).
82 That is, an organization described in IRC § 501(c)(3).
83 Reg. § 1.501(c)(3)-1(d)(2).
84 "A trust is not a charitable trust if the persons who are to benefit are not of a sufficiently large or indefinite class so that the community is interested in the enforcement of the trust" (4A Scott, *Scott on Trusts* § 372.2 at 2897).
85 Reg. § 1.501(c)(3)-1(d)(2).
86 Rev. Rul. 55-439, 1955-2 C.B. 257.
87 Rev. Rul. 64-187, 1964-1 (Part 1) C.B. 187.
88 Rev. Rul. 57-297, 1957-2 C.B. 307.
89 *Industrial Addition Association v. Commissioner,* 1 T.C. 378 (1942), aff'd, 149 F.2d 294 (6th Cir. 1945).
90 *Sound Health Association v. Commissioner,* 71 T.C. 158, 185 (1978).
91 *Geisinger Health Plan v. Commissioner,* 985 F.2d 1210, 1219 (3d Cir. 1993).
92 *Id.* at 1220.
93 See LAB 1, Q 1:1.
94 See LAB 1, Chapter 3.
95 Rev. Rul. 74-361, 1974-2 C.B. 159.
96 See LAB 1, Q 4:24.
97 Rev. Rul. 68-656, 1968-2 C.B. 216.
98 *Id.*
99 Reg. § 1.501(c)(4)-1(a)(2)(ii).
100 Rev. Rul. 81-95, 1981-1 C.B. 332.
101 Rev. Rul. 69-281, 1969-1 C.B. 155.
102 *American Women Buyers Club, Inc. v. United States,* 338 F.2d 526 (2d Cir. 1964).
103 Rev. Rul. 66-150, 1966-1 C.B. 147.
104 IRC § 501(c)(19).
105 See LAB 1, Chapter 3.
106 See *supra* note 46.
107 See *supra* note 47.
108 IRC § 4958(e)(1).
109 IRC § 6033(a)(1).
110 IRS Ann. 82-88, 1982-25 I.R.B. 23.
111 See Q 11:5.
112 Rev. Rul. 80-108, 1980-1 C.B. 119.
113 IRC § 6113.
114 IRS Notice 88-120, 1988-2 C.B. 454.
115 That is, is described in IRC § 501(c) (other than IRC § 501(c)(3)).
116 That is, an organization that is described in IRC § 527(e)(1). See Chapter 8.
117 IRS Notice 88-120, *supra* note 114.
118 *Id.*
119 *Id.*
120 IRC § 6710.
121 H. Rep. 100-391, 100th Cong., 1st Sess. 1608 (1987)).

122 See Q 13:19–13:20.
123 IRC § 501(m)(2)(A).
124 See LAB 1, Chapter 10.
125 IRC Subchapter L (IRC § 501(m)(2)(B)).
126 That is, activities described in IRC § 501(c)(3).
127 See LAB 1, Q 5:19, Q 5:21.
128 Priv. Ltr. Ruls. 9725036 and 9652026.

CHAPTER 7

1 LAB 1, Q 2:39–Q 2:42.
2 IRC § 501(a).
3 This is likewise the case with respect to political organizations (Q 8:12).
4 See LAB 1, Chapter 10.
5 That is, purposes embraced by 170(c)(4) (essentially, those referenced in IRC § 501(c)(3)).
6 IRC § 512(a)(3)(B)(i).
7 *Slocum v. Bowers,* 15 F. Supp. 400, 404 (S.D.N.Y. 1926).
8 *Broadcast Measurement Bureau, Inc. v. Commissioner,* 16 T.C. 988, 997 (1951).
9 *Id.* at 997, 1000.
10 *Id.* at 1001.
11 *Id.*
12 *Phi Delta Theta Fraternity v. Commissioner,* 887 F.2d 1302 (6th Cir. 1989), *aff'g* 90 T.C. 1033 (1988).
13 See LAB 1, Chapter 3.
14 Rev. Rul. 70-48, 1970-1 C.B. 133.
15 Rev. Rul. 80-130, 1980-1 C.B. 117.
16 Rev. Rul. 69-68, 1969-1 C.B. 153.
17 IRC § 274(a)(3).
18 Reg. § 1.274-2(a)(2)(iii)(a).
19 *Barstow Rodeo and Riding Club v. Commissioner,* 12 T.C.M. 1351 (1953).
20 Rev. Rul. 58-589, 1958-2 C.B. 266.
21 *Arner v. Rogan,* 40-2 U.S.T.C. ¶ 9567 (S.D. Cal. 1940).
22 Rev. Rul. 69-635, 1969-2 C.B. 126. E.g., *Warren Automobile Club v. Commissioner,* 182 F.2d 551 (6th Cir. 1950).
23 E.g., Rev. Rul. 69-281, 1969-1 C.B. 155.
24 Rev. Rul. 66-179, 1966-1 C.B. 139.
25 Rev. Rul. 73-520, 1973-2 C.B. 180.
26 Rev. Rul. 69-573, 1969-2 C.B. 125. E.g., *Alumnae Chapter Beta of Clovia v. Commissioner,* 46 T.C. 297 (1983).
27 Rev. Rul. 67-139, 1967-1 C.B. 129.
28 Rev. Rul. 74-30, 1974-1 C.B. 137. E.g., *Syrang Aero Club, Inc. v. Commissioner,* 73 T.C. 717 (1980).
29 Rev. Rul. 70-32, 1970-1 C.B. 140.
30 Rev. Rul. 68-266, 1968-1 C.B. 270.
31 Rev. Rul. 67-8, 1967-1 C.B. 142.
32 *McGlotten v. Connally,* 338 F. Supp. 448, 458 (D.D.C. 1972).
33 Reg. § 1.501(c)(7)-1(a).
34 "Tax Reform Studies and Proposals," Department of the Treasury (Comm. Print), 91st Cong., 1st Sess. 317 (1969).
35 *Portland Golf Club v. Commissioner,* 497 U.S. 154, 161 (1990).
36 *Id.* at 161–162 (emphasis in original).
37 *Id.* at 163 (emphasis in original).
38 E.g., *Scofield v. Corpus Christi Golf and Country Club,* 127 F.2d 452 (5th Cir. 1942).
39 S. Rep. No. 91-552, 91st Cong., 1st Sess. 71 (1969).

40 See Chapter 2.

41 E.g., *Polish American Club, Inc. v. Commissioner,* 33 T.C.M. 925 (1974).

42 Rev. Proc. 71-17, 1971-1 C.B. 683.

43 E.g., Rev. Rul. 60-324, 1960-2 C.B. 173.

44 E.g., Rev. Rul. 60-323, 1960-2 C.B. 173.

45 See LAB 1, Chapter 10.

46 *Pittsburgh Press Club v. United States,* 388 F. Supp. 1269, 1276 (W.D. Pa. 1975).

47 Rev. Rul. 74-168, 1974-1 C.B. 139.

48 Rev. Rul. 67-428, 1967-2 C.B. 204.

49 Rev. Rul. 74-489, 1974-2 C.B. 169.

50 Gen. Couns. Mem. 39343.

51 E.g., H. Rep. No. 94-1353, 94th Cong., 2d Sess. 4 (1976).

52 E.g., *Santee Club v. White,* 87 F.2d 5 (1st Cir. 1936).

53 *West Side Tennis Club v. United States,* 111 F.2d 6 (2d Cir. 1940).

54 Priv. Ltr. Rul. 7838108.

55 Gen Couns. Mem. 39115.

56 Rev. Rul. 69-527, 1969-2 C.B. 125.

57 Rev. Rul. 68-535, 1968-2 C.B. 219.

58 Rev. Rul. 68-168, 1968-1 C.B. 269.

59 Rev. Rul. 66-225, 1966-2 C.B. 227.

60 IRC § 501(i).

61 Priv. Ltr. Rul. 8317004.

62 Rev. Rul. 69-527, *supra* note 56.

63 See Q 1:5.

64 See Q 1:14.

65 IRC § 6033(a).

66 Ann. 82-88, 1982-25 I.R.B. 23.

67 IRS Notice 88-120, 1988-2 C.B. 454.

68 IRC § 6113(a).

69 IRC § 542(a).

70 Tech. Adv. Mem. 9728004.

71 IRC § 542(c)(1).

72 IRC § 170(c). Nonetheless, gifts made to an exempt social club are eligible for the annual $10,000 exclusion from the federal gift tax (Priv. Ltr. Rul. 9818042).

73 Rev. Rul. 55-192, 1955-1 C.B. 294.

74 See LAB 1, Chapter 10.

75 IRC § 512(a)(3)(A).

76 *Council of British Societies in Southern California v. United States,* 78-2 U.S.T.C. ¶ 9744 (C.D. Cal. 1978), *aff'd,* 587 F.2d 931 (9th Cir. 1978).

77 IRC § 512(a)(3)(B).

78 *Ye Mystic Krewe of Gasparilla v. Commissioner,* 80 T.C. 755 (1983).

79 *Portland Golf Club v. Commissioner,* supra note 35.

80 See LAB 1, Chapter 10.

81 IRC § 512(a)(3)(D).

82 E.g., Priv. Ltr. Rul. 8337092.

83 See LAB 1, Q 6:7–Q 6:14.

84 *Id.,* Q 6:15–Q 6:29.

85 IRC § 512(b)(13).

86 IRC § 512(b)(13)(D).

87 That is, an organization described in IRC § 501(c)(2) or (25).

88 IRC § 509(a), last sentence.

CHAPTER 8

1 IRC § 527(e)(1).

2 IRC § 527(e)(3).

3   IRC § 527(e)(4).
4   Tech. Adv. Mem. 9812001.
5   IRC § 527(e)(2).
6   See LAB 1, Chapter 5.
7   Reg. § 52.4946-1(g)(2).
8   IRC § 527(h).
9   See Hopkins, *The Law of Tax-Exempt Organizations, 7th ed.* (New York: John Wiley & Sons, 1998), Chapter 25.
10 IRC § 527(g)(1).
11 IRC § 527(g)(2).
12 IRC § 527(g)(3).
13 See LAB 1, Chapter 5.
14 Reg. § 1.527-2(c)(1).
15 *Id.*
16 Priv. Ltr. Rul. 9652026.
17 Rev. Rul. 79-13, 1979-1 C.B. 208
18 Rev. Rul. 87-119, 1987-2 C.B. 151.
19 *Id.*
20 Priv. Ltr. Rul. 9516006.
21 See LAB 1, Chapter 4.
22 E.g., Priv. Ltr. Rul. 9652026.
23 Reg. §§ 1.527-2(c)(5)(iii), 1.527-2(c)(5)(v).
24 See LAB 1, Q 10:1.
25 Reg. § 1.527-2(a)(3).
26 *Id.*
27 See LAB 1, Chapter 4.
28 E.g., Priv. Ltr. Rul. 9244003.
29 Rev. Rul. 87-119, *supra* note 18.
30 Reg. § 1.527-5(a)(1).
31 IRC § 2501(a)(5).
32 IRC § 527(a).
33 IRC § 527(b).
34 IRC § 527(b)(1).
35 IRC § 527(c)(1).
36 IRC § 527(c)(2)(A).
37 IRC § 527(c)(2)(B).
38 IRC § 527(c)(3).
39 Reg. § 1.527-3(d)(2).
40 Rev. Rul. 80-103, 1980-1 C.B. 120.
41 Gen. Couns. Mem. 39877.
42 Reg. § 1.527-5(c)(1).
43 *Id.*
44 IRC § 527(d).
45 See LAB 1, Chapter 6.
46 E.g., Priv. Ltr. Rul. 9425032.
47 IRC § 527(b)(1).
48 IRC § 11(b)(1)(D).
49 IRC § 527(f)(2).
50 IRC § 527(f)(1).
51 See LAB 1, Chapter 10.
52 IRC § 527(f)(2).
53 Reg. § 1.527-6(g).
54 Rev. Rul. 81-95, 1981-1 C.B. 332.
55 See Hopkins, *Charity, Advocacy, and the Law* (New York: John Wiley & Sons, 1992), Chapter 18.

56 See LAB 1, Chapter 5.
57 IRC § 4955.
58 E.g., Tech. Adv. Mem. 9812001.
59 That is, organizations described in IRC § 501(c)(5).
60 Priv. Ltr. Ruls. 9725036, 9652026.
61 See LAB 1, Q 4:26.
62 IRC § 527(f)(3).
63 Ann. 88-114, 1988-37 I.R.B. 26.
64 E.g., *Alaska Public Service Employees Local 71 v. Commissioner,* 67 T.C.M. 1664 (1991).
65 Reg. § 1.527-6(e).
66 Reg. § 1.527-6(e)(3).
67 FEC Advisory Opinion 1984-12.

CHAPTER 9

1   That is, an organization described in IRC § 501(c)(3).
2   IRC § 509(a). In the second sentence of LAB 1, Q 6:2, change "private foundations" to "public charities."
3   See LAB 1, Q 2:6.
4   IRC § 509(a)(1).
5   IRC §§ 170(b)(1)(A)(vi), 509(a)(1).
6   IRC § 509(a)(2).
7   IRC § 509(a)(3).
8   In LAB 1, Q 6:7, change "$167,000" to "$134,000."
9   IRC § 4946(a).
10 IRC § 4946(a)(1)(A); Reg. § 53.4946-1(a)(1)(i).
11 IRC §§ 4946(a)(2), 507(d)(2).
12 IRC § 507(d)(2)(A).
13 Reg. § 1.507-6(a)(1).
14 *Id.*
15 That is, organizations encompassed by IRC § 501(a).
16 That is, entities described in IRC § 170(c)(1).
17 *Rockefeller v. United States,* 572 F. Supp. 9 (E.D. Ark. 1982), *aff'd,* 718 F.2d 290 (8th Cir. 1983), *cert. den.,* 466 U.S. 962 (1984).
18 IRC § 507(d)(2)(B)(iv).
19 Reg. § 1.507-6(b)(1).
20 IRC § 507(d)(2)(C).
21 IRC § 507(d)(2)(C)(i)(III).
22 IRC § 507(d)(2)(C)(ii).
23 IRC §§ 170(b)(1)(D)(iii), 507(d)(1), 508(d), 509(a)(1), 509(a)(3), and IRC Chapter 42.
24 Reg. § 1.507-6(a)(2).
25 Reg. § 1.507-6(b)(i).
26 IRC § 507(d)(2)(B)(i)-(iii).
27 IRC § 4946(a)(1)(B); Reg. § 53.4946-1(f)(1).
28 IRC § 4946(b)(1).
29 Reg. § 53.4946-1(f)(1).
30 Reg. § 53.4946-1(f)(2).
31 E.g., Priv. Ltr. Rul. 9535043.
32 IRC § 4946(a)(1)(C).
33 IRC § 4946(a)(1)(C)(i).
34 See IRC § 4946(a)(3).
35 Reg. § 53.4946-1(a)(5).
36 Reg. § 53.4946-1(a)(6).
37 IRC § 4946(a)(1)(C)(ii).

38 IRC §§ 707(b)(3), 4946(a)(4).
39 Reg. § 53.4946-1(a)(6).
40 IRC § 4946(a)(1)(C)(iii).
41 Reg. § 53.4946-1(a)(3).
42 Reg. § 53.4946-1(a)(4).
43 Reg. § 53.4946-1(a)(6).
44 IRC § 4946(a)(1)(D).
45 IRC § 4946(d).
46 Reg. § 53.4946-1(h).
47 *Id.*
48 *Id.*
49 IRC § 4946(a)(3).
50 IRC § 4946(a)(1)(E).
51 IRC § 4946(a)(4).
52 IRC § 4946(a)(1)(F).
53 IRC § 4946(a)(4).
54 IRC § 4946(a)(1)(G).
55 IRC § 4946(a)(1)(H).
56 Reg. § 1.482-1(a)(3).
57 Reg. § 53.4946-1(b)(1).
58 Reg. § 53.4946-1(b)(2).
59 IRC § 4946(a)(1)(I).
60 IRC § 4946(c).
61 Reg. § 53.4946-1(g)(2).
62 Priv. Ltr. Rul. 9804040.
63 IRC §§ 4941(a), 4942(a), 4943(a), 4944(a), 4945(a).
64 IRC §§ 4941(b), 4942(b), 4943(b), 4944(b), 4945(b).
65 IRC § 507(a)(2).
66 IRC § 4962(a).
67 IRC § 4962(b).
68 IRC § 4961.
69 IRC § 4941.
70 Reg. § 53.4941(d)-1(b).
71 IRC § 4941(d)(1)(A); Reg. § 53.4941(d)-2(a)(1).
72 IRC § 4941(d)(2)(A); Reg. § 53.4941(d)-2(a)(2).
73 IRC § 4941(d)(1)(A); Reg. § 53.4941(d)-2(b)(1).
74 IRC § 4941(d)(1)(B); Reg. § 53.4941(d)-2(c)(1).
75 IRC § 4941(d)(1)(C); Reg. § 53.4941(d)-2(d)(1).
76 IRC § 4941(d)(1)(D); Reg. § 53.4941(d)-2(e).
77 IRC § 4941(d)(1)(E); Reg. § 53.4941(d)-2(f)(1).
78 Gen. Couns. Mem. 39107.
79 Gen. Couns. Mem. 39632.
80 Priv. Ltr. Rul. 9726006.
81 IRC § 4941(d)(1)(F); Reg. § 53.4941(d)-2(g).
82 Reg. § 53.4941(d)-2(b)(2).
83 IRC § 4941(d)(2)(B); Reg. § 53.4941(d)-2(c)(2).
84 IRC § 4941(d)(2)(C); Reg. § 53.4941(d)-2(d)(3).
85 IRC § 4941(d)(2)(D); Reg. § 53.4941(d)-3(b).
86 IRC § 4941(d)(2)(E); Reg. § 53.4941(d)-3(c).
87 *Madden v. Commissioner,* 74 T.C.M. 440 (1997).
88 Reg. § 53.4941(d)-2(f)(2).
89 IRC § 4941(d)(2)(G); Reg. § 53.4941(d)-3(e).
90 IRC § 4941(d)(2)(F); Reg. § 53.4941(d)-3(d).
91 Reg. § 53.4941(d)-3(d)(1).
92 Reg, § 53.4941(e)-1(a)(2).

93 IRC § 4941(e)(2); Reg. § 53.4941(e)-1(b)(1).
94 IRC § 4941(e)(3); Reg. § 53.4941(e)-1(c).
95 IRC § 4941(a)(1); Reg. § 53.4941(a)-1(a)(1).
96 IRC § 4941(a)(2); Reg. § 53.4941(a)-1(b).
97 *Id.*
98 IRC § 4941(c)(2); Reg. § 53.4941(c)-1(b).
99 IRC § 4941(b)(1); Reg. § 53.4941(b)-1(a).
100 IRC § 4941(c)(2); Reg. § 53.4941(c)-1(b).
101 IRC § 4941(b)(2); Reg. § 53.4941(b)-1(b).
102 IRC § 4941(c)(1); Reg. § 53.4941(c)-1(a).
103 IRC § 507(a)(2).
104 IRC § 4942.
105 IRC § 4942(d).
106 IRC § 4942(g)(1); Reg. § 53.4942(a)-3(a), (c).
107 Reg. § 53.4942(a)-2(c)(1), (5).
108 IRC §§ 4942(d)(1), (e)(1)(A); Reg. § 53.4942(a)-2(b)(1).
109 IRC § 4942(d)(1), (f)(2)(C).
110 Reg. § 53.4942(a)-2(c)(3).
111 IRC § 4942(e)(1)(A).
112 Reg. § 53.4942(a)-2(c)(3).
113 Reg. § 53.4942(a)-3(b)(1).
114 Reg. § 53.4942(a)-3(b)(2), (7)(i).
115 IRC § 4942(g)(2).
116 IRC § 4942(a); Reg. § 53.4942(a)-1(a)(1).
117 IRC § 4942(b); Reg. § 53.4942(a)-1(a)(2).
118 *Id.*
119 Reg. § 53.4942(a)-1(a)(3).
120 IRC § 507(a)(2).
121 IRC § 4943.
122 IRC § 4943(c)(2)(A), (3).
123 IRC § 4943(c)(2)(B); Reg. § 53.4943-3(b)(3).
124 IRC § 4943(c)(2)(C); Reg. § 53.4943-3(b)(4).
125 IRC § 4943(d)(3)(B).
126 Reg. § 53.4943-10(c).
127 IRC § 4943(d)(3)(A).
128 IRC § 4942(j)(4); Reg. § 53.4943-10(b).
129 Reg. § 53.4943-10(b).
130 IRC § 4943(c)(6); Reg. § 53.4943-6(a).
131 IRC § 4943(c)(7).
132 IRC § 4943(a)(1); Reg. § 53.4943-2(a)(1).
133 *Id.*
134 IRC § 4943(b); Reg. § 53.4943-2(b).
135 IRC § 507(a)(2).
136 IRC § 4944.
137 IRC § 4944(a)(1).
138 Reg. § 53.4944-1(a)(2)(i).
139 *Id.*
140 E.g., Priv. Ltr. Rul. 9451067.
141 Reg. § 53.4944-1(a)(2)(i).
142 IRC § 4944(c); Reg. § 53.4944-3(a).
143 Reg. § 53.4944-3(a)(1)(iii).
144 IRC § 4944(a)(1); Reg. § 53.4944-1(a)(1).
145 IRC § 4944(a)(2); Reg. § 53.4944-1(b)(1).
146 IRC § 4944(d)(2); Reg. § 53.4944-4(b).
147 IRC § 4944(a)(2); Reg. § 53.4944-1(b)(1).

148 IRC § 4944(b)(1); Reg. § 53.4944-2(a).
149 IRC § 4944(b)(2); Reg. § 53.4944-2(b).
150 IRC § 4944(d)(2); Reg. § 53.4944-4(b).
151 IRC § 4944(d)(1); Reg. § 53.4944-4(a).
152 IRC § 507(a)(2).
153 IRC § 4945.
154 IRC § 4945(d)(1).
155 See LAB 1, Chapter 4.
156 IRC § 4945(e).
157 Reg. § 53.4945-2(a)(1).
158 IRC § 4945(e); Reg. § 53.4945-2(d)(1).
159 IRC § 4945(e)(2); Reg. § 53.4945-2(d)(2).
160 IRC § 4945(e) (last sentence); Reg. § 53.4945-2(d)(3).
161 Reg. § 53.4945-2(d)(4).
162 IRC § 4945(d)(2); Reg. § 53.4945-3(a)(1).
163 Reg. § 53.4945-3(a)(2).
164 IRC § 4945(f); Reg. § 53.4945-3(b).
165 IRC § 4945(d)(3); Reg. § 53.4945-4(a)(1), (2).
166 IRC § 4945(g); Reg. § 53.4945-4(a)(3)(ii).
167 Reg. § 53.4945-4(b)(2).
168 Reg. § 53.4945-4(b)(4).
169 Reg. § 53.4945-4(c)(2), (3).
170 Reg. § 53.4945-4(c)(4).
171 Reg. § 53.4945-4(c)(5).
172 Reg. § 53.4945-4(c)(6).
173 See LAB 1, Chapter 6.
174 IRC § 4945(d)(4); Reg. § 53.4945-5(a).
175 IRC § 4945(h); Reg. § 53.4945-5(b), (d).
176 IRC § 4945(d)(5).
177 Reg. § 53.4945-6(a).
178 See LAB 1, Chapter 3.
179 Reg. § 53.4945-6(b).
180 IRC § 4945(a)(1); Reg. § 53.4945-1(a)(1).
181 IRC § 4945(a)(2).
182 Reg. § 53.4945-1(a)(1).
183 IRC § 4945(b)(1), (i); Reg. § 53.4945-1(b)(1).
184 IRC § 4945(b)(2); Reg. § 53.4945-1(b)(2).
185 IRC § 4945(c)(1); Reg. § 53.4945-1(c)(1).
186 IRC § 4945(c)(2); Reg. § 53.4945-1(c)(2).
187 IRC § 4945(i)(2); Reg. § 53.4945-1(e)(1).
188 IRC § 507(a)(2).
189 IRC § 4940(a); Reg. § 53.4940-1(a).
190 IRC § 6655.
191 IRC § 4940(e)(1).
192 That is, entities described in IRC § 4947(a)(1).
193 That is, entities described in IRC § 4947(a)(2).
194 IRC § 4947.
195 IRC § 4948.
196 IRC § 170(b)(1)(B), (D).
197 IRC § 170(e)(1)(B)(ii), although this rule is somewhat ameliorated by the special treatment accorded qualified appreciated securities (IRC § 170(e)(5)).
198 This is reflected in the recordkeeping and preparation of the private foundation annual information return (Form 990-PF).
199 Abouhalkah, "Foundations are flexing their muscles," *The Kansas City Star,* June 28, 1998.
200 Johnson, "Foundations of Power," *The Sunday Oregonian,* June 21, 1998.

CHAPTER 10

1   That is, organizations described in IRC § 501(c)(3).
2   See LAB 1, Chapter 6.
3   See LAB 1, Chapter 10.
4   IRC § 7701(a)(3); Reg. § 301.7701-2(b). These entities may include *associations* (Reg. §§ 301.7701-2(b)(2), 301.7701-3). Under certain circumstances, an entity may elect to be treated as a corporation for federal tax purposes (Reg. § 301.7701-3(a)). A business trust may be considered a corporation for federal tax purposes (Reg. § 301.7701-4(b)).
5   IRC §§ 301–385.
6   IRC § 1361(a)(2).
7   IRC §§ 1361–1379.
8   IRC § 1362.
9   IRC § 1361(a)(1).
10 IRC § 1361(b)(1)(A), (C), (D).
11 IRC § 1361(b)(1)(B), (c)(6).
12 IRC §§ 761(a), 7701(a)(2).
13 Reg. § 301.7701-2(c)(1).
14 Reg. § 301.7701-1(a)(2).
15 See LAB 1, Chapter 3.
16 *United Cancer Council, Inc. v. Commissioner,* 109 T.C. 326 (1997).
17 Reg. § 301.7701-1(a)(2).
18 *Id.*
19 IRC § 11(a).
20 IRC § 1366.
21 IRC §§ 701, 702.
22 Reg. § 301.7701-3(b).
23 IRC § 316(a).
24 IRC § 512(b)(1).
25 IRC § 512(b)(13).
26 IRC § 512(e)(1)(B)(i).
27 See LAB 1, Q 10:23–Q 10:27.
28 IRC § 512(c)(1).
29 IRC §§ 701, 702.
30 IRC § 512(b)(5).
31 IRC § 514.
32 IRC § 512(b)(4).
33 IRC § 512(e)(1)(B)(ii).
34 IRC §§ 170(e)(1), 751.
35 See Hopkins, *The Tax Law of Charitable Giving* (New York: John Wiley & Sons, 1993), Chapter 6 § 8.
36 See Hyatt and Hopkins, *The Law of Tax-Exempt Healthcare Organizations* (New York: John Wiley & Sons, 1995).
37 See LAB 1, Chapter 11.
38 *Id.,* Q 11:21.
39 Rev. Rul. 98-15, 1998-12 I.R.B. 6.

CHAPTER 11

1   IRC § 6033. This reference to *tax-exempt organizations* is to organizations that are exempt from tax under IRC § 501(a) and described in IRC § 501(c).
2   That is, organizations described in IRC § 501(c)(3), including those referenced in IRC § 501(e), (f), (k), and (n).
3   That is, organizations described in IRC § 501(c)(8), (10).
4   That is, organizations described in IRC § 501(c)(5).

5   That is, organizations described in IRC § 501(c)(19).
6   These are entities that are the subject of IRC § 4947(a)(1).
7   IRC § 266.
8   That is, organizations described in IRC § 501(c)(1).
9   IRC § 115; Reg. § 1.6033-2(g)(1)(v).
10   Rev. Proc. 95-48, 1995-2 C.B. 418, supplementing Rev. Proc. 83-23, 1983-1 C.B. 687. Illustrations of this type of affiliated tax-exempt organization are in Priv. Ltr. Rul. 9825030.
11   IRC § 6033(a)(2)(A)(i); Reg. § 1.6033-2(g)(1)(i).
12   Rev. Proc. 96-10, 1996-1 C.B. 577.
13   Reg. § 1.6033-2(g)(1)(vii).
14   Reg. § 1.6033-2(g)(1)(iv).
15   IRC § 6033(a)(2)(A)(iii); Reg. § 1.6033-2(g)(1)(iii).
16   Ann. 82-88, 1982-25 I.R.B. 23.
17   Rev. Proc. 94-17, 1994-1 C.B. 579.
18   IRC § 6033(a)(2)(A)(ii).
19   Ann. 82-88, *supra* note 16.
20   *Id.*
21   That is, organizations described in IRC § 501(c)(21).
22   That is, organizations described in IRC § 528.
23   That is, organizations described in IRC § 501(d).
24   That is, entities described in IRC § 401.
25   IRC § 6033(b).
26   IRC § 6501(a).
27   IRC § 6501(c)(3).
28   Rev. Rul. 62-10, 1962-1 C.B. 305.
29   *California Thoroughbred Breeders Association v. Commissioner,* 47 T.C. 335 (1996).
30   Rev. Rul. 69-247, 1961 C.B. 303.
31   IRC § 512(b)(12).
32   Rev. Rul. 60-144, 1960-1 C.B. 636.
33   IRC § 6072(e).
34   Ann. 96-63, 1996-29 I.R.B. 18.
35   IRC § 6033(a).
36   LAB 1, Q 6:7, Q 6:8.
37   Reg. § 1.509(a)-3(g)(1).
38   *Id.*
39   Reg. § 1.509(a)-3(g)(2).
40   E.g., Tech. Adv. Mem. 9711003.
41   See LAB 1, Chapter 6, Q 6:15–Q 6:29.
42   See LAB 1, Q 3:4.
43   See LAB 1, Chapter 11.
44   Rev. Proc. 85-58, 1985-2 C.B. 740.
45   Notice 96-30, 1996-1 C.B. 7.
46   IRC § 481(a).
47   That is, organizations described in IRC § 501(c)(12).
48   See LAB 1, Chapter 7.

CHAPTER 12

1   See LAB 1, Q 3:4.
2   See LAB 1, Chapter 10.
3   See LAB 1, Chapter 3.
4   See LAB 1, Chapter 4, Q 4:9–Q 4:14.
5   *Id.,* Q 4:15–Q 4:23.
6   See LAB 1, Chapter 5. E.g., IRC § 501(c)(3).

7   See LAB 1, Chapter 11. E.g., IRC § 512(b)(13).
8   See LAB 1, Chapter 6.

CHAPTER 13

1   IRC § 6104(e)(1).
2   IRC § 6104(d).
3   IRC § 6104(e)(1)(C).
4   IRC § 6104(e)(1)(A).
5   REG-246250-96.
6   IRC § 6104 (e)(1)(A)(ii) (not yet effective); Prop. Reg. § 301.6104(e)-1(a).
7   The rules described next are the subject of Prop. Reg. § 301.6104(e)-1(c).
8   Prop. Reg. § 301.6104(e)-1(f).
9   IRC § 6104(e)(3) (not yet effective).
10   Prop. Reg. § 301.6104(e)-2.
11   Prop. Reg. § 301.6104(e)-3.
12   Once the new law takes effect, the public inspection rules (Q 13:1) will be the subject of IRC § 6104(e)(1)(A)(i).
13   IRC § 6104(b).
14   IRC § 6104(a)(1)(A).
15   *Lehrfeld v. Richardson,* 132 F.3d 1463 (D.C. Cir. 1998).
16   IRC § 6104(a)(1)(D); Reg. § 301.6104(a)-5.
17   Reg. § 301.6104(a)-6.
18   Notice 92-28, 1992-1 C.B. 515.
19   IRC § 6652(c)(1)(C).
20   IRC § 6652(c)(1)(D).
21   IRC § 6652(c)(3).
22   IRC § 6685.
23   IRC § 6711(a).
24   Notice 88-120, 1988-2 C.B. 454.
25   IRC § 6711(b).
26   IRC § 6113.
27   IRC § 6710
28   IRC § 6115.
29   IRC § 170(f)(8).
30   IRC § 6714.

Index

INDEX

Member of the family, definition of, Q 1:26,
  Q 9:7
Membership associations, as prospective
  applicable tax-exempt organizations,
  Q 1:6
Mission societies, Q 11:3
Museums, Q 2:5

Newsletter funds, Q 8:7
Noncharitable organizations, private
  foundation grants to, Q 9:36
Noncharitable purposes, private foundation
  grants for, Q 9:37
Normally, definitions of, Q 4:32, Q 11:5

Officer, definition of, Q 1:25
Operational test, Q 3:19
Organization manager, definition of, Q 1:25

Participation, definition of, Q 1:31
Particular services, definition of, Q 5:16
Partnerships:
  and annual reporting rules, Q 12:15
  as disqualified persons, Q 9:10
  definition of, Q 3:1, Q 10:8
  exempt organizations in, Q 3:11–Q 3:21
  general, Q 3:2, Q 10:8
  information reporting, Q 3:29
  limited, Q 3:3, Q 10:8
  tax treatment of gain from sale of interest in,
    Q 10:26, Q 10:27
  tax treatment of income from, Q 10:20,
    Q 10:21
  taxation of, Q 3:5
  unrelated business income rules, Q 3:21
  use of, Q 3:4
Penalties:
  annual information returns, Q 12:17–Q 12:20
  availability of goods or services, Q 13:16
  fund-raising solicitations, Q 6:24, Q 13:18
  intermediate sanctions, Q 1:29
  private foundation rules, Q 9:20, Q 9:24,
    Q 9:28, Q 9:31, Q 9:38
  public inspection requirements, Q 13:12–
    Q 13:13
  quid pro quo contributions, Q 13:20
  substantiation rules (charitable
    contributions), Q 13:20
Per se rule, Q 3:17–Q 3:18
Political activities:
  and annual reporting rules, Q 12:12
  by political organizations, Q 8:4, Q 8:9
  taxation of, Q 8:17–Q 8:18
  by tax-exempt organizations generally, Q 8:17
Political campaign activities:
  by business leagues, Q 5:15
  by political organizations, Q 8:4, Q 8:9
  by private foundations, Q 9:34
  by social clubs, Q 7:16
  by social welfare organizations, Q 6:17,
    Q 6:33
  lobbying as, Q 8:9
Political organizations:
  contributions to, Q 8:2
  definition of, Q 8:1
  excess funds of, 8:15

expenditures for, Q 8:22
expenditures of, Q 8:3, Q 8:23
gift tax exclusion, 8:11
independent, Q 8:24
of associations, Q 5:34
primary purpose test, Q 8:10
programs of, Q 8:4, Q 8:6–Q 8:10
of public charities, Q 8:21
of social welfare organizations, Q 6:33
taxation of, Q 8:12–Q 8:16
of tax-exempt organizations generally,
  Q 8:19–Q 8:20
Preparatory time, Q 2:6
Primary purpose rule, Q 8:10, Q 12:1
Private benefit rules, Q 1:48
Private foundations:
  as disqualified persons, Q 9:10
  consequences of classification as, Q 9:40
  definition of, Q 9:1
  recipients of political organization's funds,
    Q 8:15
  rules governing, Q 9:13–Q 9:39
Private inurement:
  and intermediate sanctions, Q 1:13, Q 1:45,
    Q 1:46
  and social clubs, Q 7:7
  and social welfare organizations, Q 6:10
Public charities:
  as applicable tax-exempt organizations,
    Q 1:6
  definition of, Q 9:2
  disqualified persons with respect to,
    Q 9:3–Q 9:12
  recipients of political organization's funds,
    Q 8:15
  reporting as to status of, Q 12:16
Publicly supported charities, Q 9:2, Q 12:16
Public office, definition of, Q 8:5
Public policy doctrine, Q 6:10

Qualified charitable risk pools, Q 6:13
Quid pro quo contributions, Q 13:19

Reasonable cause, definition of, Q 1:34
Reasonable legal opinion, Q 1:34
Recognition of tax exemption, Q 4:2–Q 4:5,
  Q 5:21, Q 6:23
Reliance on rulings, etc., Q 4:22
Religious orders, Q 11:3
Rental arrangements, Q 1:18
Revenue-sharing arrangements, Q 1:13,
  Q 3:28
Rulings, Q 4:5

S corporations:
  definition of, Q 10:6
  taxation of, Q 10:10
  tax treatment of gain from sale of interest in,
    Q 10:24
  tax treatment of income from, Q 10:18
Safe harbor rule, Q 1:20
Sales transactions, Q 1:20
Sanctions:
  intermediate sanctions, Q 1:29
  private foundation rules, Q 9:14, Q 9:20,
    Q 9:24, Q 9:28, Q 9:31, Q 9:38

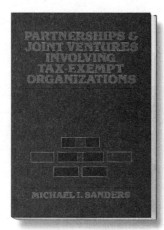

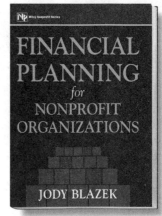